D0531823

COUNTING DOWN
BRUCE SPRINGSTEEN

Counting Down

Counting Down is a unique series of titles designed to select the best songs or musical works from major performance artists and composers in an age of de-sign-your-own playlists. Contributors offer readers the reasons why some works stand out from others. It is the ideal companion for music lovers.

Titles in the Series

Counting Down Bob Dylans: His 100 Finest Songs by Jim Beviglia, 2013
Counting Down Bruce Springsteen: His 100 Finest Songs by Jim Beviglia, 2014

COUNTING DOWN
BRUCE SPRINGSTEEN

His 100 Finest Songs

Jim Beviglia

ROWMAN & LITTLEFIELD
Lanham • Boulder • New York • Toronto • Plymouth, UK

Published by Rowman & Littlefield
4501 Forbes Boulevard, Suite 200, Lanham, Maryland 20706
www.rowman.com

10 Thornbury Road, Plymouth PL6 7PP, United Kingdom

British Library Cataloguing in Publication Information Available

Library of Congress Cataloging-in-Publication Data

Beviglia, Jim.
Counting down Bruce Springsteen : his 100 finest songs / Jim Beviglia.
p. cm.
Includes bibliographical references and index.
ISBN 978-1-4422-3065-1 (cloth) — ISBN 978-1-4422-3066-8 (electronic)
1. Springsteen, Bruce—Criticism and interpretation. 2. Rock music—United States—History and
criticism. I. Title.
ML420.S77B44 2014
782.42166092—dc23
2014000692

Printed in the United States of America

To Daniele
"May the rising sun caress and bless your soul
for all your life"

CONTENTS

ACKNOWLEDGMENTS

As someone who considers himself a fan, first and foremost, the fact that I've had the opportunity now to write books about two artists—Bob Dylan and Bruce Springsteen—who have changed my life with their music is beyond comprehension. No thanks I could ever give to the people who have helped to make this happen could ever be enough, but I'll give it my best try anyway.

Bennett Graff is my editor at Scarecrow Press, the guy who had enough confidence in this Springsteen project to give it a green light even before he knew how people would take to my Dylan book. If you're reading this book and you take notice of how well the writing flows and how there is no excess flab weighing down the prose, it's a pretty safe bet you're noticing Bennett's steady editing hand and excellent instincts taming my sometimes long-winded ranting. In addition, his coworkers at Scarecrow Press have been a great help to me every step of the way.

Springsteen fans know there are oodles of great books about his life on the market, yet I've only listed two in the bibliography. That's because those two books, and the men responsible for them, provided close to everything I needed to embark on this particular project. Early on I made the decision that since Springsteen has always been such an excellent dissector of his own songs, I would be using quotes from him to buffer my own analyses. In that respect, *Springsteen On Springsteen: Interviews, Speeches, and Encounters*, edited by Jeff Burger, has been my main source for those quotes. Mr. Burger's book depends on a lot of different interviewers, so I thank them indirectly for their fine work and

Mr. Burger personally for doing such an outstanding job of presenting and contextualizing them. Since I used many quotes from the book, I included the corresponding page numbers of the book next to those quotes as a shorthand way of citing this excellent work, while the specific information pertaining to each quote such as interviewer and publication can be found in the end notes.

As far as the facts about Springsteen's life and work, most of those I learned many years ago by reading Dave Marsh's definitive biography, *Two Hearts: The Definitive Bruce Springsteen Biography*. I've had the privilege of meeting Dave, appearing on his radio show, and keeping in contact with him for the last several years. For those who want an account of the life of Springsteen and how he came to be such a musical legend, start with Dave Marsh and you'll likely spare yourself the need to read anything else.

In terms of facts about the songs, the website springsteenlyrics.com was of invaluable assistance, especially when it came to tracking certain songs through their various incarnations. The site is run by Eddy Wehbe of Lebanon, and it's a great resource for anybody who really wants to get in-depth Springsteen knowledge. As a Springsteen nerd myself, I highly recommend it.

I have to thank my friends at *American Songwriter*, who continue to give me the chance to write for their wonderful magazine and website. My editor there, Evan Schlansky, has been a great friend to my writing and to me. The first assignment he gave me was to review *Wrecking Ball*, so maybe he had some foresight about my future involvement with Springsteen's work.

The idea for a Springsteen countdown first was indulged by Douglas Newman, who put it on a website that is sadly no longer with us but looms large in terms of its impact on my career. That list, in much truncated form from what's in this book, was spread even further by the folks at Culture Map, a website based in Houston. I also gave the list a twirl on my Countdown Kid blog, and the readers of that blog have been crucial in giving me the confidence to pursue publishing avenues for my online work.

On a personal level, there are far too many friends and family who have offered love and support over the years to possibly mention them all at once. That includes my various teachers and professors at Old Forge Elementary, Scranton Prep, and Syracuse University; with apologies to

Bruce, they gave three-minute records a real run for their money in terms of my education. My immediate family, which includes my brothers Bob and Rich; my sisters-in-law and nieces; my amazing mom, without whom I would doubtless be in some gutter; my daughter Daniele, who easily beats out Springsteen, Dylan, and all the rest in terms of being my favorite musician; and Marie, the love of my life forever, always, and beyond—well, they're the reason I do anything.

Bruce Springsteen's music is the reason this book even exists, so he obviously needs acknowledgement. It's always nice when the artists you admire are genuinely good people. I've never met Bruce, but the way he has conducted himself over the years in terms of his interaction with his fans, his thoughtfulness in interviews, and his genuine concern for his fellow man that he's demonstrated not only in his songs but also in his support for humanitarian causes makes me appreciate the man as much as I love the music. I don't know if he'll ever read this book, but if he does, I hope he gleans that much.

Finally, I'd like to thank my dad, Robert Beviglia Sr., who passed away when I was ten but remains as much a part of my life now as ever. It was my dad who encouraged me to read as many books as possible and set an example by doing it himself, so the notion that somewhere he's getting a kick out of having a kid who's written a few is the biggest reward I could ever get out of my writing.

INTRODUCTION

If you've ever seen Bruce Springsteen play live, it's likely you know what a special experience that can be. A case can be made that Springsteen is the greatest live performer in the rock era. The length of his shows, the intensity of the performances, the skill of the players supporting him, and Springsteen's force-of-nature personality make practically every one of his concerts a masterful combination of draining confession, comedic silliness, spiritual uplift, and pure exhilaration.

Springsteen has garnered such an amazing live reputation that it is the main draw for some fans who travel the world and back again, amassing impressive attendance records for his concerts. With such a devoted following, it wouldn't be surprising for newcomers to his music to think that he's an artist in the same vein as those who make records simply to use as a conduit to the live performances.

That would be a tremendous shame. Springsteen's studio work is worthy of being mentioned in the same breath as the greats of the genre. The effort he puts into his albums is unparalleled, as he forever fiddles with song selection and sequencing to ensure cohesion and maximum impact for the message he intends to deliver with each new full-length release.

Of course, those albums, and his live performances for that matter, are ultimately only as good as the songs they comprise, and that's what this project is all about. Springsteen has delivered so many amazing songs over his forty years of recording that narrowing them down to a relatively short list of one hundred songs might seem like an impossible task. Maybe, but it was also an awful lot of fun.

So let me start by explaining some of the rules that govern this humble undertaking. First of all, the songs had to be written and performed by Springsteen. Second, the ranking was made based on the official studio release of whatever song was in consideration. For example, "Because the Night" was first available in a concert performance on the *Live/ 1975–85* album, but I based its ranking here on the studio version finally released on *The Promise*.

If there was only a live version available for a particular song, which is a relatively rare circumstance, that's the version I used. If there were competing studio versions, I used the one from the original studio album. For example, the ranking of "Stolen Car" was based upon its rendering on *The River* rather than the take on *Tracks*. If a song was never released on a studio album and was eventually released in different versions, I chose the one I preferred as the basis for the ranking. (I think this only occurred with "The Promise.")

Finally, and most importantly, only songs that have been given an official release from Springsteen were considered. For all of the outtakes and cutting-room-floor demos that Springsteen has released on projects like *Tracks* and *The Promise*, fans know there are oodles more lying around in the vaults. You can hear a lot of these by searching the Internet, and some are even played with regularity on satellite radio. Yet it's my contention that if Springsteen really wanted them to be considered alongside the rest of his body of work, he would have let them see the light of day instead of locking them away, even if said lock isn't too hard to break these days.

As was the case with my book on the songs of Bob Dylan, these ranking are based on nothing but my own opinion of the merits of the songs. Chart position, the number of times a song has been played live, any kind of special place it may have in the Springsteen mythology, all of that, while it may have somehow filtered into my subconscious over the years, was excluded from my conscious decision-making process. I simply went back, listened to the entire Springsteen songbook, and started the process of separation and ranking until I came away with a Top 200. I've given essays on the Top 100; the list of the second 100 can be found in the appendix at the back of this book.

So there are the rules. Now it's time to find out which songs stand out the most in this catalog of seemingly infinite depth and brilliance. As wonderful a live performer as Springsteen has been and continues to be, he is first and foremost a songwriter and record-maker of the highest caliber, and I hope this book really puts the spotlight on that for those who may have either forgotten or are unaware of it. I highly recommend you see him live if you haven't already had the honor, but I also think that, even if you never see a show, you can listen to the songs in this list and still glean all of the beauty and truth emanating from Bruce Springsteen's rock-and-roll heart.

THE COUNTDOWN

100. "The E Street Shuffle" (from *The Wild, the Innocent & the E Street Shuffle*, 1973)

There's only one place to really begin if you're going to look back at the song catalog of Bruce Springsteen. Even though the real E Street wasn't in Asbury Park, New Jersey (it's in Belmar) and Springsteen didn't live there (David Sancious, an early keyboardist in the E Street Band who left the group before its biggest successes, did), it is still the figurative and spiritual home of all things Springsteen.

One of the recurring themes that will pop up throughout this examination of Springsteen's work is the way that his albums roughly represent a timeline in a man's life. This has created a continuity that makes his body of work more coherent than those of many of his peers, and that coherence resonates with his fans who can track the milestones and crises in their own lives through the similar ones that Springsteen's characters either celebrate or endure.

By giving these characters an address relatively early on in his career, Springsteen eased the way for this phenomenon to occur. Even though his first album included his hometown of Asbury Park in the title, the songs within didn't adhere rigidly to any sense of place. There were almost as many mentions of Arkansas as there were of Jersey.

That began to change with his second album, *The Wild, the Innocent & the E Street Shuffle*. The album's kickoff track, "The E Street Shuffle," has a lot to do with that change. In his book *Bruce Springsteen: Songs*, Springsteen copped to using the track as a kind of scene-setter. "The opening cut, 'The E Street Shuffle,' is a reflection of a community that was partly imagined and partly real," he wrote. "The cast of characters came vaguely from Asbury Park at the turn of the decade. I wanted to describe a neighborhood, a way of life, and I wanted to invent a dance with no exact steps. It was just the dance you did every day and every night to get by."[1]

There may have been no specific steps to this dance, but even those with two left feet could easily shuffle along to the funkiness Springsteen and his merry men concocted on the track. Starting with a horn fanfare to wake up the entire avenue, the song then rides through the thoroughfare on a Stax-influenced horn riff, Bruce's rhythmic guitar licks, and Sancious's underpinning clavichord rumble.

Springsteen starts his narrative off with a bang of an opening line: "Sparks fly on E Street when the boy prophets walk it handsome and hot." The nifty internal rhymes and nimble street jargon are emblematic of what's to come in the song as he lays out some of the major players while crafting an overview of the entire scene along the way.

His main characters, Power Thirteen and Little Angel, have names that sound like they came from a Springsteen name-generating machine set on stun. As Power scuffles with the cops and Angel keeps herself busy with some of E Street's other male denizens ("Everybody form a line"), the songwriter subtly creates a world that seems alternately fantastic and lived-in all at once.

Springsteen's career-long fascination with dreams begins in earnest as well on this album. In "The E Street Shuffle," "those sweet summer nights turn into summer dreams." Indeed, those dreams will get battered around a bit on the disc's subsequent songs, but here, in the beginning of this tour of this wild, innocent place, they are still immaculate.

In creating this semi-mythical home base, Springsteen was doing what literary icons like Faulkner, Twain, and many others have done by setting disparate works in recurring settings. This trick also allowed Bruce the opportunity to do little call-backs in his songs. Think of the way that "The Promise" acts as a semi-sequel to "Thunder Road," or how the "The Last Carnival" rounds out the story begun in "Wild Billy's Circus Story."

It's hard to imagine all of that occurring had Springsteen not had the wherewithal at such a young age to attempt this ploy. Actually, it was a bold thing to do considering that he had no way of knowing his career would last past that album. "The E Street Shuffle" is essentially the beginning of that through-line that continues to wend its way through the man's fabulous catalog.

What a soulful, fun beginning it was. And while Power Thirteen and Little Angel don't seem savvy enough to have made it this far, it's good to know that there are plenty of quasi-fictional denizens of E Street still doing the Shuffle as their primary source of enjoyment and method of survival.

99. "Easy Money" (from *Wrecking Ball*, 2012)

Many of Bruce Springsteen's characters have been tempted to the wrong side of the law to rectify desperate financial straits. Way back on *Born to Run*, the two small-timers in "Meeting across the River" debate a little job that involves carrying "a friend" in their pockets to get it done properly. In "Atlantic City," the hard-luck narrator promises his beloved that things will start to change once he does a "little favor" for some random guy.

So in many ways, there is precedent for "Easy Money," the second song on Springsteen's 2012 album *Wrecking Ball*. And yet the newest version of the get-rich-quick scammer in the Boss's songbook is a decidedly different kind of cat. Whereas the previously mentioned characters seemed somewhat nervous and ambivalent about the decisions they were making and only drifted to the dark side because they had no other options, the narrator of "Easy Money" seems to have no reservations about the actions he is about to take.

This attitude is seconded by the robust, positively gleeful music that Springsteen chooses to accompany this fellow on his sinister rounds. Set to a booming drum loop, "Easy Money" is a celebratory Irish jig. Soozie Tyrell's violin is meant to make you dance and not weep, while the "la-la-la" backing vocals and Springsteen's whoops toward of the end of the track serve to exacerbate the entire party atmosphere.

Such brazen music is fitting considering the way that the protagonist boldly flaunts his intentions. He's not exactly clandestine in his dealings, even inviting his better half along for the ride. At least the guy in "Atlantic City" told his girl to meet him after the fact; this guy tells his woman to put on an attention-grabbing red dress to join him on his adventure.

Of course, Springsteen isn't telling a tale of two grifters just for the heck of it. He's using these characters to portray in miniature the kind of large-scale theft that goes on every day in America. That point becomes clear in the second verse, when the narrator promises his victim that his downfall will come with little fanfare: "There's nothing to it mister, you won't hear a sound / When your whole world comes tumbling down." As a matter of fact, the only sound that's audible in the background is the laughter of the "fat cats" who can appreciate such conscience-free ruthlessness.

If such behavior is allowed by the captains of finance and industry who often run roughshod over the wants and needs of ordinary citizens, Springsteen seems to be saying, then why shouldn't those ordinary citizens react in kind with the same kind of callousness? Without defending the actions of this guy, Bruce is drawing a very powerful parallel between the character's disregard of law, decency, and other human beings and that same disregard exhibited by men and institutions infinitely more powerful who cause consequences exponentially more catastrophic.

Wrecking Ball succeeds in large part because of the way that Springsteen marries his social concerns to such vigorous music. His previous forays into topical material, like *Nebraska* or *The Ghost of Tom Joad*, were usually folk-music based, which certainly suited the subject matter. Yet the thunder and fire evident in many of the better songs on *Wrecking Ball*, while inherent in the lyrics, only truly emerges when the thrilling music draws it out.

As a result, a song like "Easy Money" gains a variety of dimensions. It is, on its surface, a small-scale story, but the pounding drums and Ron Aniello's boisterous production won't allow it to stay on that level. The song rises and widens in order to meet the scope of the problems that it addresses.

"I got a Smith & Wesson .38," Springsteen sings toward the end of the track. "I got a hellfire burning and I got me a date." It's never clear whether this guy is pushed to this life of crime by his circumstances or whether he simply sees it as upholding the example set by those much higher on the pay scale.

What unites him with the other would-be criminals in Springsteen's songs is his belief in a better time to come once the deed is done. "Got me a date on the far shore / Where it's bright and it's sunny," he promises. Whether or not the couple in "Easy Money" ever gets to that far shore is irrelevant. What matters is that they think that getting there by any means necessary is, as the fat cats have shown them, the American way.

98. "Lucky Town" (From *Lucky Town*, 1992)

When Bruce Springsteen chose to release the albums *Human Touch* and *Lucky Town* simultaneously in 1992, he essentially decreed that those albums would forever be linked. If he had the chance to do it all again, it's conceivable that he might choose differently because the two albums are actually vastly different.

Whereas *Human Touch* was recorded over a long period of time, *Lucky Town* was dashed off in a matter of weeks. *Human Touch* featured a bevy of studio musicians working, or, perhaps more accurately, struggling, to bring Springsteen's vision to life. *Lucky Town* was pretty much a solo affair, with drummer Gary Mallaber usually the only accompanist to Bruce playing all other instruments.

Most important of all, *Lucky Town* contains, on the whole, a much better selection of songs. Many credit that to the fact that the material is much more autobiographical in nature than any other previous Boss release. Springsteen himself made a similar assertion in a 1992 *Rolling Stone* interview. "But with *Lucky Town*, I felt like that's where I am," he said. "This is who I am. This is what I have to say. These are the stories I have to tell. This is what's important in my life right now."[2]

Still, many of those autobiographical songs hew a bit too closely to Springsteen's life to make them truly transcendent. Songs like "Better Days," "Living Proof," and "Local Hero" are fascinating portraits of the man at a turning point in his career and life, but the effort to put them across seems strained, as if he wants to get so much out of his system that he can't possibly fit it into the boundaries of a song.

The title track, on the other hand, is a different animal. Here is a song that not only gives an accurate rendering of the songwriter at that point in his life but also touches on themes and experiences that his listeners can more readily appreciate.

To further the point, the experience described in "Local Hero," that of Springsteen seeing a black-velvet portrait of himself in a store window, is comical and meaningful only if you know the context of his life and history. You don't have to know a thing about Springsteen to identify with the narrator of "Lucky Town"; you just need to have struggled through some hard times even as you still burn with the desire to get things right.

Another thing that separates the song from some of the other material on the album is the toughness of the music. Many of the other tracks mentioned above go for a kind of gospel release, Springsteen yearning for a catharsis that comes at the cost of musical subtlety. "Lucky Town" plays it far straighter: a grinding, bluesy rhythm accentuated by Springsteen's skewed-angle guitar licks. It's leaner and meaner, yes, but it also effortlessly creates the impact that the other autobiographical material huffs and puffs to achieve.

The minor keys keep things from ever getting too light-hearted, yet the chorus delivers a modicum of triumph over the narrator's malaise. What stands out in this guy's tale is his indefatigable spirit. When he gets hemmed in by life, he heads out to an unknown destination: "Out where the sky's been cleared by a good hard rain." If his past was a bit of a confused mess ("I had some victory that was just failure in deceit"), his present doesn't care to dwell on it ("Tonight I'm steppin' lightly and feelin' no pain").

This is not pie-in-the-sky optimism that he displays. It's more accurate to say that he's rough and ready for whatever crosses his path, hoping for the best while steeled for the worst. And considering he's already been through the mill, it doesn't seem like anything will slow him down for too long. "When it comes to luck you make your own," Springsteen sings with a defiant snarl in his voice, following it up with his statement of purpose: "Tonight I got dirt on my hands but I'm building me a new home."

Those sentiments are as inspirational to Springsteen's listeners as they were specifically meaningful to him when he wrote the song. "Lucky Town" may indeed have been born of Springsteen's own restless search for a figurative home at the time. What makes it stand out is how his audience can all dwell comfortably there as well.

97. "Two Hearts" (from *The River*, 1980)

Not for nothing has Bruce Springsteen often interspersed bits of Marvin Gaye and Kim Weston's hit 1965 duet "It Takes Two" in his live versions of "Two Hearts." The sentiments of the songs are strikingly similar. You could easily imagine some of the lines sung by Gaye and Weston (which were written by Mickey Stevenson and Sylvia Moy) sliding right into

Springsteen's song, in particular, "One can stand alone in the dark / Two can make the light shine through."

"Two Hearts" is one of the standouts of *The River*, Springsteen's 1980 behemoth of a double-album. It was on that album that the Boss finally loosened the tight thematic reins found on his previous few albums and let some good-time songs through to keep company with tougher, darker material.

"Two Hearts" contains elements of both of those approaches in its DNA. On the one hand, it speaks of broken hearts and makes reference to the personal stubbornness that inevitably transforms into loneliness. Yet the narrator has come to the realization that he can change all of that, that he can indeed make the light shine through the darkness that once enveloped him. He just needs a copilot.

This is the E Street Band at their tightest. One of the other novelties of *The River* was the preponderance of terse, punchy pop songs over the longer, wordier, and more musically ambitious compositions that populated albums like *Born to Run* and *Darkness on the Edge of Town*. It was the album when the band showed they could play with restraint just as well as they could play with grandeur.

"Two Hearts" is a fine example of that. It keeps a rapid pace throughout, egged on by drummer Max Weinberg's sharp snares. No instrumentalist steps to the fore, yet the combo comes together to keep the momentum at a breathless level until it finally comes to a crashing halt less than three minutes after it began.

Springsteen frames the song in terms of a loving relationship that makes the difference in the life of a lonely person, but he never specifies whether it's a romantic relationship or a friendship that can do the job. Reading the lyrics, one might assume it is indeed a romantic love that is at the crux of the song. Listening to it creates another impression entirely.

That's because the harmony vocals of Steven Van Zandt are so integral to the song's success. Van Zandt has rarely been given center stage instrumentally on a Springsteen song, yet throughout the band's time with Bruce, Van Zandt has found subtle ways to make a major impact. As just two of multiple examples, he was the one whose suggestions ultimately molded the immortal riff at the heart of "Born to Run" into its legendary form, and he was the one who figured out how the horns should sound on "Tenth Avenue Freeze Out."

More importantly, he has been one of the main sounding boards for Springsteen when it comes to choosing material and shaping songs. That's why, even if the evidence isn't always tangible, it's hard to imagine the E Street Band without Van Zandt. His musical partnership and longtime friendship with the leader of the band, therefore, can't possibly be ignored when considering the line "Two hearts are better than one," especially as he bellows it out in high harmony above the Boss.

Even in up-tempo, quick songs like this one, Springsteen has a way of referring to the common themes that hang over his work. The way he writes about dreams, for instance, is often a good emotional barometer for the overall tenor of his material at a given time.

In "Two Hearts," the narrator realizes that his dreams are only useful when they're pushing him in the right direction. His "childish dreams" of "tough guy scenes" are only leading him down a path to isolation. So he follows the advice of Corinthians to "put away childish things," which he sums up in an excellent couplet: "Someday these childish things must end / To become a man and grow up to dream again."

What that grown-up dream entails, "Two Hearts" suggests, is the blessing of going through this hard world with somebody else by your side to endure it and make it easier to bear. Or, as Marvin and Kim put it simply way back in the day, "It takes two, baby / Me and you." Insert your own special someone into that equation, Springsteen suggests, be it a friend or a lover, and that light shining through will be golden.

96. "Livin' in the Future" (from *Magic*, 2007)

When you think of the songwriting output of Bruce Springsteen, you don't necessarily think of it as being subversive. This is not to say that Springsteen is a timid songwriter. It's just that he usually doesn't cloak his message. If he has a serious message to deliver, there is usually some serious music to accompany it. Likewise, he'll usually conjure music upbeat and joyous whenever he wants to put across something lighthearted in nature.

"Livin' in the Future" is an exception to that rule. If you could somehow remove the lyrics from the song and listen to it as an instrumental, you might think it was a sequel to "Hungry Heart." It has the same kind of swagger and brio, right from Clarence Clemons's boisterous opening solo through the key change at the end that heralds the "la-la-la" backing vocals. Only Danny Federici's urgent organ solo suggests any mood other than pure glee.

The song comes on 2007's *Magic*, which was the second album that Springsteen did with the reunited E Street Band and the second that was produced by Brendan O'Brien. The first was *The Rising*, an album that lumbered at times under the weight of its 9/11–themed material, but one that also found the band and its leader struggling a bit with how to translate their classic sound into a modern setting.

Magic was on much firmer footing because it wasn't afraid to reach back for some classic E Street tropes like Roy Bittan's scene-setting piano, Federici's instinctive fill-in-the-blanks organ work, and, of course, Clemons blowing through the proceedings like a force of nature. If the songs are there, those elements are timeless.

With all of these colorful signposts in place on "Livin' in the Future," it would be natural for Springsteen fans to expect something similarly buoyant from the lyrics. Maybe he would add a few tinges of wistfulness to the story, à la "Glory Days" or even "Girls in Their Summer Clothes," which also can be found on *Magic*, but certainly nothing too downcast, right?

At several points during the song, the lyrics to this fascinating, under-rated track fall into line. The first verse, in particular, seems like the narrator is trying to use the music to take the sting out of his relationship blues. He gets a letter that indicates that his lover has departed the premises without any intention to return. The mood gets a shade dark when he mentions "the taste of blood on your tongue," but then the chorus comes around and that's easily swept aside.

In the second verse, however, there are signs that there are things afoot that are far direr than just the lament of a broken-hearted fool. Gunpowder-and-gray skies block a dirty sun as the narrator wakes up on Election Day, the first signal that the political may be muscling its way into the personal. Even then, the sight of the girl walking back into town diverts attention from this brief turn of events.

By the time the bridge comes around, though, the portents of something more sinister than a break-up can no longer be ignored. "The earth it gave away," Springsteen sings, "the sea rose toward the sun." That could be just poetic license used to indicate a general topsy-turvy, but it's more likely he is referencing the danger of global warming.

The ante gets upped as Springsteen rails on: "My ship liberty sailed away on a bloody red horizon / The groundskeeper opened the gates and let the wild dogs run." Human rights replaced by institutionalized chaos: that's the terrible bottom line here. In that context, Federici's solo seems like a desperate cry for help.

Our hapless protagonist finally begins to admit that the problems are way beyond his control. "Tell me is that rollin' thunder," he asks, "or just the sound of somethin' righteous goin' under?" It becomes clear that the refrain ("We're livin' in the future / And none of this has happened yet") is a bit of intentional ignorance that he has to perpetrate just to face this frightful scenario.

There is no rule that says that you have to hear "Livin' in the Future" in this way, of course. You can just sing along and use the song as a four-minute respite from the bigger picture it subtly implies. Yet Springsteen cleverly puts doubt into our heads as to whether that "la-la-la" refrain is a celebratory release or the final howls of the damned.

95. "Mansion on the Hill" (from *Nebraska*, 1982)

There are lots of rock artists who have produced great albums in their careers, but the ones that ascend to exalted status in the rock pantheon usually have an album somewhere in their catalog that has a great story behind it as well, almost giving it the aura of myth. Think of the way the Beatles quit touring and created fictional versions of themselves to produce *Sgt. Pepper's Lonely Hearts Club Band*, or the way Bob Dylan shelved a finished version of *Blood on the Tracks* on the brink of its release so he could re-record half the material.

For Bruce Springsteen, the album that stands out as a special one in terms of the story behind its recording would have to be 1982's *Nebraska*. Springsteen famously demoed all the songs on a four-track recorder before eventually deciding that the material should be released as it was first laid to primitive cassette tape. His acoustic guitar, whining harmonica, and howling vocals perfectly captured the isolation and desperation hidden just below the surface of these slice-of-life narratives.

Casual fans might think that this choice was a bit of genius foresight by Springsteen, but, in truth, it was sort of a last resort. After all, he did indeed take the material into the studio where the E Street Band took their best crack at whipping it into rock-glory shape. But the efforts were futile. Chuck Plotkin, the engineer who helped turn Bruce's homemade cassette tape into a listenable LP, explained in Dave Marsh's Springsteen biography *Two Hearts: The Definitive Bruce Springsteen Biography* that, no matter what the band tried, the essence of the songs was best revealed in the initial versions. "The stuff on the demo stuff was astounding," he said. "It was an incredibly evocative piece of work. And we were losing more than we were picking up."[3]

It's interesting to think of what some of the songs might have sounded like in full-band versions (and Springsteen has provided many clues with his live takes of the songs with the band over the years). Yet it's difficult to imagine "Mansion on the Hill," one of the standout tracks on *Nebraska*, in any other way than in the quiet reading he gives it on the album. Maybe the band could have given the song a country-tinged arrangement à la "Factory," but they likely would have run the risk of trampling the delicacy that makes the original such a wonder.

Hank Williams had a song called "A Mansion on the Hill," and it's most likely that Springsteen was aware of it when he created this track. Whereas in his early years Springsteen's songwriting was almost wholly influenced by the rock, R&B, and Top 40 that amazed him as a kid, the post–*Born to Run* period found him expanding his source material, from literature to cinema to roots-based music. As a result, there's a high probability that a country classic like Williams's song would have filtered into his imagination.

There is, however, a marked difference between the two songs. In Williams's song, the woman inside the mansion is a character to be pitied, for the life she has chosen is loveless and isolated. By contrast, the narrator of Springsteen's "Mansion on the Hill" looks up at the titular place with envy and wonder, knowing that the inhabitants exist in a world that he can't possibly ever inhabit.

Or could he? The irony of the song is that Springsteen would eventually know the wealth that is implied. During the *Born in the U.S.A.* tour, he rhapsodized about just that fact to a Minnesota audience. "This is a song about when I was a kid," he said. "My father was always transfixed by money. He used to drive out of town and look at this big white house. It became a kinda touchstone for me. Now, when I dream, sometimes I'm on the outside looking in—and sometimes I'm the man on the inside."[4]

Springsteen's inner child tells the story in straightforward but subtly telling fashion. Note how the mansion towers over the "factories and the fields," suggesting that the workers in those places will always be subordinate to the elite. In the same way, those iron gates that the child notices are impenetrable barriers that forever deny those lower classes entry.

Since the song is written from a child's point of view, or at least the view of a man looking back to his childhood, the lyrics don't judge, and Springsteen makes sure that his vocal is filled with the guileless awe of youth. "Mansion on the Hill" is one of those *Nebraska* songs that just couldn't possibly be improved by any other rendering, as it vividly evokes a nightmare of ruthless class systems via the untarnished innocence of a young boy's dream.

94. "Valentine's Day" (from *Tunnel of Love*, 1987)

Pigeonholing Bruce Springsteen albums is usually an exercise in folly. Like many of the best songwriters, Springsteen often demands a certain thematic unity from his full-length albums. Yet he is too well-rounded a writer to ever deliver something that is so narrow in scope that it would not allow for some contrast and variety.

When you talk about Springsteen's albums in terms of those that hew the closest to a specific theme, it's most likely that *Tunnel of Love* will enter the discussion pretty quick. While the album was actually recorded before his separation and eventual divorce from first wife Julianne Phillips, its focus on the difficulties of maintaining a loving relationship certainly foreshadowed those real-life events.

Yet if you're going to label *Tunnel of Love* a "divorce album," then how can you account for the fact that the final track, a position of great importance on an album in that it is the closing statement to a listening audience, is "Valentine's Day," a song about the power that love possesses that can redeem even the most long-gone soul?

The sequencing was a counterintuitive move by Springsteen that works only because it isn't a drastic departure from everything that precedes it. Had "Valentine's Day" been as gooey a love song as the title might suggest, the effect would have been too jarring and would have come off as disingenuous.

But it isn't. It is a realistic depiction of the priority of love in someone's life. The song in no way mitigates the struggle and toil that it takes to keep two people together when the pressures of the outside world invade and their own inner natures interfere. What it does suggest is that backing down from that struggle and toil is a far bigger mistake than taking it on and coming up short. In other words, the reward far outweighs the risk.

Springsteen plays all the instruments on the track; coming on the heels of the band's success with *Born in the U.S.A.*, it's sometimes easy to forget that the follow-up was essentially a solo affair. The track he creates is full of circular patterns that individually repeat and collectively intertwine. As gentle as the music is with its gently strummed acoustic guitars, ambling bass lines, and sighing synthesizers, the arrangement, in conjunction with the repetitive melody, evokes the effect of someone running in place, struggling against the confines of an endless reverie.

There is also a nifty contrast between this lulling music and the urgency displayed in the lyrics. The first verse depicts a man speeding home in his car with a heart pounding practically out of his chest in an attempt to get back to his girl. While this manic drive symbolizes the enormity of the feelings he has for this woman, the sheer desperation of it implies the possibility that she might not be there when he gets back.

In the second verse, the man testifies to his own desire for a family life similar to the one that his friend has cultivated for himself. This domestic bliss enthralls him now far more than any romantic tale of lone wolves: "They say he travels fastest who travels alone / But tonight I miss my girl mister tonight I miss my home."

And yet he is still out there on the highway, as lonely as it might be, for reasons he can't quite explain. This bit of doubt and fear ties into the themes expressed more overtly in some of the darker songs on *Tunnel of Love*. "What scares me is losin' you," he sings, but the moment of truth will be when he decides whether or not he can confront this fear or whether he will run from it and wander so far down that highway that he might not ever return.

Luckily, this character triumphs in the song's thrilling final lines. Those Springsteen dreams, ever fickle, here play a benevolent role, scaring the protagonist straight by revealing that his deliverance isn't waiting on some untraveled road. It's actually right there beside him. He makes his choice: "So hold me close honey say you're forever mine / And tell me you'll be my lonely valentine."

Maybe that's not the way you'd expect an album that's so brutally honest about romantic anguish to end. Yet "Valentine's Day" works as the closer for *Tunnel of Love*, and on its own, because of its clear-eyed insistence that love is always worth the pain.

93. "Jackson Cage" (from *The River*, 1980)

As metaphors go, comparing life to a prison is not exactly a novel ploy. Yet Bruce Springsteen skirts any worries of cliché thanks to the incisive lyrics and fierce music he and the E Street Band manage on "Jackson Cage," a powerhouse, three-minute rocker found on *The River*. That album is so sprawling that certain songs get lost in the shuffle, but this one is so well-executed and forceful that it's not likely to be forgotten by anyone who has heard it.

In many ways, the song's themes and concerns make it a lyrical cousin to the nakedly personal, psychologically intense songs on *Darkness on the Edge of Town*, the predecessor to *The River*. Yet the song sounds of a piece with the album it inhabits because of its more colorful sound palette, as opposed to the starker, darker textures that define *Darkness*.

The song is part of the brilliant opening side of the double-album. Springsteen's previous albums had thematic unity in mind when they were sequenced, but *The River* takes you on more of an all-encompassing ride. Side 1 starts with the power pop of "The Ties That Bind," rolls into the swaggering, raucous, comical "Sherry Darling," surges into the fiery rock of "Jackson Cage," keeps up the pace even as it lightens the mood a tad with "Two Hearts," and then closes out with the somber, broken "Independence Day." It's a tour de force in five songs, with three sides still to go. Feel free to praise Springsteen on his knack for sequencing a live set for maximum impact, but don't sleep on his ability to do the exact same thing on his studio albums.

"Jackson Cage" is the perfect third hitter in that Murderer's Row of a lineup because it can do a little bit of everything. It has the muscle of a great rock song while still maintaining the melodic punch of the best pop. In addition, the instrumentalists are all at the top of their game in the service of lyrics that effortlessly hum within the musical framework while telling a compelling and resonant story.

You could pretty much laud every member of the E Street Band that participates here. Special mention goes to Max Weinberg for the galloping drumbeat that propels the song. Springsteen takes a quick harmonica solo, but otherwise the players subordinate the spotlight for the greater good. Steven Van Zandt's harmonies, which play a bigger part on *The River* than on any other E Street album, give the sense that there is an alliance of friends ready to help the stymied protagonist, a sliver of hope.

Springsteen was likely referencing Jackson, New Jersey, a town very near his hometown of Freehold, in the song title, but the specific place is really immaterial. The setting could be any town whose fortunes have crumbled to the point that its inhabitants have little chance to thrive without finding a way out.

It's clear that the woman the narrator attempts to encourage here is hemmed in by forces she can easily feel even if she can't identify them. Springsteen never indicates whether she is married, either to another man or to the narrator, or not, but that's ultimately immaterial. What's important is the inertia that creeps up and keeps her from enjoying the only life she's ever going to get.

The narrator is sympathetic enough to understand that her problems are not entirely of her own making. Springsteen's imagery could make even the heartiest of souls cower: "Every day ends in wasted motion / Just crossed swords on the killing floor." Yet he's also trying to light a fire under her. "Are you tough enough to play the game they play / Or will you just do your time and fade away?" he sings in the chorus.

He can ask that question because he's been forced to answer it himself. Springsteen wisely brings her interrogator into the action, which keeps the song from being condescending to this tragic woman. The narrator also dreams of a better life, only to be reminded over and over how far from reality those dreams are. It's enough to make anyone participate in their own figurative incarceration, "'til you become the hand that turns the key down in / Jackson Cage."

Springsteen leaves open the possibility that these characters can still make an escape. The punch of the music is such that it could surely explode the "Jackson Cage" into rubble. The tragedy is that these souls might be so battered that they might not know enough to step into their freedom.

92. "A Good Man Is Hard to Find (Pittsburgh)" (from *Tracks*, 1998)

When you think of Bruce Springsteen and songs about Vietnam, "Born in the U.S.A." is likely the first one that comes to mind, and rightfully so. It is, after all, one of the great anthems of Springsteen's career and one of the fiercest castigations of that conflict and its aftermath ever put on record.

Many casual fans might overlook "A Good Man Is Hard to Find (Pittsburgh)," which is a shame, because it's excellent in its own right. Considering that it was included on *Tracks*, Springsteen's mammoth four-CD collection of cutting-room-floor material from 1998, it's understandable why a song as restrained and unassuming as this one might be somewhat forgotten.

The song was recorded for the *Born in the U.S.A.* album, as were about seventy other songs or so during that humongous overtaking. Whether it was ever a close contender for the album is a matter for those who were in on that selection process, but it seems most likely that this was one of Bruce's "notebook" songs that he decided to pull out during a random 1982 session and give it a go. It never even reached B-side status like "Shut Out the Light," another trenchant Vietnam-themed outtake.

Musically, the song is a far cry from the tracks the band ended up producing for *Born in the U.S.A.* That album was full of glossy, very of-its-time productions, with synthesizers and booming drums as Springsteen attempted to stay current in the MTV era. By contrast, "A Good Man Is Hard to Find" is a very natural-sounding country throwback, distinguished by Roy Bittan's Nashville chords. As such, there's no threat of it ever sounding dated, a problem that befalls some of the productions that did make the album.

It also attacks the Vietnam topic in a much different way than the "Born in the U.S.A." single. That song was very much about the bigger picture, even as Springsteen told the story from the perspective of a veteran who's struggling to make sense of his postwar life. "Good Man" is the specific tale of a war widow, and it never tries to tackle any of the outlying issues concerning the war itself. In fact, it need not have even been about the Vietnam War, since the destructive effect of wars in general is its intended target. Vietnam just happened to be the relevant war in the time frame that Springsteen was writing the song in—the early 1980s.

In fact, the only time that a specific war is even mentioned is in the first verse when the narrator combines the weather in the woman's hometown of Pittsburgh with the rainy skies in Saigon. The mention of Saigon quickly inserts the context into the listener's head, which is all that

Springsteen wants out of it. From there, he can go about his business of telling a very personal story.

Springsteen also sets the song at Christmas time, further bringing home the tragedy of this woman's loss. In the second verse we find out that she has a daughter as well who will grow up without her father: "Now there's a little girl asleep in the back room / She's gonna have to tell about the meanness in this world."

The woman that Springsteen portrays here clearly has a strong will, strong enough to realize that she doesn't want a lesser man to replace the one that she's lost. Yet she still craves the human companionship that comes with having someone: "Just somebody to hold her / As the night gets on." As the refrain makes clear, finding even that solace is next to impossible since all possible suitors will be compared to her dead husband.

For most of the song, Springsteen refrains from making any outward commentary because it would somehow interrupt the fragile tale he's telling. In the final verse, he gets in a quick but effective shot at what a waste this loss is, just as all other losses like it, by putting it in the mind of his protagonist. "Well she thinks how it was all so wasted," he sings, "and how expendable their dreams all were."

"Expendable" is a word that often gets thrown around in times of war, though those making the battle decisions would never dare to openly use it when describing the soldiers doing the fighting. Springsteen exposes this hypocrisy by spotlighting the uncounted collateral damage of war in "A Good Man Is Hard to Find (Pittsburgh)" and comes away with an underrated gem in the process.

91. "Working on the Highway" (from *Born in the U.S.A.*, 1984)

The "New Dylan" tag that eager record executives and music journalists hung on Bruce Springsteen in the early days of his career was always wrongheaded, but marketing shorthand won out over common sense for a while. As time passed, the differences between the two men became so increasingly clear that there might have been a bit of an overcorrection in the old point of view, with people assuming that Springsteen actually had little in common with Bob Dylan.

One thing that Springsteen and Dylan certainly share is the urge to constantly tinker with their material, although even in that department they do things in different ways. Dylan first and foremost messes with his lyrics until they get to a point where he's happy with them (although sometimes they never reach that point, even if the rest of the world might think they're brilliant). As for his music, he might tinker with arrangements, tempo, and instrumentation, but the core of the song usually goes unchanged from its original incarnation.

Springsteen, on the other hand, has been known to change everything about a song, stripping it of its essential meaning in the process to replace it with an entirely different one. You might be able to recognize snatches of lyrics or a chord change here and there from one take to the next, but otherwise the two versions (or however many versions he runs through) will be totally disparate.

It can be fun to scramble around the Internet for these alternate versions, but ultimately what you'll find is that Springsteen's instincts are generally right about the changes made. One fascinating transformation that serves as an informative example of how Springsteen hews his material to the album he's in the process of making is the one that eventually created "Working on the Highway" from *Born in the U.S.A.*

Most folks know the song from the version on that album, where it falls into line with some of the other good-timey tracks such as "Darlington County" or "Glory Days." Marrying a roller-rink sound to hand claps and a guitar rhythm reminiscent of the Eddy Cochran rock classic "Summertime Blues," "Working on the Highway" is an irresistible, candy-colored throwback that can't help but make you smile even as the story within the song ends with the narrator hopelessly stuck in prison.

What might strike some as surprising is that "Working on the Highway" first found life as a track written during the period when Springsteen came up with the songs for his solo masterpiece *Nebraska*. Trying to imagine the "Darlington County" that we all know in that setting is difficult; perhaps he could have turned it into an "Open All Night"–style acoustic rave-up, but it's still an odd fit.

Instead, the impetus for "Darlington County" was a soft folk number called "Child Bride." The tempo is drastically slower, the melody is different, and there is no sing-along chorus as would be found on the *Born in the U.S.A.* take. The story is essentially the same: A hard-working yet foolhardy fellow gets mixed up with the wrong girl and ends up in the hoosegow for his trouble.

What "Child Bride" brings to the forefront that stays relatively hidden in "Working on the Highway" is the fact that the reason he ends up in jail is because the girl is underage. "Working on the Highway" gives clues to that fact but never says it explicitly, to the point where you can imagine his imprisonment was the result of her father having connections. In "Child Bride," it's right there in the title and in the line "Well they said she was too young."

The earlier version is an excellent song that would have worked on *Nebraska* with a little bit more editing. Springsteen had the wherewithal to not only see that it wouldn't fly on *Born in the U.S.A.* as it was, but also to recognize that there was a kernel of something in there that could be reconstituted to fit in with all of the crowd-pleasers on that record.

The final result is a sugar rush of a song, one that doesn't let us get too down about this character's dire straits, because he doesn't seem to be too depressed about it himself. He's just back where he started, getting up every day to work. He even finds a buddy in the warden.

With those chirping keyboards and flickering guitars, "Working on the Highway" sounds like a guy making the best of a bad situation. Springsteen, the tinkerer, certainly made the best out of the pitch-black early incarnation of the song.

90. "The Ties That Bind" (from *The River*, 1980)

One of the interesting things that happened on *The River* was how Springsteen tightened up the music of many of the album's most accessible songs while lightening up the lyrics. This was a bit of an about-face from *Darkness on the Edge of Town*, where the music he created was as stark and as relatively simplistic as anything he'd ever recorded, while the lyrics were mostly dark and smothering.

The River quickly announces its intentions to change Springsteen's modus operandi with its very first song. "The Ties That Bind" comes bursting out of the gate with a circular guitar riff that borrows from the Searchers' "Needles and Pins," with hints of the Byrds' 12-string elegance and the interweaving guitars of Keith Richards and Brian Jones from early Rolling Stones records thrown in for good measure.

Many folks notice the strong British Invasion influence on the song, but "The Ties That Bind" also harkens back to 1970s power-pop mavens like Big Star and Badfinger in the way that it feels meticulously constructed yet still punchy and powerful. Everything that's played by the instrumentalists feels like it's a hook, especially Max Weinberg's stuttering drum beat in the bridge and Clarence Clemons's sax solo, as colorful as always but perhaps more precise that what he was usually called upon to produce.

Springsteen's fascination with pop radio growing up as a kid in the 1960s took a while to manifest itself in his music. He couldn't be as succinct as those classic hits on the early albums because his lyrics demanded scope and breadth from the music. On *The River*, the straightforward meanings of many of the songs allowed him the ability to make those classic sounds his own.

Although it is, by the intention of its creator, an album that veers all over the place in terms of its topics and subject matter, *The River* does have a few themes that crop up throughout several different songs. One is the need for companionship to navigate an unforgiving world. "Two Hearts" and "Out in the Street" certainly make compelling cases for trading in isolation for a connection with others. "The Ties That Bind" makes roughly the same point, but it does so with perhaps more of an awareness of the darkness that can envelop those who don't make that swap.

"The Ties That Bind" features an extremely clear-headed narrator, one who has probably reached his wisdom the hard way by committing the same mistakes that he wishes the girl he's addressing can avoid. This is a girl who's been burned by others in the past, so she wants to hide away from it all and avoid the hurt. Springsteen has an answer for her in the bridge: "I would rather feel the hurt inside, yes I would darlin' / Than know the emptiness your heart must hide."

He also castigates her for falling for the notion that being tough and unfazed is the proper way to deal with pain. "You're so afraid of being somebody's fool," he sings, "not walkin' tough baby, not walkin' cool." This front can only last so long, as the next lines make plain: "You walk cool, but darlin', can you walk the line / And face the ties that bind."

As in "Two Hearts," the narrator admits to having dealt with his own lone-wolf tendencies and to the fact that he's having trouble practicing what he is preaching. Note that in the last verse he says, "We're runnin' now" and not "You're runnin' now." Yet what matters is that he realizes that any type of attempt to escape is folly, that the inevitability of the truth will envelop them both: "We're runnin' now but darlin' we will stand in time / To face the ties that bind."

Springsteen sings at song's end that "The Ties That Bind" can neither be broken nor forsaken, stretching out the syllables as if pulling at the ties to prove their elasticity. His point, embellished by the thrillingly no-fat musical onslaught, is that once you accept the necessity of these bonds, you can also begin to reap their benefits.

89. "This Life" (from *Working on a Dream*, 2009)

"This Life" appears on an album that, upon its release in 2009, was met with less than the usual slam-dunk reaction from critics concerning a Bruce Springsteen disc. This is not to say it was trashed, but the reviews tended toward measured praise instead of unmitigated gushing. In much the same way, it feels like the album doesn't have a very high standing among some Springsteen fans.

That's odd because it's an excellent album, and even though it's barely more than a half-decade old, it already feels like the most underrated Springsteen album ever. So what is it that hampers the reputation of *Working on a Dream*? The fact that it was released not too long (by modern album-cycle standards anyway) after 2007's *Magic* might be one problem. There is also the fact that the title track, which served as the lead single for the album and thus the example of what fans could expect from it, was a bit pedestrian. Maybe Springsteen's Super Bowl appearance in the same month as the album's release—which drew a lot of attention to his back catalog but shoehorned "Working on a Dream" awkwardly in among the evergreens—didn't do it any favors either.

The most likely reason, however, seems to be the album's apparent lack of a thematic hook, which maybe fooled people into thinking it was slight. Yet the hook was there, if a bit hard to spot at first. *Working on a Dream* is an album about growing older, if not downright old, and the attendant heartbreaks and triumphs that go with that stage of life.

Very subtly, a continuum runs through the songs. "Outlaw Pete" tells the tale of an outlaw who has outlived everything but his enemies. "Queen of the Supermarket" is about a middle-aged dude obsessing over both a checkout girl and a shopping mecca in almost equal measure. "The Wrestler" spotlights a guy facing the autumn years in isolation due to his own self-destructive tendencies. And "The Last Carnival" is about death.

In between these extremes are a bunch of love songs—including "This Life"—of a finer vintage than one might expect from rock music. Springsteen makes the daring assertion in these songs that romance actually gets better with the passage of time. To drive home his point, he coats these songs in the glow of the Golden Age of rock and roll.

Springsteen had started down this path on his previous album *Magic*, with songs like "Girls in Their Summer Clothes" and "Your Own Worst Enemy" that featured classic melodies and production. *Working on a Dream* ups the ante on this style. In the case of "This Life," the obvious touchstone is *Pet Sounds*–era Beach Boys, from the watery intro to the "ba-ba-ba" backing vocals that bring the song home.

Speaking of which, the walled vocals in the chorus have a stirring effect. Sculpted harmonies have never been Springsteen's stock and trade, but he and the band execute them beautifully on this and a few other songs from *Working on a Dream*. It makes sense because such a technique is very era-appropriate, maybe not for 2009 but for 1964, which is the rough date for the head space that Bruce seemed to be occupying during the making of this record.

In the manner of so many great love songs, the celebration of the relationship at the core of "This Life" is made more meaningful by the hardships that have been overcome by the narrator to get to that point. If you know what the dark side is like, a dark side that is represented by the universe's unforgiving, vast blackness of space that ruled this guy's life prior to the big bang of romance, it makes the eventual arrival in the light that much more glorious.

Springsteen deftly contrasts poetic descriptions of the cosmos with simple, earthly pleasures like a nighttime car ride. This is not an unrealistic depiction of a loving relationship, mainly because the songwriter admits to the way that even the most heavenly aspirations get derailed by life's messier aspects: "We reach for starlight all night long / But gravity's too strong."

Yet these realities are trivial compared with the living dream of this love story. The narrator is young enough at heart to refer to her as "The beauty in the neighborhood," the one who transcends all of the earthly bonds: "This lonely planet never looked so good."

The refrain is blissfully optimistic about how long this pair will stay together ("This life and then the next") while the narrator's final words

("My universe at rest") suggest that his striving is done, not because his heart has stopped beating, but because it has found its home.

Beautiful sentiment and beautiful music pours out of "This Life." It's time to give the song and the album that produced it their due.

88. "We Take Care of Our Own" (from *Wrecking Ball*, 2012)

Bruce Springsteen's hardcore fans tend to have an unwavering faith in the ability of their musical hero to deliver the goods every time he comes out with a new release. Yet it's likely that even the most diehard Boss backers had to be a tad worried about what Springsteen would produce when it was announced that he would have a new album titled *Wrecking Ball* coming out in early 2012.

The last Springsteen album had been *Working on a Dream*, released three years prior to that in 2009, and it included what would essentially be the last performances by the most well-known and enduring lineup of the E Street Band. Keyboardist Danny Federici died in April 2008 but had played on the *Working on a Dream* sessions. Saxophonist Clarence Clemons died in June of 2011, and his work can be found on just two of the songs on *Wrecking Ball*.

While Federici was no less essential to the band's musical chemistry, the loss of Clemons—who is on a short list of the best saxophonists in rock history, served as onstage foil for Springsteen, and whose status on E Street ranged beyond iconic to practically mythological—seemed like an event which could forever alter Springsteen's musical output. Certainly he would still go on writing songs and producing albums, but would it ever be quite the same again?

With that context looming over its release, the importance of "We Take Care of Our Own"—the first single off *Wrecking Ball*—being an effective song can't be overstated. Had Springsteen come out with something tentative or the least bit unsure of itself, those predicting doom and gloom for his future career path would have had a crucial piece of evidence in their favor. It might have been overwhelmingly difficult to counteract that perception with subsequent songs and albums.

From the booming drums and instantly memorable guitar riff that open the song, "We Take Care of Our Own" quickly soothed all doubts. It's a fist-pumping, foot-stomping, cathartic blast of rock and roll, and while it might have a modest ranking on this humble list, it certainly places in the Top 10 in terms of the most important songs of Springsteen's career.

Springsteen made a cagey move by releasing the song as an introduction to *Wrecking Ball*, an album that is a bit of a departure from his signature sound with its fascinating mixture of antiquated song styles and ultra-modern production techniques. Even though "We Take Care of Our Own" is essentially a two-man studio job by Springsteen and producer Ron Aniello with some help from backing vocalists and Soozie Tyrell on violin, it sounds like it's an E Street Band track. As such, it was a great way to ease the world into the headier and off-kilter creations that awaited them on the album that contained it.

If there were any thoughts that the losses he had suffered in his band would somehow mellow the fire of Springsteen's message, this song doused them in a hurry. "We Take Care of Own" is full of classic Springsteen themes, themes that are hammered home time and again on *Wrecking Ball*: frustration at broken promises, bewilderment over what America has become, and resilience in the face of all that.

Springsteen presents the song as a quest by the narrator to find his home, a futile task since his home is now unrecognizable to him. The landmarks he once knew by heart have been forever altered by the actions of those calling the shots. In particular, the line "From the shotgun shack to the Super Dome" specifically references what Springsteen clearly sees as a particularly heinous betrayal: the reaction (or lack thereof) by the federal government to the devastation of Hurricane Katrina.

This quester spends the second half of the song asking a series of questions in the hope that someone can direct him to the rights and ideals for which his country once stood. He repeats his final question twice for emphasis: "Where's the promise from sea to shining sea?" Without that promise, he implies, anyone who sings "America the Beautiful" is lying through their teeth.

Springsteen wants the refrain to be ironic—more empty words coming from the mouths of those who can't possibly be believed. Yet in the midst of that powerful music, a more positive way to listen to it is to change the identity of those speaking the words. If you imagine the refrain "We take care of our own" to be a pact between Springsteen and all of his fans in E Street Nation who believe in the same things for which he has spoken so eloquently in his career, it becomes clear that the promise can be believed as long as you're counting on the right people.

That's a message that's classic E Street, which is why "We Take Care of Our Own" had to be reassuring and comforting to fans still mourning two of that avenue's most respected residents.

87. "Open All Night" (from *Nebraska*, 1980)

Even on an album as focused in its intensity and moodiness as *Nebraska*, it's good to have a change of pace here and there. Yet it's a tricky endeavor to try and introduce levity to a collection of songs so unrelentingly bleak. You run the risk of shattering the mood and taking the listener out of the experience entirely.

Springsteen manages this delicate balancing act ingeniously on the rollicking "Open All Night." His strategy is to pump the music full of energy and vigor in the service of a character who has a different perspective than the rest of the folks who populate the album even as he's beset by the same stifling, no-way-out existence.

Taking his electric guitar out of the holster, Springsteen creates an amalgam of Jerry Lee Lewis's whooping rockabilly and Chuck Berry's rat-a-tat verbal and guitar assault, with a little dose of the late 1950s novelty hit "Beep Beep" by the Playmates thrown in there too. It all adds up to a breathless sprint that mirrors both the frantic pace of the narrator's all-night drive and the antic output of his overloaded mind.

The set-up is pretty simple: A guy stuck on a night shift decides to make an overnight car ride to get back to his girl. Yet as the old saying goes, it's the journey that's important, not the destination. That's probably why Springsteen ends the song without the reunion for which the narrator is so eager. The implication is that this frazzled fellow, even if he gets to the girl sometime after we stop eavesdropping on his journey, will always be on one high-speed chase after another because behind the wheel is the only place where he can maintain the illusion that he has some control in his life.

That's why his description of the tune-ups he does on his car is far more detailed than the one he gives of the girl. As a matter of fact, what he remembers of their initial meeting, other than her big brown eyes, is a road map and fried chicken. This girl is ultimately just an excuse to get him out on that highway.

If you're listening to *Nebraska* for the first time, you might get a bit of déjà vu when you get to "Open All Night." That's because there are lyrical similarities between that song and "State Trooper," which precedes it on the album. Yet even with those lyrical callbacks and the fact that both songs profile a late-night drive, Springsteen manages to evoke completely different moods with the two songs. The protagonist of "Open All Night" ultimately seems harmless and fun; the protagonist of "State Trooper" is a powder keg.

Even though it is more light-hearted in tone than other songs on the album, "Open All Night" doesn't skimp on the pressures and hardships endemic to *Nebraska*. The narrator is stuck in a job he clearly hates, and his beloved Wanda was unemployed when he met her. Yet even as he sprinkles in enough of these downers to keep things honest, Springsteen clearly doesn't want things to bog down too much here.

After all, there's fun to be had in the sights and sounds of the road. The same things that set the late-night driver to a dangerous boiling point in "State Trooper" only serve to make the narrator of "Open All Night" rev his engine a little bit more here. This guy doesn't have the time to brood. He only has time to make some feverish descriptions of the scenery flying by him at breakneck speed: "New Jersey in the mornin' like a lunar landscape."

In the closing moments, the narrator asks the wee-hours DJ to "deliver me from nowhere." We leave him whooping and hollering out as "Open All Night" fades out. Notice that it doesn't come to a halt, which is fitting for the profile of a character who doesn't even want to slow down, let alone stop. At blinding speed, he can avoid seeing the truth that he's just another lost soul on an album full of them.

86. "Straight Time" (from *The Ghost of Tom Joad*, 1995)

It's a counterintuitive notion that someone who served time in jail might be anything less than thrilled to be free. Yet Bruce Springsteen handles "Straight Time," from *The Ghost of Tom Joad*, so adeptly that he convinces you that, for the hard case within the song, freedom's just another word for nowhere to go.

The Ghost of Tom Joad is often thought of in the same vein as *Nebraska* when Springsteen's albums are compared in that they are both moody affairs full of folk-based, topical songs. One major difference is that *Joad* actually contains a few band performances interspersed throughout the songs that feature just Springsteen on acoustic guitar and vocal.

Those band songs, for the most part, hold an advantage over the acoustic solo songs on the album because they have a bit more melody. On the acoustic songs, Springsteen seems so focused on the stories that he's telling that the tunes can seem like afterthoughts. On songs like "Straight Time," the interplay between the instruments creates some extra added atmosphere and inspires Bruce to break out of any monotonous tendencies.

In the case of "Straight Time," the atmosphere conjured by the assembled band, which features E Streeter Danny Federici on keyboards and longtime collaborator Soozie Tyrell on violin, is one of creeping dread. The song never breaks out of that tension, leaving the listener expecting the worst after the song concludes.

That's the perfect musical setting for the protagonist of "Straight Time." By singing the song in the first person, Springsteen allows us to get inside and see what makes this guy tick, and it's not pretty. Despite his efforts to walk "the clean and narrow" in the time since he was released from prison, his worst self continues to pull him back into a criminal's life: "In the darkness before dinner comes / Sometimes I can feel the itch."

The people that surround him don't believe in his reformation, which only serves to push him further back to the dark side. His uncle, who still revels in crime, bribes him into recidivism. His wife can't shake the feeling that he'll return to his previous ways, even as she tries to hide it: "Mary's smiling but she's watching me out of the corner of her eye." All this leads him to believe that any dreams of a different life on the outside were unrealistic. "Seems you can't get any more than half free," he ponders.

Any uncertainty about where this is all headed is laid to rest as the song wends toward its conclusion. "In the basement huntin' gun and hacksaw / Sip a beer and thirteen inches drop to the floor," Springsteen sings. The way that the act is described makes it seem like the protagonist had no free will about reconfiguring the gun to better suit criminal purposes; the excess barrel just falls to the floor as if it had a mind of its own. It's a clever way for Springsteen to evoke the restlessness and inner void that drives this character to what will likely be a calamitous fate, one that will bring all his loved ones down with him.

"Straight Time" is one of the few songs on *The Ghost of Tom Joad* that doesn't delve into a specific social issue. Songs like "Sinaloa Cowboys," "Balboa Park," and others on the album are so tied to their specific, overarching topic that they can come off sounding like lessons rather than story songs. "Straight Time" avoids this pitfall both through its subtle musical flavorings and by the way Springsteen creates a compelling character and makes his story somehow relatable even to those in his audience who have never thought of committing a crime in their lives.

We leave this character on his pillow dreaming, "driftin' off into foreign lands." The methods that he'll use to get to such far-off places are no longer in doubt. His sentence to "Straight Time" is clearly just about to end.

85. "Tunnel of Love" (from *Tunnel of Love*, 1987)

"It oughta be easy ought to be simple enough / Man meets woman and they fall in love." That all-important couplet from Bruce Springsteen's 1987 song "Tunnel of Love" is the view that most people have about relationships until they learn otherwise, usually the hard way, that it's rarely simple or easy.

Most times it's infinitely the opposite, full of complexity and difficulty, a notion upon which Springsteen expounded for an entire album, one which features "Tunnel of Love" as the title track. The song followed its equally clear-eyed predecessor "Brilliant Disguise" into the Top 10 in 1987, proving that Springsteen's popularity was such at the time that he could infuse the typically cheery environs of pop radio with ambivalent sentiments like those found in the two songs and still ride high in the charts.

It helps that "Tunnel of Love" is such a dynamic track. Back when Springsteen embraced the synthesizer and other glossy sounds on *Born in the U.S.A.*, he generally used them to brighten the musical colors on songs like "Dancing in the Dark." "Tunnel of Love" was recorded featuring many of the same techniques, but with an ear toward evoking moods like doubt and anguish.

Roy Bittan's synthesizers do a lot of the work in conjuring those aforementioned moods, with help from Max Weinberg's effects-laden drums that practically crash right through the walls of the "Tunnel of Love." Nils Lofgren, who usually subsumes his guitar wizardry within the bigger picture of the E Street Band, gets a rare chance to solo on a

Springsteen record here. The wild, squalling notes that he plays captures the unease of the narrator.

In the extended instrumental coda, Patti Scialfa lets loose with some powerful belting that compliments the thrust of the music. These elements unite on a shimmering, animated recording that still sounds good today even considering the very of-its-time approach.

Another factor that helps the song's accessibility is the way that Springsteen lets the metaphor drive the message and not the other way around. His descriptions of the carnival atmosphere are so vivid that you feel like the ride that couple is taking is real and not just symbolic. That allows the song to work not just as a dissection of relationship turmoil but also as a detailed slice of life.

As the couple descends into the "Tunnel of Love," they endure a barrage of sights and sounds that uncannily mirror the different touchstones of the romance upon which they are about to embark. The presence of the fat man unnerves them at the start, but that's quickly replaced by sensuality and sexual connection: "I can feel the soft silk of your blouse / And them soft thrills in our little fun house."

Yet these pleasures of the flesh only serve to distract from deeper issues that must be resolved, issues that quickly rear their head in the next figurative stop on the ride: "Then the lights go out and it's just the three of us / You me and all that stuff we're so scared of." This tunnel creates equal parts wonder and fear within its passengers.

In the bridge, the journey continues with mirrors that distort the images of the couple. Although they find it humorous at the time, this little pit stop is Springsteen's way of warning about the possibilities of romantic partners hiding away their true selves and presenting skewed images to their partners (a phenomenon that "Brilliant Disguise" describes in painful detail).

The last stop that Springsteen describes is perhaps the most harrowing: "There's a room full of shadows that get so dark brother / It's easy for two people to lose each other." This room is emblematic of the unforeseen circumstances, the hard times, the perilous pitfalls that crop up in the midst of any relationship. Perhaps human nature is wired so that each person tries to deal with these situations on their own; Springsteen is suggesting that the best way to combat the shadows is to huddle even closer together.

In the closing verse, Springsteen sums up the ride succinctly and pointedly: "But the house is haunted and the ride gets rough / And you've got to learn to live with what you can't rise above." This is perhaps the most pessimistic stance he takes in the song since it makes no mention of any of the positive aspects of love, only the obstacles that must be either overcome or endured.

That doesn't exactly seem like any kind of joyride. Springsteen's "Tunnel of Love" seems more like a test of bravery and resilience, something that, if you're lucky, you survive with your wits and heart intact.

84. "Across the Border" (from *The Ghost of Tom Joad*, 1995)

On an album filled with desperation and death, "Across the Border" finds a sliver of life-affirming hope in the wilderness. It may be only wishful thinking, but it is powerful enough as a state of mind to propel the song's characters high above the unconscionable sorrow of their daily lives, if only for as long as the thought lasts.

"Across the Border" is a change of pace from the seemingly bottomless well of sorrow and pain that permeates *The Ghost of Tom Joad* and makes it an easier album to appreciate than love. Springsteen certainly wanted the album to serve as a wake-up call for those either unaware of the social problems being described or simply too selfish to care about them. Yet "Across the Border" suggests that not even man's most insidious sins can kill the spirit of those who stay pure in their minds and hearts. That kind of uplift is well-earned after all the hardship that precedes it on the album.

Springsteen spoke about the effect he wished the song to have in a 1995 interview with *Mother Jones* magazine. "I got to the end of the record, and there had been a lot of mayhem," Springsteen said. "I wanted to the leave the door open, so I wrote 'Across the Border.' That song is a beautiful dream. It's the kind of dream you would have before you fall asleep, where you live in a world where beauty is still possible. And in that possibility of beauty there is hope" (216).[5]

The open-hearted vibes within the lyrics extend to the music. This is another case where a song from *The Ghost of Tom Joad* benefits from a full-band arrangement rather than a solo take with guitar and vocal. "Across the Border" actually starts with Springsteen alone before building in lovely grace notes like Soozie Tyrell's violin and Danny Federici's accordion. Springsteen delivers some impassioned harmonica that surges and sighs amid the wistful chord changes.

As the song begins, it seems like it could be another of Springsteen's treatises on immigration; there are several of those tucked among the narratives on *The Ghost of Tom Joad*. Yet it becomes clear soon enough that the narrator is only describing his ideal trip, the one he plans to make if only within the safe corridors of his heart. He describes this place to his beloved as if trying to convince her of the reality of this place that seems too good to be true.

The details are all almost impossibly idyllic. There are Edenic scenes of green and gold pastures, azure skies, aromatic blossoms, and ever-present waters that run from muddy to clear and cool but always replenish the soul. But more important than the sights, sounds, and smells are this paradise's healing powers. "Pain and memory have been stilled," he sings, which is in stark contrast to their condition in their current location: "We'll leave behind my dear / The pain and sadness we found here."

This optimism might seem misplaced or naïve considering that the perfection of the intended destination can't possibly be realized on Earth. (As the Eagles once sang, "You call some place Paradise / Kiss it good-bye.") Springsteen defends himself against these charges with a simple question that reaches to the core of the human spirit: "For what are we / Without hope in our hearts?"

It's a question that's best left rhetorical because the answer is too terrible to contemplate. It also seems like piling on to mention that there are clues in the lyrics that hint that this narrator is singing the song from a point of separation from the love he's addressing. Perhaps it's because he's about to cross over the border between life and death, a journey with no return ticket.

We're probably better off just riding along with the loveliness of the vision until it finally dissipates than contemplating the final outcome. In the dying embers of the dream, the man sings, "I know love and fortune will be mine / Somewhere across the border." How or if he gets there is unimportant. What's important is that hope in his heart, inextinguishable even if his promised land is ultimately exposed as the fantastic creation of a pipe dream.

83. "Growin' Up" (from *Greetings from Asbury Park, N.J.*, 1973)

To be honest, "Growin' Up" isn't recorded very well. The second song off Bruce Springsteen's debut album, *Greetings from Asbury Park, N.J.*, falls victim to the same mushy, washed-out sound that befalls several other tracks on that record. Only David Sancious's piano, stately in the intro, jazzy in the middle, rises above the murk.

Then there's that title. When you hear that a song is going to be called "Growin' Up," your immediate thought is that it's going to be filled with life lessons from someone too stuffy and self-righteous to realize the glorious foolhardiness of youth. As Bob Dylan famously sang in "My Back Pages," "I was so much older then, I'm younger than that now." Why would any rock and roller sing about going in the other direction?

It may have some strikes against it, but "Growin' Up" pretty much obliterates all objections on the strength of Springsteen's unapologetic gusto. It's as if he was making a preemptive strike against those who might have mistaken his relatively unironic stance for squareness. After hearing all he brings to this early classic, even the most jaded cynics had to admit that the kid had serious talent.

The song even got an early stamp of approval from no less of an iconoclast of cool than David Bowie, who cut a strutting version of the song in 1973, just a few months after its release on *Greetings from Asbury Park, N.J.*, featuring Ronnie Wood on his guitar. "Growin' Up" was recorded too late for inclusion on Bowie's 1973 covers-album *Pin Ups*, although it would be added years down the road in a deluxe version of the album. In any case, hearing Bowie sing about being "the cosmic kid in full costume dress" makes it seem like Bruce was ghostwriting the song for the Thin White Duke.

As for the concern that the song might be humorless and didactic based on the earnest title, Springsteen blows that out of the water pretty early. Anyway, he's not talking about growing up and learning lessons; he's talking about growing up in defiance of lessons. The title turns out to be the most ironic thing about the song because the narrator, whose point of view probably mirrors that of the songwriter pretty closely, actually celebrates foolishness and reckless abandon, notions which are antithetical to maturation. If anything, this character rebels with extreme prejudice against the idea of growing up.

Springsteen adds a patina of science fiction to the song to give the narrator's exploits a spin that's larger than life. In three verses, he is alternately a Mad Max–style nomad wandering through a wasteland, a crazed bomber pilot, and a space traveler. And Springsteen's fancy word-play, leaping tall buildings and stunning innocent bystanders, makes for pretty good patter for his journey.

This was the early, wordy Springsteen, of course; "Growin' Up" was written back in 1971, when he was just twenty-two, so the lack of a filter is understandable. Yet the overexuberance works for the song's subject matter, and hidden among the piles of words is some effortlessly impressive technique. Springsteen has admitted to not being much of a reader in the early days of his career, yet a line like "I hid in the clouded wrath of the crowd," with its subtle rhyme and fascinatingly imagery, sounds like it could have sprung from the pen of a poet from the Elizabethan era.

The fantastic nature of the lyrics is the hook, but what really elevates "Growin' Up" are the flashes of insight into what makes this guy tick. Sure it's fun to get carried away in phrases like "jukebox graduate" or wonderfully polysyllabic lines like the killer opener, "I stood stonelike at midnight suspended in my masquerade." But if lyrical dexterity were the only quality the song had to offer, it would have been impressive but hollow.

Luckily, Springsteen includes quick but telling glimpses of vulnerability and heartbreak to humanize this guy. There is both triumph and tragedy in his story ("I swear I lost everything I ever loved or feared"), but what's striking is how he keeps stubbornly forging ahead into the breach. "I was open to pain," he says early on, suggesting that the best parts of life are only available to those willing to endure the worst. It's a theme Springsteen would tease out further on some of his classic albums still to come in the decade.

No matter the pain, what's essential about him remains unscathed: "I strolled all alone through a fallout zone and came out with my soul untouched." As the song wraps up, Springsteen sings the refrain twice. The first ends on a minor chord, suggesting the tribulations the character has experienced, while the second time around the major chord resolves the matter and brings our hero's wild-and-wooly journey to an end.

We know it's only a temporary respite since Springsteen proves that his version of "Growin' Up" is not a transformation to some staid existence but rather a sustainable state of mind whereby one takes on every obstacle at full speed. Forty years or so since he first wrote the song, Springsteen can still sing about that state of mind and sound gloriously authentic.

82. "I'm on Fire" (from *Born in the U.S.A.*, 1984)

Only four songs in Bruce Springsteen history ever reached higher in the U.S. pop charts than "I'm on Fire," which burned its way to a #6 ranking in 1985. Those four songs were "Hungry Heart," "Dancing in the Dark," "Glory Days," and "Brilliant Disguise."

The aforementioned songs that barely outperformed it were either anthemic in nature or exquisitely crafted with mass consumption in mind. Compared to them, "I'm on Fire" can seem like little more than an afterthought of a song. It's barely more than two-and-a-half minutes long, most of which consists of a repetitive guitar-and-drum rhythm borrowed whole hog from Johnny Cash's signature boom-chicka-boom sound. (Cash would later do an excellent cover version of the song.) Roy Bittan's mournful synthesizer fills in the gaps.

Lyrically, the song is also extremely minimal and simplistic, at least until the final verse when Springsteen ratchets up the intensity a bit. Certainly it doesn't have, nor was it trying to have, the kind of depth possessed by many songs throughout Springsteen's career which are not nearly as well known.

The easy answer as to why "I'm on Fire" created such an impact was that it was released at the absolute apex of Springsteenmania. It was the fourth of a ridiculous seven Top 10 singles that would emanate from *Born in the U.S.A.*, which also spawned a massive tour that would bring Springsteen to huge audiences all over the world. It was the kind of wave that could sweep a fun but relatively minor track like "I'm Goin' Down" into the Top 10, which is jaw-dropping when you consider "Born to Run" only hit No. 23.

Another possibility to consider is that the song was buoyed by an extremely popular video which included Springsteen acting rather than just performing in a clip for the first time. Directed by John Sayles, the "I'm on Fire" video features dialogue before the music even begins, a relatively novel concept at the time, and focuses on the budding attraction between Springsteen's auto-mechanic character and a high-society woman who brings in her car.

Springsteen actually acquits himself quite well in the video (maybe a little better than in the "Glory Days" video, where his portrayal of a fading ex-jock comes off as a bit deranged in the closing scene). He and Sayles were trying for something that complements the song rather than spells it out, which is a good thing because Springsteen literally in flames might have been a nightmare for the insurance companies.

While it's certain that all of this tangential stuff aided the popularity of "I'm on Fire," any opinion that posits that they are the only reasons for the song's success is misguided. While it may not have the ambition or sweep of some of Springsteen's bigger shots, the song does what it sets out to do in succinct and effective fashion, leaving an impact that long outlasts the song's modest length.

What set "I'm on Fire" apart from the rest of Springsteen's recorded catalog to that point was the unblushing focus on sexual desire. Prior to the song, Springsteen tended to refer to sex only as a minor part of his characters' existence, as in the closing moments of "Jungleland." If he did put a major emphasis on it within a song, he usually did it through innuendo so blatant it was more comical than sexy (as in "Ramrod" off *The River*).

There is little doubt that the narrator of "I'm on Fire" is deadly serious about his intentions. Springsteen sings with coiled tension in his voice throughout, not releasing it until the "whoo-whoo" falsetto he unleashes in the fade-out. Those opening verses are simplistic because the character doesn't need to extrapolate. I want you bad and I'm a better lover than the guy you're with: That's the essence of the first part of the song, and it doesn't get much more direct than that.

In the final verse, Springsteen allows himself a little leeway to describe the depth of this guy's passion, the rambling lines providing effective contrast to the terse declarations from earlier in the song. "Sometimes it's like, someone took a knife baby edgy and dull and cut a six-inch valley through the middle of my skull," he sings. "At night I wake up with the sheets soaking wet and a freight train running through the middle of my head."

His desire, when unfulfilled, equals torment. "Only you can cool my desire," he admits. "I'm on Fire" tiptoes the fine line between that kind of desire and debilitating obsession, something that even those secure in loving relationships can feel. That kind of relatability, along with the song's effortless sexiness, is why its popularity justly outweighs its modest scope.

81. "Terry's Song" (from *Magic*, 2007)

Bruce Springsteen has never been the kind of artist who deals in hidden tracks, the songs that aren't listed in the CD credits but turn up unexpectedly after the conclusion of what was supposed to be the closing track. Not that there's anything wrong with the tactic when deployed correctly, but Springsteen has never needed such a sly tactic to deliver the goods to his audience.

He made an exception for *Magic*, his excellent 2007 album. After all the songs were recorded and most of the packaging had been completed, Terry Magovern, Springsteen's longtime personal assistant, passed away in July of that year. Springsteen gave the eulogy at his funeral and delivered a new song as a tribute to his friend. That song, "Terry's Song," was then rushed onto the album as the hidden track that comes after the conclusion of "Devil's Arcade."

Springsteen also included a page in the liner notes of *Magic* that briefly summed up his relationship with Magovern, whom he had known since the latter worked in a New Jersey bar where Springsteen played all the way back in 1972. "His presence and spirit have been an unspoken part of my music for the last two decades and will continue to be," Springsteen wrote in the liner notes. "Terry, when they built you brother, they broke the mold."[6]

That last line serves as the touching refrain to "Terry's Song." Springsteen played all the instruments himself for the version that appears on the album, adding mournful piano to folky guitar strumming to create a track that's both sober enough to fit the occasion and loose enough so as not to be a total downer. His impassioned harmonica playing clearly seems to contain every bit of experience the two men shared together over the years.

Tribute songs are a tricky bit of business for even the best songwriters because they run the risk of being so overly fawning of their subject matter that the object of the tribute doesn't seem like a real human being anymore. That's why there are more well-intentioned clunky ones than genuinely good ones by a pretty good margin.

Springsteen avoids this trap by focusing on the uniqueness of Magovern over anything else. He manages this via a laundry list of some of the world's miraculous manmade wonders, such as the *Titanic*, the Eiffel Tower, and the *Mona Lisa* among others, ultimately surmising with each one that, if they made it once, they can certainly make it again. His friend, however, is a creation that can't be duplicated: "And sometimes something comes along and you know it's for sure the only one."

Springsteen avoids this trap by focusing on the uniqueness of Magovern over anything else. He manages this via a laundry list of some of the world's miraculous manmade wonders, such as the *Titanic*, the Eiffel Tower, and the *Mona Lisa* among others, ultimately surmising with each one that, if they made it once, they can certainly make it again. His friend, however, is a creation that can't be duplicated: "And sometimes something comes along and you know it's for sure the only one."

Springsteen doesn't shirk from his own heartbreak at the loss of his pal. "They say you can't take it with you, but I know that they're wrong," he sings. "'Cause all I know is I woke up this morning, and something big was gone." Yet he also refrains from sanctifying his friend, which he implies isn't what Magovern would have wanted anyway: "And I know you'll take comfort in knowing you've been roundly blessed and cursed."

If there is a bit of wishful thinking that Springsteen indulges in, it's when he imagines his buddy entering the afterlife without the afflictions of advancing years upon him: "Gone into that dark ether where you're still young and hard and cold." The unknown that awaits after death may be daunting, but Springsteen paints his friend as being rough and ready for the challenge.

Like all great eulogies, "Terry's Song" manages to both do justice to the memory of the deceased and provide comfort to those in mourning. It's likely that a great number of eulogists who know Springsteen's work have likely borrowed a few lines or ideas from the song since its release. In that way, his song transcends its very specific intent and becomes something that anyone who has lost a loved one can borrow in their own time of need.

80. "The Wish" (from *Tracks*, 1998)

One of the underrated reasons that Bruce Springsteen has such a devoted fan base is the way that his song catalog seems to offer up something for just about every one of life's occasions. For example, the previous essay on this list about "Terry's Song" talked about how the song can be an excellent starting point and source of ideas for anyone who has to write a eulogy for a loved one.

"The Wish" fills in its own very specific niche, one that doesn't get too much attention from songwriters but is desperate for quality candidates. You see, there is a dearth of well-written, non-sappy, cool songs that can be used as the song played when a groom dances with his mother at a wedding. That's where this special tribute by Springsteen to his mom Adele comes in very handy.

Anyone who has been to a lot of weddings will recognize the usual easy-listening candidates for this important role such as "Wind beneath My Wings." Rock artists have been sadly lacking in this department. Certainly anyone choosing either of the searing songs titled "Mother" by John Lennon or Pink Floyd is trying to make a point about his childhood wholly inappropriate for the festive occasion.

Why there are so many good father-daughter songs and so few mother-son songs is a topic for the psychologists to explore. What's important here is that Springsteen came to the rescue, as usual, by writing a very personal song, one of the most nakedly autobiographical that he's ever written, that somehow can work for any grateful groom who really wants to honor a good mother for all that she's done for him.

Springsteen recorded the song during the *Tunnel of Love* sessions in a solo performance save for the help of studio drummer Gary Mallaber. Yet you get the feeling listening to the song that there was never any intent by him to include it on an album full of dark treatises on relationship troubles. This was simply a gift to his mom that only made the light of day when he included it on *Tracks* in 1998.

Of course, Springsteen's songs about his sometimes fractious relationship with his father growing up are some of the most memorable in his career. Yet there is just this single charming song about his mom. In an interview with Charlie Rose around the time that *Tracks* was released, he tried to explain why.

"My mother was very consistent and we had a relationship that was easier to understand," he said. "It was nurturing and there was faith involved and support and a lot of giving love. That was something I shied away from writing about. I think it's easier to write about your dad in rock and roll than about your mother" (268).[7]

It's a good thing that Springsteen overcame that reticence because "The Wish" is one of the most charming combinations of songwriting and performance that he has ever delivered. You can tell that the song means a lot to him in the almost sheepish way he squeezes in "It's overdue" when in the last verse he talks about finally writing a song for Adele. Even for a guy as ready to bare his emotions in his songs as Bruce is, his heart is further out on his sleeve here than ever before.

The fine details he's able to recall from his mother's daily routine and the night when the two of them stood outside looking at the guitar that she would eventually buy him for Christmas show just how cherished these memories are to him. What's even more vital is how well his mother protected him and steered him toward a better life. "If pa's eyes were windows into a world so deadly and true," he sings, "you couldn't stop me from looking but you kept me from crawlin' through."

It's likely that those lines resonate with a lot of folks who have similar relationships with their own parents. The song's specific references to Springsteen's rock-star good fortune help to personalize matters, but "The Wish" understands and pays homage to the selfless sacrifice and unwavering support that all of the best mothers provide.

Springsteen eventually offers Adele her own dance as the song progresses, warning her at the end that "if you're looking for a sad song, well I ain't gonna play it." Those grooms looking for the right musical thanks to give to their moms on their most important day can't do much better than "The Wish." While you're at it, just bring a boom box to play Bruce's wonderful version and save money on the band.

79. "Outlaw Pete" (from *Working on a Dream*, 2009)

Bruce Springsteen made a bold choice by making "Outlaw Pete" the lead-off track for his 2009 album *Working on a Dream*. It's rare that an artist as advanced in his career as Springsteen can release a song that genuinely sounds like nothing they have done before, but "Outlaw Pete" manages to be just such an outlier.

Such a drastic departure doesn't necessarily have to lead to something that's artistically effective, of course, and it seems that "Outlaw Pete" is a bit of a polarizing song among the rabid Springsteen faithful. Some fans took to derisively labeling it "Out to Pee" for the way that a segment of the crowd would head for the bathrooms whenever the E Street Band trotted it out on the tour supporting *Working on a Dream.*

If there are fans who have dismissed this fascinating track, they should reconsider. "Outlaw Pete" is full of musical daring, and it works lyrically whether you choose to hear it as a well-told tall tale of a legendary bandit or as a metaphor for the way that the tentacles of the past relentlessly spread into the present and the future.

Springsteen referenced the latter reading in a 2009 interview with *Observer Music Monthly.* "The past is never the past," he said. "It is always present. And you better reckon with it in your life and in your daily existence, or it will get you. It will get you really bad. It will come and devour you, it will remove you from the present. It will steal your future and this happens every day."[8]

That quote shows that Springsteen feels that the old William Faulkner maxim ("The past is never dead. It's not even past.") doesn't quite go far enough to explain the danger of it all. The title character in "Outlaw Pete" is emblematic of this, a man whose attempt to put his heinous past behind him is nothing but a fool's errand.

The music that accompanies Outlaw Pete on his journey is one of Springsteen's most ambitious concoctions. It's a heady combination of Ennio Morricone spaghetti-western ambience and progressive rock drama. The song alternately recalls some of the more ornate productions of Jeff Lynne for ELO and the over-the-top thrills of modern rock adventurers Muse.

If nothing else, the song takes you on a ride, and even if it occasionally makes you queasy, it's never less than invigorating. There are powerful hooks at every turn, from the elegiac guitars to the darting strings. It's all very cinematic, which makes sense in a song that plays out like some bizarre Western.

In the early stages of the song, Springsteen describes Pete in such a way as to make him seem like the Paul Bunyan of banditry, weaving exaggerated tales of both his criminal behavior as a child and his supernatural defiance of heavenly figures. The tone gets more realistic when Pete gives up his life of crime to settle down with his new wife and child on an Indian reservation. From that point, Springsteen's tale plays out like a thriller, especially with the introduction of the bounty hunter Dan.

Dan represents the righteous revenge that Pete has coming to him, and even as the bad (or badder) guy wins the showdown, Dan's dying words ring with icy truth that Pete cannot deny: "We cannot undo these things we've done." So Pete rides off alone and takes a header with his horse off a mountain.

That strange finish is just another one of the daring turns this song takes. It's as if Springsteen started off writing a John Ford movie and it transformed into one directed by David Lynch. The refrain "Can you hear me?" becomes especially haunting at song's end, since Pete is now an apparition calling from limbo to warn the living against repeating his mistakes.

Those who feel "Outlaw Pete" is too much of a departure for Springsteen might not be listening closely enough. After all, the street races and gang fights that filled his early narratives were always larger than life; "Outlaw Pete" just offers that grandiosity in a different setting. You could even say that the ambiguous ending, whereby no one can be sure of Pete's fate, is a throwback to the way that Zero and Blind Terry disappeared into the night way back when.

In any case, Springsteen's ambition is part of what makes him such an enduring artist. Experimental curve balls like this exciting track are testaments to his refusal to live off past glories. After all, as "Outlaw Pete" clearly shows, a healthy relationship with the past is integral to peace of mind in the present.

78. "Secret Garden" (from *Greatest Hits*, 1995)

The *Greatest Hits* album that Bruce Springsteen delivered in 1995 was long-awaited and yet was almost instantly a disappointment to critics and fans alike. First of all, the title alone painted Springsteen into a corner. It suggested that song selection would be tied to chart status and, if that were the case, half of the album should have come from *Born in the U.S.A.*

Instead, the "hits" portion of the album consisted of fourteen of Springsteen's most well-known classics, but including no songs from his first few albums while tacking on "Human Touch" and "Better Days" was a huge folly. Admittedly, creating a compilation for an artist whose albums are so coherent and thematic in nature is a hard job, and it's always better to stick with the original LPs for the true essence of Bruce, but *The Essential Bruce Springsteen*, which came out a few years down the road, is a much more comprehensive and representative sampler.

Springsteen also garnered a lot of publicity for the album by recording four new songs with the E Street Band in a sort of mini-reunion. All of these songs were solid, with "Murder Incorporated" rocking pretty righteously; "Blood Brothers" providing decent nostalgia; and "This Hard Land" adding some heartland credibility, albeit in a fashion perhaps a smidge too heavy-handed.

Ironically, the only one of these tracks that really soars is "Secret Garden," which has less of a band feel than any of the other songs recorded for the project. Perhaps that's because the song was left over from an unreleased solo album that Springsteen prepped but then scrapped circa 1994, a year before *Greatest Hits* was released.

Whereas the other new songs on the compilation sounded a bit derivative of past triumphs, "Secret Garden" wore its modern, adult, contemporary garb with pride. Built around a swirling three-note electronic keyboard riff from Danny Federici that both represents the way the narrator gets spun around and around by the object of his affection and creates an effective hook, the track weaves a gentle spell that's embellished by Springsteen's restrained yet sturdy vocal.

The lyrics have a similar vibe to Billy Joel's "She's Always a Woman," although they lack the aftertaste of subtle sexism that dogs that track. The narrator is focusing on a single woman but it's pretty clear that she represents all women in their unknowable splendor. One might think there were sexual connotations to the title "Secret Garden," but that's probably off-base because the narrator admits that intimacy of that kind is available to a suitor with the right moves. Yet the garden itself is unreachable.

Springsteen suggests that there are times when a woman will let you into the deepest corners of her heart and soul, and yet she can still keep something elemental locked away from even the most ardent pursuers. That part, he sings, "will always stay / a million miles away."

"Secret Garden" got an unexpected boost in popularity when it was used in the film *Jerry Maguire*, which prompted an enterprising DJ to splice bits of the film's dialogue into the finished recording. Springsteen graciously allowed this to happen and it did wonders for the song, which soared into the Top 20 two years after its initial release.

That version is an interesting trivia footnote, but it's best to stick to the original track. That way there is no distracting from the song's secret weapon: Clarence Clemons's beautiful saxophone solo to close out the song. In the liner notes to *Greatest Hits*, Springsteen writes simply of "Secret Garden," "Men + women . . . + the Big Man sweeter than ever."[9] That's really all you need to know about this lovely ballad, a song that can boast it is indeed a greatest hit and not be second-guessed at all.

77. "Because the Night" (from *The Promise*, 2010)

Like most great songwriters, Bruce Springsteen has spun some tunes that others turned into hits. "Fire" by the Pointer Sisters and "Light of Day" by Joan Jett were two among several that cracked the charts, and there have been numerous others that have been among the most popular songs for the artists who have recorded them.

The most successful of these cover versions of Bruce songs tend to be the ones that weren't first recorded and released by Springsteen. He has always had a backlog of material that results from his selectivity during the album-making process, and he's been generous about loaning those songs out.

Without the definitive Springsteen stamp on a song, cover artists are much freer to shape the song without having to live up to the original. Once he has put out his own take, perhaps the only alternative for a prospective cover artist to make an impact with a Springsteen song is to radically change it, as Manfred Mann did with "Blinded by the Light," but that's a tricky act to pull off.

Perhaps the most iconic Springsteen cover is Patti Smith's "Because the Night." Springsteen claimed in interviews around the time that Smith's hit version came out that all he had written was the title and Smith did the rest, but that was false modesty. In actuality, it seems from tapes of the *Darkness on the Edge of Town* sessions that Springsteen had the musical structure of the song intact along with the refrain. Only pieces of lyrics in the verses were missing.

Whatever the case, the song proved to be an anthem that didn't compromise the raw power of Smith's music but still was accessible enough for the pop masses to digest. And it is a fantastic performance that Smith delivers on her version, her vocals imbuing the lyrics with the anguish and desperation that shadow the kind of intense desire that the lyrics express.

Springsteen's studio take on the song with the E Street Band, which didn't see the light of day until the *Darkness* odds-and-ends collection

The Promise was released in 2010, pretty much sticks to the lyrics that Smith wrote. In concert, however, Springsteen has always toyed with the lyrics a bit, creating an angle about the protagonist's work life that suggests that his passionate moments with his lover provide an antidote to the banality of his modern life. Smith's take doesn't include any of that, implying that the passion is the sum total of her protagonist's existence.

It makes for an interesting contrast when comparing the two, but the song works in either version. That's because the lyrical trivialities aren't the elements that separate "Because the Night" from other rock songs expounding upon such a fiery romance. What really counts is the drama and the urgency inherent in the musical structure, which is Springsteen's most crucial contribution.

Since Smith's single borrows heavily from the arrangement used by the E Street Band, it's safe to assume that Springsteen engineer Jimmy Iovine, who was producing Smith's album *Easter*, simply brought the tape that Bruce provided for him and asked Smith's group to mimic it. The quiet-loud dynamic that the E Street band captures on the take found on *The Promise* and in a slew of live performances is expertly aped by Smith and company.

From that lonely piano to the tango-like rhythmic surge in the chorus and bridge to the key change in the closing moments, it is a thrilling track, one that captures all the reckless excitement and dangerous emotion that the lyrics suggest. Springsteen's version also benefits from the presence of Clarence Clemons blowing through the proceedings like a brass hurricane, so you have to score one for the E Street Band there if you're going to play the comparison game.

Still, the studio version of the song that Springsteen and the band performed and then locked away until *The Promise*, on which this ranking is based, is a tad restrained compared to some of the electrifying live performances that have made this song such a concert favorite. It's rare that Springsteen gets to play guitar hero in the studio, but concert readings of "Because the Night" allow him to unfurl and reflect the lustful energy of the words in the furious squalls of his axe.

Had Springsteen kept the song for a bit longer, worked the lyrics into shape, and released it on his own, it seems a safe bet that he would have had a hit single of his own on his hands. The fact that the song brought out the fire in a relatively mannered performer like Natalie Merchant of

10,000 Maniacs, who delivered a fine hit cover of their own in 1993, shows just how durable a construct it is.

All other versions, even his own, aside, Springsteen certainly found the perfect performing vessel for the song in Smith. No matter who plays and sings it, "Because the Night" is a powerful portrayal of the blurred lines between love and lust and of the yawning chasm that can envelop a person when all-consuming passion goes unfulfilled.

76. "Point Blank" (from *The River*, 1980)

One thing that's been lost in the CD era is the way that vinyl albums allowed artists to sequence two individual sides. Or, in the case of a double-album like Bruce Springsteen's *The River* from 1980, four sides.

Springsteen used the first songs on these sides as a way of telegraphing the kind of variety that would be evident in the entirety of the music. Three of the sides start with energetic rockers ("The Ties That Bind," "Hungry Heart," and "Ramrod") that really get the blood flowing. But side three, or the first side of the second album, starts off with the decidedly downcast "Point Blank."

The River was, after all, an album of stark contrasts, as Springsteen for the first time in his career tried intermingling the dark and the light. As he told interviewer Robert Hillburn, deciding to throw all of these conflicting emotions on one album was a hard concept for him to grasp. "I wasn't ready for some reason within myself to feel those things," he said. "It was too confusing, too paradoxical. But I finally got to a place where I realized life had paradoxes, a lot of them, and you've got to live with them."[10]

Such a thoughtful approach meant that there was a little something for everyone on the album. If you wanted to have a good time, "Ramrod" and "Sherry Darling" were always available to you. If you wanted to wallow, there were certainly those kinds of depths that you could plumb on the album as well. And those depths certainly don't get much lower than in "Point Blank."

Springsteen had tested the song two years earlier on the road during the tour following *Darkness on the Edge of Town* (you can hear it on the show from Houston included with *The Promise* box set); "Point Blank" certainly shares the kind of bleak outlook that was prevalent on that album. Yet the song was transformed both musically and lyrically in the time period between conception and execution, and that process was yet another example of how Springsteen's perfectionism with his material reaps great rewards.

In terms of the music, Springsteen always had the jazzy, nightclub feel for the song in place, but the earlier live versions included a section where the musical intensity ratchets up a bit with louder guitars and drums before returning to the quieter parts. By the time "Point Blank" made it to *The River*, it stayed quiet and sad all the way through, leaning heavily on Roy Bittan's insinuating piano part while the other instrumentalists just added subtle accents. This was the right choice, because there is no respite from the deluge for the character at the heart of the song, no chance for release, so it makes sense that the music should reflect that.

Lyrically, those early live versions made the drug use of the protagonist a much more explicit issue than it would be in the recorded version. The more crucial change came in the involvement of the narrator. He was more of an objective commentator on the proceedings in the song's earliest incarnation. In that way, "Point Blank" was an effective character sketch but maybe not much more.

In the version on *The River*, the narrator is much more a part of the girl's life, an ex whose pain at the way that she allows herself to be victimized is just as much a part of the song as the girl's downward spiral. "I was gonna be your Romeo you were gonna be my Juliet," he remembers, before comparing that idyllic vision to the reality: "These days you don't wait on Romeos you wait on that welfare check."

The narrator's deeper stakes in the song also clear the way for the memorable denouement. A long, detailed memory of the pair dancing, with all the sights, sounds, and emotions flooding back to the narrator, is contrasted to the previous night when he sees the girl hiding in the shadows "like just another stranger waitin' to get blown away."

As Dylan once sang of one of the denizens of "Desolation Row," "her sin is her lifelessness." Springsteen has his own plainspoken yet equally impactful take on the end result of that kind of yielding: "You wake up and you're dying / You don't even know what from."

The narrator's heart is broken here not just because he is separated from the girl but because she has been irrevocably altered by her willingness to take the easy way out and not fight against the nameless "They" that oppress her. "Point Blank" is the compelling, cautionary flip side to some of the more rousing songs on *The River*, proof that Springsteen's quest for a more balanced album could produce riveting results.

75. "Tougher Than the Rest" (from *Tunnel of Love*, 1987)

The touchstone album in rock history to which Bruce Springsteen's *Tunnel of Love* is most often compared is *Blood on the Tracks*, the 1975 masterpiece from Bob Dylan. This is because both albums are, in large part, meditations on doomed romance and both were written prior to the divorces of the artists who wrote and recorded them.

Neither of those two outstanding albums would be quite as affecting as they are if they had consisted of only one-sided diatribes or endlessly gloomy complaints. For example, *Blood on the Tracks* includes, among all the sadder stuff, the relatively hopeful (title notwithstanding) recap of an affair "You're Gonna Make Me Lonesome When You Go" and the rollicking Old West parable "Lily, Rosemary and the Jack of Hearts."

Providing this type of balance to a thematically unified album is a tough task because you run the risk of putting in a song for balance that ends up interrupting the album's flow. Springsteen himself made this mistake on the otherwise excellent *Wrecking Ball* with the sore-thumb outlier "You've Got It."

Tunnel of Love is handled much more nimbly in terms of the change-of-pace songs. "Tougher Than the Rest" is a prime example of a song on the album that alters the tone without breaking the spell. That's because even though it is a more optimistic view on potential romance, it's still realistic about the pitfalls and heartbreaks that hang heavy over some of the disc's more painful tracks.

There is an irresistible swagger to the music that immediately grabs the listener's attention, right from the one-two bass-snare drumbeat that will vibrate your innards in the best possible way. Springsteen's efficient, rumbling guitar solo captures the Sun Records feel of the entire recording, which is accentuated by Danny Federici's moody organ work. Bruce's harmonica solo at the end breaks out from the tempered feel of the rest of the recording with some serious emoting.

Springsteen's vocal here is right on point as well, steady and reassuring, which is just what the object of his romantic pleas would want to hear. In a way, he comes off like a gunslinger of a suitor, albeit the veteran type à la Clint Eastwood or Tommy Lee Jones, who doesn't say too much but gets his point across nonetheless.

Love is a process of elimination in the hardscrabble world of these characters: "Well 'round here baby / I learned you get what you can get." He is pitching this woman on a possible romance by telling it like it is, not like it should be. That credibility is the product of experience ("Well it ain't no secret / I've been around a time or two"), but it's what separates him from the rest of the rabble ("Maybe your other boyfriends couldn't pass the test"). Heck, the guy paraphrases Johnny Cash ("And it's a thin thin line / But I want you to know I'll walk it for you any time"), so there is little doubt as to his fortitude and spirit.

Over and over in the song, the narrator takes the measure of this girl to see if she too can withstand what's ahead of them should they proceed. "If you're rough and ready for love," he assures her, "Honey I'm tougher than the rest." "Tougher" here doesn't mean a guy who can beat up everybody else in the room. It refers to someone who can hold on through the inevitable hard times that are bound to ensue if this one-night stand leads to something more permanent.

Songs like this one are sneaky difficult because they can easily cross over into macho posturing, a fate that befell some of the songs on *Human Touch*. "Tougher Than the Rest" walks the line just right, however, giving hope that these two might just be sturdy enough for the future. After all, no one ever said that the *Tunnel of Love* can't have a few hard-earned smooth rides along with the inevitable derailments.

74. "With Every Wish" (from *Human Touch*, 1992)

Everything is relative, of course, and a lot of rock albums would pale in comparison to the standout LPs that Bruce Springsteen has released with regularity throughout his career. So maybe it's not fair to pick on *Human Touch* too much for being the weakest of all Springsteen's full-lengths, but it's impossible to deny.

There are many issues that keep the album from ever reaching the heights that so many of its predecessors and followers in the Springsteen catalog have reached. For perhaps the first time since his first two albums, the production (shared on the album by Springsteen, Jon Landau, Chuck Plotkin, and Roy Bittan) was not up to speed. It's probably the only Springsteen album that sounds clunky, with some songs coming off as undercooked ("Gloria's Eyes") and others seeming unbearably glossy ("Real Man").

You also get the feeling that Springsteen, who in the past had been so unerring about song selection and cohesion on his records, got a bit confused about what kind of album he was trying to make. At times, *Human Touch* feels like it wants to be a throwback soul album, but it never commits itself to that too long before returning to sterile modern rock. As a result, it's a little bit of everything but not enough of anything.

Fans have always been quick to blame the so-called Other Band, the studio pros that Springsteen used in lieu of the E Street Band (with the exception of Bittan) on the album, but in truth, that loose assemblage of musicians, which included on most tracks bassist Randy Jackson of *American Idol* fame and drummer Jeff Porcaro from Toto, acquit themselves well for what they're given. In truth, they weren't given enough because this is Springsteen's weakest collection of songs ever.

That's the main problem with *Human Touch*, but this being Springsteen, there's no way that he would come up completely empty. "With Every Wish," for example, is an underrated beauty, one that manages to sidestep many of the aforementioned problems that dog the album and benefits from a lovely bit of feigned autobiography by the songwriter.

There was likely never a time when Springsteen went cat-fishing in the swamps of Jersey as a boy. Yet the opening tale works as a parable about the dangers of going after what you want before realizing the consequences of getting it. That extends to the second verse, when the narrator talks about falling in love with his dream girl, only to have the relationship implode due to his jealousy and meanness. "Bobby, oh Bobby, you're such a fool," is the woman's reply, and it's clear that this guy, looking back, can understand that she was right.

All through his retrospective journey, the narrator is joined by the gorgeous, muted trumpet of Mark Isham. Isham is known for his movie scores in addition to his instrumental work, and his playing here gives the song a cinematic feel, lifting it out of its bare-bones folk-song structure into something more mysterious and magical.

After the lessons learned in the first two verses, you might think that the narrator would become tentative about leaping headlong into the unknown. Yet one of the themes that keeps popping up in the songs on this list is the necessity of fighting for the life you want instead of letting past failures and hardships become a self-fulfilling prophecy. So it makes sense then to hear the narrator once again excited about the possibility of a new romance with a girl "with a look in her eyes."

As he drifts along in the same mystical river that washed over him as a kid, he understands that caution can be practiced without lapsing into despair. "And though my heart's grown weary and more than a little bit shy," he sings, "tonight I'll drink from her waters to quench my thirst."

Throughout the song, the refrain warns, "With every wish there comes a curse." In the closing moments though, Springsteen sings, "With every wish . . . " and leaves the other part out. As Isham's trumpet goes gliding skyward, the final impression that "With Every Wish" leaves is one of hope, tempered and measured, but hope nonetheless. That's a classic Springsteen message in the midst of the rare album when that message got muddled.

73. "From Small Things (Big Things One Day Come)" (from *The Essential Bruce Springsteen*, 2003)

Upon its release in 1998, it was commonly assumed that *Tracks*, a three-CD exhumation of the outtakes, excess songs, alternate versions, and other ephemera from Bruce Springsteen's songwriting career, was a pretty comprehensive and definitive sweeping of the Boss's cutting-room floor. Yet subsequent years have proven that assumption to be off-base; heck, the guy gave us two CDs of extras from a single album a few years back (*The Promise*, which went deep into the *Darkness on the Edge of Town* sessions), so it's clear that the vaults are bottomless with this guy.

For fans seeking out some quality songs on a relatively unheralded release, they should check out the three-CD 2003 compilation *The Essential Bruce Springsteen*. The first two discs are highlights from his studio albums, but the third disc, originally released in a so-called Limited Edition but now readily available at most major online sites, collects some excellent songs that fell through the cracks.

Some were songs that Bruce did for movie soundtracks ("Dead Man Walkin'," "Missing"). Others became live classics over the years but had never been released ("Trapped"). In the case of "From Small Things (Big Things One Day Come)," the rollicking rocker that opens this set of oddities, it's one of those songs that first gained recognition through the cover version released by another artist.

British roots-rocker Dave Edmunds was introduced to Springsteen backstage at a Bruce show one night and was handed a tape by the Boss of "From Small Things," a song that he felt would fit Edmunds well. The rockabilly track was definitely right in Edmunds's wheelhouse, and it became both a highlight of his 1982 album *D.E. 7th* and a staple on compilations and retrospectives of this renowned artist.

Springsteen recorded his own version back in 1979 during the making of *The River*. Other than a little big-band coda tacked on by Edmunds to pad the running time a little bit, the respective versions are quite similar, both leaning heavily on the inviting, Chuck Berry–influenced groove and the tongue-in-cheek lyrics.

In the liner notes to *The Essential Bruce Springsteen*, Springsteen writes of the song, "I busted out my Gretsch 'country gentleman' guitar and the band drove the hell out of it in a take or two."[11] The edginess and vitality of the recording certainly can be attributed to the raw power that the band emanates, especially with Springsteen wielding that guitar with unstoppable force. Just the way he barks out the count-in indicates that the track is going to be a rip-snorter.

The song upends expectations at practically every turn. Even the title is ironic in a darkly comic sort of way since the "big things" that the girl at the heart of the story perpetrates are the abandonment of her kids, the cuckolding of her husband, and the murder of her new lover. It's also a bit of a twist on traditional gender roles that it's the woman who's doing the cheating and the killing throughout the song while the man sits at home, ever-faithful no matter how poorly he gets treated. Considering all the songs that Springsteen recorded for *The River* that centered on women who were beaten down by the drudgery of their lives, maybe this was a bit of wish fulfillment on his part.

Springsteen adds fun details throughout in much the same way Berry would to his classic ramblers. The "all-night hamburger stand" where the girl works even seems like a knowing throwback to that 1950s era of cars and girls that Berry brought to life so expertly. Springsteen seems to be sending up his own image as a writer of car songs a bit as well; the girl takes this automobile fetishism to the extreme when she gives the reason for offing her beau: "And when they caught her all she said was she couldn't stand the way he drove."

There's no real moral to this story, but that's fine because you wouldn't want anything weighing down the reckless fun of it all. Springsteen does his job on "From Small Things (Big Things One Day Come)" so well that you can practically see the poster for the movie version of this sizzling piece of pulp fiction.

72. "Downbound Train" (from *Born in the U.S.A.*, 1984)

Bruce Springsteen filled up an album with hard-luck tales of delusion and defeat in 1984, yet ended up with not just the biggest hit of his career but also one of the biggest hits of all time. The album was *Born in the U.S.A.*, and Springsteen pulled off this sleight of hand by couching the downcast stories in effervescent music.

It's a pattern that repeats itself all through the album. Things don't go very well for the guys at the heart of "Darlington County" and "Working on the Highway," but you'd never know it from the light-hearted melodies and ebullient arrangements. "Dancing in the Dark" and "Glory Days" are relentless in their depictions of midlife crises and still they paraded through the Top 10. The title track was the biggest trickster of all, making fans feel patriotic about the United States with the music while castigating the country in the lyrics.

Such tactics are delicate and can only be pulled off by the nimblest of songwriters, a group that certainly includes Springsteen. The one song on the album where he chose to simply allow the darkness of the lyrics to fully invade the music as well is "Downbound Train." It's a pretty bleak affair, although Springsteen and the band make it palatable with a compelling performance.

Born in the U.S.A. is the first album where Springsteen made heavy use of synthesizers, but he did it in such a way that it didn't betray the inherent earthiness of his music. The title track is just the most celebrated example. On "Downbound Train," the way the synths are played by Roy Bittan manages to add interesting shades to the song without allowing things to get too bright and take the sting out of the words.

Springsteen explained this technique to UK magazine *International Musician and Recording World* in a 1984 interview. "Like on 'Downbound Train,' it can sound pretty haunting," he said, describing the synthesizer. "It gets this real austere sound, and I liked that. A little bit of coolness" (139).[12] That coolness perfectly plays off the minor keys and ominous guitars within the song.

"Downbound Train" was originally included as one of the demos that became *Nebraska*, where it was performed at a much faster pace. It's one of the few survivors of the so-called Electric Nebraska sessions, whereby Springsteen attempted to beef up those stark demos with a full-band sound. What's interesting is that the subject matter, a man pushed to the limit by his dwindling work opportunities and the seemingly bottomless despair of his surroundings, could easily have fit in on 2012's *Wrecking Ball*, an album released thirty years after the song was written. Come to think about it, maybe depressing is a better way to describe that phenomenon than interesting.

The narrator quickly lets us in on his situation in the first few lines with his use of the past tense: "I had a job, I had a girl / I had something going mister in this world." What follows are descriptions of a never-ending series of occupations and of his constant torment, the whistle in his ears pushing him deeper and deeper into the depths of his misery even as he hallucinates the kiss of his ex-lover on his lips.

Speaking of hallucinations, the elongated final verse plays out like a fever dream that is representative of this character's tortured state of mind. It's possible to take it literally, since it's never expressly said that it isn't really happening, in which case the narrator would have to live within running distance of where the woman lives even though they're separated by an entire forest. It's more likely though that this guy's mind is playing tricks on him, buffeted as it is by the pressures of his life.

In any case, the build-up to the climax is painfully suspenseful, as the low whine of the keyboards hints to us that there is no chance for a happy reunion despite the man's insistence on her need for him. Instead, he ends up at his former home only to find it empty, at which point he collapses pitifully in tears.

Springsteen wisely realized that this was a tale that no amount of chiming organs or whooping and hollering could, or should, for that matter, ever lighten up. This "Downbound Train" may not ever stop its descent, and what really makes the song so potent is the realization that this poor soul isn't the only rider.

71. "The Hitter" (from *Devils and Dust*, 2005)

Anyone who thinks that Bruce Springsteen has mellowed somewhat as the years have passed would be hard-pressed to explain the severity and grit contained within 2005's "The Hitter." The song may not get the recognition of other songs because it's featured on *Devils and Dust*, an unheralded album in Springsteen's canon, but it demands your attention and commands your respect and fear when you hear it, much like the title character.

Springsteen wrote the song all the way back in 1995 during the tour supporting *The Ghost of Tom Joad*, only to come back to it and others written at the same time for *Devils and Dust*. In the case of "The Hitter," Springsteen fans have to be grateful for his reclamation project.

The song features a title character as nasty and unredeemable as perhaps any in the Springsteen catalog, a statement made truer when you include only those whom Bruce inhabits in their respective songs in the first person. "The Hitter" is reminiscent of something Randy Newman would have written in his heyday, a portrait of an unlikable, moral-free character whose powerful story still deserves to be told.

Sung by Springsteen in tones that barely get above a mumble in a flatlining melody that is prevented from getting too dull by the string accents in the margins, "The Hitter" tells the tale of a man whose only method of communication is brute-force violence. This beast didn't just emerge from nowhere as a battering ram of a human being, though; he had to have come from somewhere, which is why Springsteen frames his story around a visit home to his estranged mother so he can rest for the night.

Utilizing the freedom of the folk-song structure and the length of the song, Springsteen is able to really delve deep into this fellow's psyche. Forced from home at a young age and quickly hounded by the law, he finds that he has a talent that makes him useful to those much better off than him in society: "I knocked the men down, I did what I did, it come easily / Restraint and mercy, Ma, were always strangers to me."

The barbaric nature of the fights lets us in on the fact that the song is set in a bygone era of unregulated brawls. Our antihero rises to the level of champion only to take a dive for the money offered to him. When he throws the fight, he betrays his boxing skill, the one thing in his life that has been good to him, and at that moment whatever hope or fire still burning within him dies: "As they raised his arm my stomach twisted and the sky it went black."

It's at that point that he attempts to justify himself to his mother, but his words ring hollow until he takes her to task for her own betrayal of him so long ago. "Ma, if my voice now you don't recognize," he says, "then just open the door and look into your dark eyes." The implication is that his sins are hers as well.

Notice that the mother never actually opens the door in the song, even after all of the imploring done by her son. Whether he is even at her door or is just punch-drunk and hallucinating in the rain is certainly up for debate. What is for certain is that we leave him searching out yet another fight. Only his boxing takes place now, just as it did when he was a youth, outside the ring in the alleys and fields where there is no referee and no judge, just two men beating each other until one can no longer stand.

This is a song that's not for the timid of spirit. But it is songwriting of the highest order nonetheless. That's because Springsteen manages to elicit, if not sympathy, at least some understanding for "The Hitter," which is more mercy than the character would ever show to his unfortunate opponents.

70. "Ain't Good Enough for You" (from *The Promise*, 2010)

The premise behind *The Promise*—the 2010 reissue of *Darkness on the Edge of Town* that came with, among other cool extras, two CDs' worth of unreleased material from those sessions—was to show what might have been in the career of Bruce Springsteen. He is an artist who has accomplished huge mainstream success without ever compromising the purity of his artistic vision; in other words, he did it the hard way. *The Promise* is a look at an alternate universe where Springsteen would have simply given the people what they thought they wanted, as opposed to the way he's done it his entire career, which is to give the people what they didn't realize they wanted.

While some of *The Promise* is devoted to different versions of the songs that would populate *Darkness on the Edge of Town*, there is also a slew of poppy, crowd-pleasing songs that were either recorded during that time period or at least started before Springsteen and company went back in and cleaned them up for the 2010 release. These are the songs that likely could have slid right up the pop charts in 1978 alongside those of contemporaries like Billy Joel and Bob Seger and others of their ilk who enjoyed far more chart success than Springsteen, at least pre–*Born in the U.S.A.*

Yet those who would contest, based on the evidence presented on *The Promise*, that Springsteen could have guided his songwriting talent with the pop charts as his first priority and not lost the essence of what makes him great are probably off-base. What you get, for the most part, from those tracks is a strong sense of songcraft and pop-music history, but nothing really revelatory or unique.

As a result, most of the lighter songs from *The Promise* come off as fun and well-done but lacking consequence or impact. Springsteen seemed to be alluding to this in a 2010 interview shown on the Australian TV show *Sunday Night* when he defended his ultimate song selection for *Darkness*.

"It's frustrating that we made so much music that I was constantly rejecting," he said. "But I had good reasons, and in the end I think the choices I made were right. But at a very young age, I had a sense of purpose and of what I wanted the band to be about. I had a certain essential kind of record that was simply going to take me a while to get through. And a part of the process was I wrote a lot of music, you know, and then I culled it down to the toughest things I had and that's what became *Darkness on the Edge of Town*" (371).[13]

In other words, some of the songs left out lacked that toughness and essential quality. "Ain't Good Enough for You," however, may not have fit in with *Darkness*, but it's the one unreleased track from *The Promise* that marries easy accessibility with Springsteen's unique spark.

While it borrows a bit from the rhythm and blues of Springsteen favorite Gary U.S. Bonds and recalls some of the piano-driven pop that was a chart mainstay circa 1978, those influences are all fully filtered and come out firmly on E Street. Roy Bittan's piano has rarely been so recklessly tuneful, while the street-gang, call-and-response backing vocals take us back to "Spirit in the Night."

If there's one aspect of Bruce Springsteen's songwriting that is constantly underrated, it's the sense of humor that he displays in so many of his songs. Even though "Ain't Good Enough for You" is ostensibly the lament of a hapless guy in over his head with a girl he can't ever satisfy, there never seems to be too much at stake. After all, if this girl leaves him, he might be heartbroken for a while, but he'd better off in the long run.

Still, you get the sense that she's not going anywhere because she gets off on torturing this poor devil. Her complaints run the gamut from his lovemaking style to the loudness of his car. "Logic defies how you got stuck with me," he sarcastically whines, his most ardent entreaties constantly rebuffed: "End of the night I lean in for a kiss / Here comes the pitch, swing and a miss." Even name-dropping Jimmy Iovine doesn't do him any favors.

The whole thing swings and sways in all the right places as we the listeners laugh while this guy cries. It's clear the song would have landed with a thud on *Darkness*, and, as good as it is, it falls a bit short of the sublime raucousness of the similar "Sherry Darling," which probably kept it off *The River*. Yet "Ain't Good Enough for You" was always good enough to keep from falling through the cracks in the Springsteen songbook for too long. It's a blast and could have been a big hit, but it's also essential, and that's what really counts.

69. "Radio Nowhere" (from *Magic*, 2007)

"Is there anybody alive out there?" It's a question that Springsteen has asked tour audiences time and again in a way to elicit even louder cheers from already-deafening crowds. It's also a way for him to ask those people to commit to being in the moment, rough and ready, vigilant and responsible, engaged and invigorated not just there at the concert but in their lives once they leave the show and beyond.

The question takes on a much different tone in "Radio Nowhere," the firecracker opening track from Springsteen's 2007 album *Magic*. It is less a rallying cry in the song than it is a desperate plea from a lost soul who's trying to ascertain if he's the last person in the universe with the pulse and drive to recapture what has been lost in the modern wasteland we call Earth, or if he still has some kindred spirits somewhere in the night feeling the same hunger for connection.

"Radio Nowhere" was perfectly timed to answer any lingering doubts about Springsteen's viability as a rock-and-roll icon at that point in his career. He's been on such a great run of albums since *Magic* that it's easy to forget that his recorded output had been in a bit of swale right before the album's release.

That lull (and again, this discussion is relative to Springsteen's own career, with the acknowledgment that many artists would give anything to release music of the quality that Bruce did from 1992 to 2007) began with the somewhat disappointing double shot of *Human Touch* and *Lucky*

Town. Barring *The Ghost of Tom Joad* and *Devils and Dust*, which were more folk than rock and were generally seen as subordinate in that respect to the staggeringly great *Nebraska*, the only rock album released in that long span by Springsteen was *The Rising*, which earned him a lot of praise but doesn't hold up that well in retrospect, seeming more honorable than inspired.

So "Radio Nowhere" coming out of the box with such purpose and renewed energy seemed to be a good sign that Springsteen had recaptured whatever rock mojo he might have lost, and the music that he's released since then bears that out. This was he and the E Street Band at their blunt-force toughest, a quick reminder that the group could snarl and sting as well as they could swagger and sway.

The opening guitar riff is like an immediate punch in the face, cutting into Brendan O'Brien's dense production like a meat cleaver. Yes, those chords are similar to 1980s one-hit-wonder Tommy Tutone's "867-5309 (Jenny)," but that's really where that similarity ends. Tutone's song was New Wave chunky; "Radio Nowhere" is a blistering assault. All the needles seem to be pushed well into the red, with even Clarence Clemons's familiar sax made to sound serrated as it tries to answer the narrator's call in the wilderness.

Way back on *Nebraska*, Springsteen had characters in songs like "Open All Night" and "State Trooper" bemoaning the sad state of the radio dial. On "Radio Nowhere," the lone rider in the night takes this obsession with hearing good music to the extreme. He uses the music as a beacon, so he's rudderless when he can't find it: "I was tryin' to find my way home / But all I heard was a drone." Over and over, he cries, "I just want to hear some rhythm," as if his heart will only start beating properly with some accompaniment.

On the surface, "Radio Nowhere" is effective as a complaint about the homogeneity of modern music and the radio stations that play it. Not for nothing is Springsteen's narrator "searchin' for a mystery train," a reference to the iconic rock-and-roll song that carries the origins of the genre in its DNA. Yet the song is far more than just a plea for good tunes, because the music he craves represents the fading vestiges of purity and truth in a world full of artificiality and misdirection.

Springsteen talked about the song to *Rolling Stone* and explained how he was using an extreme setting to make a point about his job as an artist. "It's an end-of-the-world scenario—he's seeing the apocalypse," he said.

All communications are down: "Trying to find my way home / All I heard was a drone bouncing"—trying to connect to you. It comes down to trying to make people happy, feel less lonely, but also being a conduit for a dialogue about the events of the day, the issues that impact people's lives, personal and social and political and religious. That's how I always saw the job of our band. That was my service. At this point, I'm in the middle of a very long conversation with my audience.[14]

That conversation is far too profoundly entrenched at this point to ever be interrupted by even the gloomiest of future predictions for the music business as we know it. Yet "Radio Nowhere" hints that there is a lot more at stake here than just the absence of some great songs when you're driving late at night. What's in danger of being lost in a world full of noise is the human interaction and connection that sustains us all. When those lines become hopelessly crossed, Springsteen suggests, the gulf stretching out to the nearest living soul may become too daunting for even the most fearless traveler to cross.

68. "Adam Raised a Cain" (from *Darkness on the Edge of Town*, 1978)

When a child first catches adults out—when it first walks into his grave little head that adults do not always have divine intelligence, that their judgments are not always wise, their thinking true, their sentences just—his world falls into panic desolation. The gods are fallen and all safety gone. And there is one sure thing about the fall of gods: they do not fall a little; they crash and shatter or sink deeply into green muck. It is a tedious job to build them up again; they never quite shine. And the child's world is never quite whole again. It is an aching kind of growing.[15]

Based on the way that Bruce Springsteen has written about the relationship between father and son in many of his finest songs, you might assume that it was the Boss himself who gave the above quote. It actually comes from John Steinbeck's *East of Eden*, which is a sort of retelling of the biblical tale of Cain and Abel, which itself partly inspired "Adam Raised a Cain," Springsteen's searing rocker from *Darkness on the Edge of Town*.

It just goes to show that the subject matter has been popular for time immemorial and still no one has come anywhere near understanding its vast complexities. That didn't stop Springsteen from trying though, which is a good thing for his fans in this case. "Adam Raised a Cain" is as hard, dark, and true as anything Springsteen has ever written.

In a 1978 interview with *Creem* magazine, Springsteen was asked if he was indeed getting downright biblical with his listeners in the song. "I did read the Bible some," he said. "I tried to read it for a while a year ago. It's fascinating. I got into it quite a ways. Great stories. Actually, what happened was I was thinking of writing that particular song, and I went back trying to get a feeling for it" (86).[16]

He may have gone back to the oldest book there is to get a feel for the story, but the musical setting in which he placed it was vividly modern. The flickering electric guitar that starts the song eventually builds into anguished squeals in the solo. Even with the hard-rock trappings of the guitar, Garry Tallent's bass line is inherently soulful, keeping things from getting too sludgy. The backing vocals sound like they're emanating from some ghostly chain gang.

It's probably a bit of a stretch to look at the musical landscape at the time and say that this was Springsteen's answer to punk. While he may have been attempting a bracing kind of sound, the musicality of the song is just as much a part of its success as its raw power. Maybe a better comparison would be the primal-scream rock that John Lennon undertook on his *John Lennon/Plastic Ono Band* album. Springsteen's raspy howls certainly recall Lennon's wild screaming on that landmark record.

"Adam Raised a Cain" begins with a baptism, but what the narrator realizes is that the rite that is supposed to introduce a child to religion instead simply begins the suffering he was preordained to feel. It's a suffering that will be passed along to him by his father, bound as they are by their familial connection: "With the same hot blood burnin' in our veins."

The song struggles with the notion that a son should naturally follow his father. "They fit you with position and the keys to your daddy's Cadillac," he sings, a Cadillac that might as well be the black one carting your body away from the church for the meager opportunity such a life will afford. After all, this father's life is not one anybody in their right mind would ever want to live: "Daddy worked his whole life for nothing but the pain."

Such a life breeds resentment that builds up until it explodes onto others in the vicinity: "Now he walks these empty rooms looking for something to blame." The narrator can't make sense of why it happens, but to paraphrase another *Darkness* song, at least he has his facts straight at the end: "You're born into this life paying for the sins of somebody else's past."

Much of what makes *Darkness on the Edge of Town* such a striking album is its fearlessness in detailing the bleaker aspects of life, "the dark heart of a dream" as it's so hauntingly described here. If it all begins with children and parents, then that dark heart beats most purely in "Adam Raised a Cain," a song where a son goes wallowing into the "green muck" that Steinbeck described and comes up a little wiser and a lot dirtier.

67. "One Step Up" (from *Tunnel of Love*, 1987)

The title of this track from the sublime *Tunnel of Love* is a bit misleading, pretending in a way that the second half of the phrase ("two steps back") doesn't exist. That makes it completely appropriate, because a song about two people clinging to a spent marriage should have a title that's in denial.

Certainly the two participants in "One Step Up" are kidding themselves in their hope that their relationship will somehow reboot and reach the kind of heights it once scaled. The woman is deluded in thinking that their fairytale lives can ever be restored. The man is deluded in thinking that he can make things right simply by putting in the work and going through the daily drudgery of their lives.

It's a bit of a miracle that this song, as unflinchingly honest as it is about detailing a relationship in the midst of implosion, snuck into the Top 20 back when it was released. That says something about Springsteen's towering popularity at the time, the afterglow of *Born in the U.S.A.* still bathing the darker material on *Tunnel of Love*.

Yet credit also goes to Springsteen for doing a fine job of creating music on this solo recording that both suits the lyrics and makes a subtle impression on its own. The instruments, for the most part, are trapped in patterns, like the folk riff of the acoustic guitar and the thumping timpani drum beat. It's a musical microcosm of the hamster-wheel lives that the protagonists are living, going around and around, never progressing, inevitably regressing. Only the distant, mournful guitar in the breaks tries to let its pain be known to the world.

Everything in this guy's life has broken down in one way or another. Utilitarian products like the car and the furnace make his day a chore, while metaphorical joy-givers like singing birds and wedding bells are notably absent. Note that the bride is at the church, but the fact that the bells have been stilled suggests that her groom has checked out on the big day.

The narrator tells his story from a bar stool, which, along with Springsteen's emerging twang and the little Nashville twists in the tune, gives "One Step Up" the sheen of a country weeper on its surface. Yet Springsteen goes deeper than the average tear-in-my-beer clichés and really cuts to the splintering heart of the relationship.

What really seems to be killing the narrator is the redundancy of it all; he bemoans how the story replays itself night after night, from the fights to his eventual escapes to the bar. He's honest enough to look in the mirror and see his faults, but he seems to lack the drive to do anything about them.

The last verse is a real gem, Springsteen capturing the rollercoaster ride going on in this guy's mind and heart with chilling accuracy. First, he explores the notion of adultery with a stranger giving him the eye: "Mmm she ain't lookin' too married / And me well honey I'm pretendin'."

Yet even as he admits this, he recounts a dream from the previous night that seems to be a memory of better days when the two were inseparable: "We danced as the evening sky faded to black." As the intermingled, wordless voices of Springsteen and Patti Scialfa coo through the fade-out in "One Step Up," we can only guess if he made his way across the bar to the stranger or, inspired by the dream, paid his tab and headed home. In either case, it seems like a no-win for him, just one more delusion for the road.

66. "Linda Will You Let Me Be The One" (from *Tracks*, 1998)

Bruce Springsteen is known for writing so many songs for his albums that no full-length album, no matter how much it's elongated, could ever contain them all. That didn't happen, however, with the album that many regard as his all-time classic, for there are very few extra songs known to exist from the *Born to Run* sessions.

By all accounts, these sessions were pressure-packed for Springsteen, since he was in danger of being labeled a flop and possibly even being dropped from his record deal if the album didn't outperform its two predecessors. Add in the fact that there were time constraints to deliver the album, and it's understandable that he couldn't afford the luxury of writing dozens of songs. He had to get the ones he had written just right.

History proved that he did just that, but there is one especially fascinating excess song that emanated from that time that eventually showed up on *Tracks*. "Linda Will You Let Me Be The One" shows Springsteen and the E Street Band honoring his classic pop influences while still imbuing the song with the kind of tragic romanticism that was his calling card circa 1975. It's a beautiful and haunting song, simple yet as deep as the gash of a broken heart.

The most obvious touchstone for the recording is "Be My Baby," the classic hit by the Ronettes that was produced by Phil Spector. It's become a misleading cliché of sorts to refer to *Born to Run* as Springsteen's Wall of Sound album in reference to the famously dense and lush productions that Spector favored in his early 1960s heyday. In truth, only the title track really pays that kind of obvious homage to Spector; the rest of the album glides between driving rock, aching balladry, and soulful exultation, sometimes all within the course of a single song, but there are not really too many Spectorian touches to be found.

"Linda Will You Let Me Be The One," had it made the album, certainly would have made those references to Spector's influence on the proceedings more accurate. It mimics the oft-copied "Be My Baby" rhythm, while Roy Bittan's staccato piano overlay also harkens back to that inimitable portrait of teen romance. Danny Federici's organ glides subtly in whatever open spaces it can find, and all the instrumentalists make way for Clarence Clemons's powerful sax solo.

This is yet another example of the E Street Band borrowing from an iconic recording without being too slavish to it, keeping the band's chemistry and personality intact in the process. Springsteen does the same with the lyrics; the chorus is essentially Eddie asking Linda to be his baby, but the verses allow for the kind of poetic exposition that Springsteen pulls off with ease.

Springsteen has always had a soft spot for characters who act out, even if impulsively and foolishly, as opposed to those who let their surroundings dictate their situations, those who "stand back and let it all be," as he famously sang in "Jungleland." Eddie is definitely one of those favored aggressors, doing everything to the extreme, whether he's fighting or crying or slashing Linda's name in her father's car seat.

The descriptions, as usual, are fantastically evocative, such as Eddie "walkin' like an angel in defeat." Once again, we're in a larger-than-life, West-Side-Story world of gangs and forbidden romance, but the quieter moments make it all relatable, like the way Eddie hides his weary body from the rain in a church basement or how he wraps Linda's scarves around him to feel close to her in his lowest state.

For all of these grace notes, the most potent moments in the song come during the refrains, Springsteen inhabiting this James Dean–like character to ask Linda, with touching vulnerability, if she'll join him in his wild exploits. The question is never answered, but those wistful chord changes lead us to believe it might not ever happen, maybe because Eddie's dangerous life might expire before it can occur, maybe because Linda can't stand the pain this love would no doubt cause.

That's just one more way "Linda Will You Let Me Be The One" splinters off from its main influence. Those classic pop songs always expected an affirmative answer that would last forever, but "Linda Will You Let Me Be The One" expects nothing more than fleeting joy before the tragic part of this romance takes hold.

65. "American Skin (41 Shots)" (from *Live in New York City*, 2001)

"American Skin (41 Shots)" is relatively rare in the Bruce Springsteen catalog in that only a live version is available at this time for his fans to purchase. Springsteen wrote and began performing the song in 2000 while on his reunion tour with the E Street Band, eventually releasing it on the *Live in New York City* CD that came out in 2001. He did complete a studio version, but that was only released as a promotional copy.

That's not the only unique aspect of this haunting and brave song. It's maybe the only time that Springsteen has ever released a song related directly to a current event. He has written scores of songs that delve into topical issues, but these are generally less specific in nature and not usually tied to a single event.

In the case of "American Skin (41 Shots)," the subtitle refers to the number of gunshots fired by four New York City police officers at unarmed West African immigrant Amadou Diallo on February 4, 1999, killing him. The officers allegedly mistook Diallo's reaching for his wallet for the possibility that he had a weapon and responded with the gunfire. The four officers were found innocent of murder charges by a jury; New York City later paid a $3 million settlement to Diallo's family.

When news of Springsteen's new song leaked in 2000, he was greeted by a mixture of praise and outrage. Considering that it had only been performed in certain cities, many of those who were critical had not actually heard "American Skin (41 Shots)" before speaking out. Had they listened, they would have heard a song that doesn't take sides but rather assesses the perspectives of all of the participants to see why such a tragedy had to happen.

For those who were willing to come down hard on Springsteen, they should compare his approach to the one taken by Bob Dylan in his own songs based on current events. Dylan fudged the facts surrounding the cases behind "The Lonesome Death of Hattie Carroll" and "Hurricane" and did so unapologetically in his efforts to prove the case of the side he favored. The resulting songs are extremely powerful and persuasive, even as they inevitably anger many listeners who take the other side.

Springsteen's approach refrains from placing blame. In the first verse, he depicts a grief-stricken officer praying for the life of the victim of this tragedy. In the second, he imagines a mother warning her young son on the proper way to deal with police officers if confronted by them to prevent any tragic misunderstandings.

If Springsteen proceeds with caution in his lyrics, he doesn't hold anything back musically. Partly reminiscent of the arrangement of Jimmy Cliff's "Trapped" that has become such a live staple of the E Street Band, "American Skin" builds from an ominous keyboard riff into a full-fledged band attack as the song progresses. The performance on *Live in New York City* is a juggernaut, from Springsteen's anguished guitar solo to Clarence Clemons's quiet saxophone benediction to close out the song.

One thing that Springsteen has in common with Dylan's approach is that just as Bob never had to mention that Hattie Carroll was a black woman, Bruce never mentions how racial tensions are at the heart of his song. In his book *Bruce Springsteen: Songs*, Springsteen wrote about the main message that should be taken away from "American Skin": "Here is what systemic racial injustice, fear, and paranoia do to our children, our loved ones, ourselves. Here is the price in blood."[17]

In "American Skin," that blood doesn't just belong to the victim; Springsteen sings, "Baptized in these waters / And in each other's blood." It is an all-inclusive, terrible rite that we share when tragedies like the one that befell Amadou Diallo take place, when death results from the wrong answer in a game of chance: "Is it a gun, is it a knife / Is it a wallet, this is your life."

"American Skin (41 Shots)" doesn't rank higher on this list because it's probably too emotionally raw to be as artful as some of Springsteen's very best, but the thoughtful and empathetic spirit of the song along with the wonderful performance carry it a long, long way. Sometimes the job of an artist goes beyond pleasing an audience to challenging them, making them reflect on painful truths and divisive issues, risking controversy and the potential alienation of part of that audience in the process. That's where integrity comes into play, and there are few musicians in the ballpark of Bruce Springsteen in that department.

In the *Live in New York City* version of the song, Springsteen asks the crowd for quiet at the beginning. Maybe he knew that he could get everyone in that crowd to hear his important message to help tip the balance against those who might never listen.

64. "Happy" (from *Tracks*, 1998)

Bruce Springsteen has often in interviews half-jokingly referred to the relatively poor reception of his 1992 albums *Human Touch* and *Lucky Town* received as a time when he finally started writing happy songs only to have his audience dislike them. Although there is probably something to what Springsteen is implying since, other than perhaps the Beatles, it's hard to name any rock legends who recorded upbeat songs as affecting as downcast ones, it's also true that Springsteen didn't quite rise to the occasion with his best material on these albums.

Had he written a few more happy songs as lovely and deeply felt as "Happy," he might have earned a better reaction to those albums. The song languished until appearing on *Tracks* in 1998, where it immediately stood out as one of the prettiest love ballads that Springsteen has ever created.

The *Tracks* liner notes list the song as having been recorded in January of 1992, which, if correct, means that the song was a little late to have been considered for inclusion on *Human Touch* or *Lucky Town*. However, the band and production personnel and the location of the recording suggests that the liner notes may have been mistaken and that the song was actually recorded a year earlier in the early stages of the *Human Touch* sessions.

If that's the case, it makes "Happy" one of the few occasions when Springsteen probably made a poor selection in terms of choosing songs for an album. Including such an optimistic yet not overly sappy view of romance would have made a nice contrast to some of the macho rockers on the album (in addition to providing a counterpart to the similarly themed "If I Should Fall Behind" on *Lucky Town*).

Sitting on top of a comfortable bed of keyboards provided by Roy Bittan, Springsteen begins by listing some of the crutches that people use to get them through their existence: wealth, drugs, even religion, the latter a bit of an eye-opener from a guy who has always exuded in his songs a pretty powerful faith.

Echoes of that faith return in the second verse with an image of an idyllic family home protected by angels. Even that perfection is hounded by shadows: "At night I feel the darkness near." In that context, his love represents not just happiness, but also deliverance from this darkness.

Notice how the bridge finds Springsteen, one of rock's great dreamers, presenting his reveries almost as if they were traps into which one can fall unsuspectingly. "Lost in a dream, you caught me as I fell, now / I need more than just a dream to tell." He is stripping away all his old attachments, tangible and intangible, for full immersion in his newfound joy.

The last verse is a beauty, as Springsteen describes the self-destructive dance done by men and women who can't escape the prison of selfishness that has confounded couples for ages. This pair won't make the same mistake: "Lost and running 'neath a million dead stars / Tonight let's shed our skins and slip these bars."

In the chorus, drummer Shawn Pelton strikes his timpani in a way that recalls Roy Orbison's "Crying." Surely Springsteen intended the similarity to show the fine line between the bliss his protagonist is feeling and the polar opposite that's always lurking. Maybe that hint of the unfortunate flipside is why "Happy" succeeds on a level that Springsteen's other "happy" songs from that era can't quite match. The glimpses of the darkness make the light seem that much more radiant.

63. "We Are Alive" (from *Wrecking Ball*, 2012)

Springsteen's knack for sequencing his albums with the deftest touch possible clearly hasn't abandoned him after forty years of recording. To wit, consider his 2012 album *Wrecking Ball*, a fierce cry for justice and accountability for the brazen wrongdoers in the United States and an exhortation for those on the wrong end of the stick to stay vigilant and strong.

The obvious way to end the album would have been a song that summed up all of the tumult, anguish, and soul-deadening suffering that the rest of the album had detailed. Instead, Springsteen delivers "We Are Alive," a song that mines a powerful vein of hope in a graveyard, of all places.

Wrecking Ball is a revelatory album for a number of reasons, not the least being that, so many years into his career, Springsteen found a new musical avenue to tread. On his 2006 side project *We Shall Overcome: The Seeger Sessions*, Springsteen delved deep into the roots of folk music. On *Wrecking Ball*, he took those vintage sounds and wedged them into anachronistic settings full of samples and loops. The result was a marriage of the old and the new that made Springsteen sound as vigorous as he had in three decades.

"We Are Alive" is an excellent example of some of that alchemy, albeit one that leans further to the "old" side of the equation than other tracks on the album. But the experimental nature of it is in keeping with the rest of the songs, as the track combines banjo, mariachi horns, whistles, and handclaps into a thrilling stew, with a dash of Johnny Cash's "Ring of Fire" thrown in for good measure.

This is more than just a ghost story or a campfire yarn that Springsteen is telling to scare us at the end of a harrowing album. "We Are Alive" is a story of the resilience and persistence of the dead in terms of their lingering influence on the living. The song also endeavors to clarify the message we should be receiving when we cup our ears and arch our heads to hear their faint cries.

Springsteen places his magical graveyard right at the foot of Calvary Hill, suggesting that the eternal life of these dead is not the result of black magic but rather the product of faith. Their intent is not to haunt or burden the living, but to inspire: "To carry the fire and light the spark / To stand shoulder to shoulder and heart to heart."

The second verse is a roster of martyrs whose earthly lives were spent in pursuit of some sort of ideal, the kind of ideal betrayed time and time again by nefarious characters in other songs on *Wrecking Ball*. The railroad workers, civil rights advocates, and struggling immigrants are all contained beneath this umbrella, all united in their corporeal final resting place.

But what rests in the graves isn't important anyway, as the bridge suggests: "Let your mind rest easy, sleep well my friend / It's only our bodies that betray us in the end." That reassurance goes a long way toward salving the wounds that the living have been enduring for the entirety of the album.

Springsteen often utilizes a portentous dream to deliver his ultimate point within a song, but in the case of "We Are Alive," his protagonist wakes up to his moment of truth. He finds himself buried, and as he describes his terrifying surroundings and tries to extricate himself, the stomping backbeat presages joy rather than terror. Sure enough, he finally hears the voices of his dead brethren, and "the earth rose above me / my eyes filled with sky." The chorus comes around one more time, promising that "our souls and spirits rise," before Springsteen whistles that indestructible Cash hook one more time as the song and album end.

"We Are Alive" is really ingenious in terms of the different ways it can be heard. One can hear the chorus as the dead showing the kind of zest for life that Springsteen has always saved for his favorite characters, the same kind of spirit that those who are indeed still alive need to show in their darkest times.

Or that chorus can be Springsteen's way of giving voice to those who have been marginalized and trivialized throughout the album's previous songs, a kind of wish fulfillment on his part that those people will indeed rise from their figurative graves and reclaim the inner fire that not even the lowliest of scoundrels could ever extinguish.

In short, "We Are Alive" answers a question that Bruce has been asking of his crowds in concert for years. It turns out there are more people alive out there than you think; they just need to be reminded of it once in a while.

62. "Cover Me" (from *Born in the U.S.A.*, 1984)

There is an inherent bias that some connoisseurs of the best rock music have against hit songs. The feeling is that the songs that break out of the pack and make it big might have done so by appealing to the lowest common denominator, thereby allowing them to reach the biggest possible audience. In many cases, this is hogwash, but you'll often hear folks who dearly love an artist say something to the effect that "the hits are the weakest songs on the album."

For an artist like Bruce Springsteen whose main concern has always been creating the best possible albums and, for the most part, letting the chips fall where they may in terms of hit singles, it's understandable that he might be swayed by a similar bias. *Born in the U.S.A.* represented a slight change in his hardness toward songs ready for mass consumption, but Springsteen didn't change his mind easily.

Two Hearts: The Definitive Bruce Springsteen Biography, Dave Marsh's definitive biography of the first thirty years of Springsteen's recording career, does an exhaustive and outstanding job of recounting the seemingly endless process of recording and choosing the songs that went on *Born in the U.S.A.* Apparently the big sticking point was Springsteen's reluctance to include several songs that he considered a bit lightweight but that producer Jon Landau and engineer Chuck Plotkin heard as surefire hits.

Chief among these was "Cover Me," a song that Springsteen originally wrote with the intent of giving it away to pop-disco megastar Donna Summer, who was then at the acme of her popularity. When Landau heard the finished product, he immediately stepped in and urged Bruce to keep the song. Springsteen relented and eventually donated another song, "Protection," to Summer, but he still failed to see the merits of "Cover Me" for months until eventually relenting to the opinions of those working with him.

Whoever ultimately swayed him, he or she or they deserve a lot of credit for bringing this crunching rocker to the fore. Springsteen must have come around as well, since he chose the song for the second single off the album. This was a crucial choice, one Springsteen had bungled in the past.

Back in 1980, Springsteen made his deepest ever (at that time) dent on the pop charts with "Hungry Heart" to introduce *The River* to the world.

It was his first incursion into the Top 10, but for the follow-up single, he chose the relatively pedestrian soul ballad "Fade Away," which only made it to No. 20 and squandered the momentum that "Hungry Heart" had built. It's conceivable that the selection kept *The River* from attaining the kind of sales and widespread popularity that would elude Springsteen for another four years.

By contrast, "Cover Me" managed to keep the ball rolling after "Dancing in the Dark" kicked off *Born in the U.S.A.* by being Springsteen's biggest hit single ever (reaching #2 on *Billboard.*) "Cover Me" came right back at No. 7, which was all the more impressive considering that Springsteen made no video to accompany the song, a rarity in those days of MTV's dominance over the music scene.

It's easy to hear why the song was a smash. The rat-a-tat guitar rhythm that Springsteen fashioned for the song is a hook that keeps on giving throughout the entirety of the track. He adds to that with one of his most powerful and concise guitar solos in the break, accentuating the song's inherent urgency.

Maybe Springsteen was concerned originally by what he perceived as the simplicity of the lyrics. The words may lack fanciness, but they more than make up for it with the primal need they express. When you connect their directness with the force with which Springsteen sings them, a line like "Well I'm looking for a lover who will come on in and cover me" takes on all the meaning in the world.

The power in the song lies in the way it reveals how a good relationship can stem any tide and solve any problem, at least temporarily. The blindness Springsteen describes is actually love's bliss, the ability to shut out the rest of the world, even with "the wild wind blowing." Yet the desperation of the music hints that such a port in the storm isn't easy to find and is even harder to maintain.

So we can forgive Springsteen's initial reticence to unleash this powerhouse on the world. The important thing is that he came around to "Cover Me," a hit single as worthy as any deep cut, in time.

61. "Factory" (from *Darkness on the Edge of Town*, 1978)

Bruce Springsteen's first three albums were populated with a lovable but motley crew of big-hearted gang members, teenage femme fatales, and other spectacularly romantic rogues who lived lives that seemed to consist only of wild summer nights. The only folks who seemed to have jobs in his songs, legitimate jobs anyway, were the cops who tended to rain on everybody's parade.

On *Darkness on the Edge of Town*, all those wonderfully unburdened kids had to grow up and get a job, and it wasn't pretty. Most of the songs on the album made passing reference to some sort of job or work that the protagonists had to endure. The resulting shift in the tone of the music on the album was telling, as Springsteen veered from florid, almost operatic arrangements to stark, guitar-driven cries of raw pain.

"Factory" is the poster child for the drudgery that Springsteen's suddenly employed characters are forced to face. The only difference in this case is that the protagonist is not the one doing the work; he is actually remembering the harsh working life of his father. And without making any kind of editorial comment on it, the narrator still manages to make it harrowingly clear that it is a life he wishes to avoid at all costs.

Springsteen was writing autobiographically in "Factory," reflecting on his father's own experience. In a 1998 television interview with Charlie Rose, Springsteen contrasted the fulfilling work experience he witnessed his mother have with the debilitating conditions that his father suffered at his factory job. As opposed to his mother who "walked with tremendous pride and enormous strength" to and from work each day, his father's work "was involved with pain," Springsteen explained; "He lost a lot of his hearing when he worked in a plastics factory" (274).[18]

So it is that in "Factory," Springsteen sings, "Factory takes his hearing." Yet note that he completes that line by singing, "Factory gives him life." That's the dichotomy that Springsteen is attempting to reconcile as an adult songwriter so many years after he witnessed it all as a child. Yes, it was a terrible job that his father had to do, but at least it gave him a purpose while he had it. In that same interview with Rose, Springsteen said of his dad, "He struggled to find work and go to work. The regulation of behavior that work provides wasn't a big part of his life, and that was painful for everybody involved."

In other words, you're damned if you do and damned if you don't. The faceless working men who populate "Factory" at least have reliable jobs, but what is the price they pay? They must travel "through the mansions of fear, through the mansions of pain." On their way out, "men walk through these gates with death in their eyes."

But theirs is not the only suffering in this song. In the final verse, as the men complete their working day, Springsteen anticipates what lies ahead: "And you just better believe, boy, somebody's gonna get hurt tonight." The implication is that when these men get home to their family, all the innumerable slights and pent-up rage that built up over the course of their long shift will manifest themselves in violence against their wives and children.

It's not a pretty story, but it's notable that Springsteen did not use on this particular track the kind of arrangements he favored throughout *Darkness on the Edge of Town*. Most of the album is comprised of raw, howling rock, only occasionally prettied up to signify the slightest tinges of hope. "Factory," on the other hand, is a country ballad, the first time ever on record that the E Street Band had taken their cues from Nashville instead of New York or Detroit.

They took to the new challenge with aplomb. In particular, Roy Bittan on piano and Danny Federici on organ are wonderful here. The chemistry between the two in terms of knowing when to step up to be the focus and when to back off and let the other emerge is nothing short of magical. In their soulful exchanges, the two prove that pain and sorrow can be expressed with elegant restraint, as opposed to the forceful musical emoting that the other songs on the album favor.

Springsteen efficiently expresses the mind-numbing, soul-crushing mundaneness of working at a job like the one he describes here. In three short verses, he covers an entire day of work and all of the subtle defeat that goes with it. Note how he sings, "The working, the working, just the working life," repeating that word three times to drive home the endless, repetitive cycle of waking, working, and suffering.

In many ways, the men in "Factory" never really reach the end of the day since their work haunts every moment of their dreary existence. Springsteen does these men great honor by exposing their jobs as the slow deaths that they are.

60. "Nebraska" (from *Nebraska*, 1982)

It's easy to look back at it now and see that Bruce Springsteen's decision to release his original acoustic demos as the album *Nebraska* was the proper choice to serve those songs, but at the time it had to have been a difficult choice. After all, 1982 was an era when popular music was focused on the bright and brassy, all the better to translate to the music videos that were beginning to overwhelm the scene.

Remember that this was a time well before the whole "unplugged" movement made an album like *Nebraska* a badge of credibility for rock artists rather than the serious departure that it was back in 1982. Not to mention the fact that Springsteen was essentially taking one on the commercial chin for his legacy, sacrificing the possibility of hit singles and big album sales and doing so on the heels of *The River*, which was his biggest success in those two departments.

But really, how else could a song like "Nebraska" possibly be rendered? Only the Woody Guthrie modesty of the folk melody and the harmonica wheeze that seemed like wind on the infinite plains could possibly have fit. Yet Springsteen had to commit to songs like these in the face of commercial pressures and audience expectations, so for that he can't be commended enough.

He also deserves credit for diving into subject matter so dark. Like an actor who plays the role of a serial killer, it had to be somewhat daunting for Springsteen to slip inside the mind of serial killer Charles Starkweather, who, at age nineteen, killed eleven people in a 1957–1958 killing spree in Wyoming and Montana, ten murders of which came in the company of his fourteen-year-old girlfriend Caril Ann Fugate.

Springsteen realized that there is worth in such an exercise that goes beyond morbid curiosity. It serves as an object lesson to warn against what happens when some members of society, for whatever reason, become detached from the fabric of that society. "That whole *Nebraska* album was just that isolation thing, and what that does to you," he told the UK magazine *International Musical and Recording World* in 1984. "And when that happens, there's just a whole breakdown. When you lose that sense of community, there's some spiritual breakdown that occurs. And when that occurs, you just get shot off somewhere where nothing seems to matter" (134).[19]

The easiest way to write this song would have been to do so from a third-person perspective, allowing for an omniscient narrator to detail and condemn the horrendous acts Starkweather committed. But using that approach wouldn't have brought much more to the table than that which could have been gleaned from media reports. By imagining the thought process of that individual, however misguided and askew it might have been, Springsteen tries to put a finger on the reasons such a person would snap. The eternal question "Why would someone do such a thing?" is the question he's trying to answer.

He does this by skimping on the details of the crimes. In fact, the way that Springsteen's Starkweather describes them in the song, it makes it seem like he was a passive bystander to these murders, that they were almost beyond his control: "Me and her went for a ride, sir, and ten innocent people died."

Springsteen did his due diligence and researched the story, but his imagination provides the most illuminating components of the song, with a little help from a classic American writer. As he told Will Percy of *Double Take* magazine in 1998, Springsteen drew on the influence of Flannery O' Connor's stories for the entire *Nebraska* album. "She got to the heart of some part of meanness that she never spelled out, because if she spelled it out you wouldn't be getting it," he said of O'Connor. "It was always at the core of every one of her stories—the way that she'd left that hole there, that hole that's inside of everybody" (247).[20]

That "meanness" comes out of Starkweather's mouth at the end of "Nebraska" when he's asked for his motives: "Well, sir, I guess there's just a meanness in this world." That void so prominent in O'Connor's stories is a part of Springsteen's song as well because he refuses to provide Starkweather with any easy answers.

Springsteen doesn't let off Starkweather easy; his selfishness to the end and lack of remorse for his victims come through in the way his only concern on the electric chair is whether or not Fugate will join him there. But Springsteen dares to hint at a larger malaise particularly harsh on twisted individuals already teetering on the edge, a malaise that continues to infect the country to this day. It's what makes "Nebraska" so terribly relevant more than a half-century since the killer at the heart of the song died for his crimes.

59. "Ricky Wants a Man of Her Own" (from *Tracks*, 1998)

Bruce Springsteen has written, recorded, and released many songs that cut to the heart of the emotions and desires roiling deep inside of us. Through his music, he has eloquently elaborated on some of the most pressing social issues of our time. He has also bestowed upon us some of the most memorable characters in the history of rock music, characters who sometimes come from the wells of his imagination and sometimes serve as a proxy for what's going on in his own life.

All that is true about Springsteen, but very few artists have been able to create so many songs that are pure, unadulterated fun as he has over the years. That fun is evident in the performances that Springsteen and, in most cases, the E Street band give on these songs, and it rubs off on the listeners who get to enjoy them. So it is that a seeming throwaway like "Ricky Wants a Man of Her Own" can rank so well on this distinguished list of songs among some of its more proper siblings.

One of the things that separates Springsteen from many of his contemporaries and puts him in the same league as the Dylans and Beatles of the world is his ability to strike a balance between the serious and the silly. Sometimes he does this within the course of a single album, à la *The River*. At other times, he records fun songs that don't fit the tone of a specific album, but, thankfully, collections of excess material like *Tracks* allows them their proper time in the spotlight.

Springsteen, who was a devout fan of rock and roll and the other genres of music that feed into it long before he ever got a chance to play, has always understood the value of such songs, even if it doesn't always seem that way based on the earnest tone of some of his LPs. In a 1999 interview with *Mojo* magazine tied into the release of *Tracks*, Springsteen explained how his favorite record at the time played into "Ricky Wants a Man of Her Own" and other songs of its ilk recorded in 1979. "One of my favorite records that summer was the Raspberries *Greatest Hits*," he said. "They were great little pop records, I loved the production, and when I went into the studio a lot of things we did were like that. Two-, three-, four-minute pop songs coming one right after another."[21]

While Springsteen may not have captured that kind of power-pop pristineness for which the Raspberries were known, recording a bunch of songs with little or no forethought to their feasibility as album cuts brought out the inherent catchiness in his writing. If you're looking for comparisons for "Ricky Wants a Man of Her Own," it falls somewhere between the Farfisa-drenched early songs of Del Shannon and colorful novelty hits like "Judy in Disguise."

Danny Federici's organ has rarely been so chirpy and cheeky, while the rest of the band plays loose and stays tight all at once. Springsteen plays the role of a benevolent older brother who has the wherewithal to realize that his sister's burgeoning teenage independence cannot be contained, a fact that her parents are either reluctant or just too plain ignorant to accept. And that independence means romance, only it's not a boy that she's seeking, it's a man.

All of the typical signs of rebellion are there, from time spent either in the bedroom away from the prying eyes and ears of parents or going out at all hours of the night, to jeans that are way too tight, to the girl's embarrassment at having to be dropped off by her dad. Accompanied by just Max Weinberg's peppery drum beat, Springsteen sums up her sassy attitude in the final verse with two lines that are probably familiar to addled parents everywhere: "Well my folks say, 'Son talk to her, she'll listen to you.' / Yeah, she listens real nice and she does what she wants to do."

That slice-of-life situation makes this blast of a track relatable even as you're bopping your head along to the beat. In other words, it's fun, but it's not mindless. "Ricky Wants a Man of Her Own" may not try to save the world, but it makes the world a more pleasurable place to be for the duration that it struts across the speakers.

58. "Devils and Dust" (from *Devils and Dust*, 2005)

Devils and Dust might be the most unheralded album in the Springsteen catalog, a solo album that has a randomness to its construction that might be its best asset. You never know what you're going to get from one song to the next, a quality that gives away the fact that the album was a loose collection of songs taken from different periods of songwriting by Springsteen.

There's a meditation on the Son of God's relationship with his mother ("Jesus Was an Only Son") and a pretty vivid description of a rendezvous with a prostitute ("Reno"). "The Hitter" is a character sketch of a man whose skill is mercilessly pummeling people, while "Matamoras Banks" is filled with empathy for a doomed immigrant. Contrasts like that are all over the disc.

It's a rollercoaster lineup, where the variety becomes almost a theme in itself. Yet the album hangs together in the way the lyrics, regardless of their topics, are uniformly thoughtful, and in the way the subtle musical adventurism keeps it from being pegged solely as another Springsteen folk album. All of which makes the title track a perfect representative for the album as a whole.

"Devils and Dust" likely would have worked as a simple folk song, but Springsteen and producer Brendan O'Brien had something a bit more dynamic in mind. As a result, what begins with Bruce strumming intently and singing in his huskiest voice blooms into something that incorporates live and pre-programmed drum beats, sighing strings, and even some horns. Instead of having to rely on Springsteen's lyrics for all the heavy lifting, "Devils and Dust" builds tension and drama through these instrumental tactics, forming a one-two punch with the potent story.

Although there is no outright mention of a specific war, the timing of the song's release and some implications in the lyrics place the soldier at the heart of "Devils and Dust" squarely in Iraq. The first two lines are an immediate reference to the ambivalence at the heart of that conflict: "I got my finger on the trigger / But I don't know who to trust." That's a powder keg of a conundrum if ever there were one.

The narrator refers to someone named Bobbie in the first verse. This could be a comrade in arms or, based on the spelling, a girl to whom he is attached. If the latter is the case, the whole song can be read as a letter home from a terrified soldier well in tune with his conflicted emotions. It doesn't really matter either way, since the narrator's damaged soul is the real concern for Springsteen.

Springsteen references the same hypocrisy that Bob Dylan noted in his own anti-war lament ("With God on Our Side") many years ago with the line "I got God on my side." This frightened soldier asks a question that has no answers: "What if what you do to survive / Kills the things you love?" In other words, what if the necessities of enduring battle strip you of your humanity, your faith, your inner spark for life?

This is a legitimate question for a soldier in a just war. It takes on nightmarish ramifications if the foundation for the war in question is flimsy at best and nonexistent at worst. "It's take your God-filled soul," Springsteen sings, "and fill it with devils and dust." Out with the good and in with bad, with no chance for the good to reenter.

Now take that tarnishing of this single soldier's soul and multiply it by every man in the midst of the battle. Their collective finger stays on the figurative trigger long after the actual fighting is done, ever poised for the kill shot. "Devils and Dust" does a marvelous job of detailing the horrendous folly of a specious war by getting inside the battered brain and scorched soul of one man fighting it.

57. "Wreck on the Highway" (from *The River*, 1980)

Death was not an uncommon topic in the songs of the early days of Bruce Springsteen. On his debut album, bodies were all over the pavement in "Lost in the Flood." Although we never get to witness the funeral, we can assume from the ambulance pulling away at the end of "Jungleland" that the Magic Rat has met his untimely end. In "Zero and Blind Terry," recorded in the early days but unreleased until *Tracks*, the hero and hero-ine are caught in the crossfire of a gang fight and are represented at song's end by Springsteen as ghostly figures watching over the streets they once prowled.

Those deaths were like movie deaths, the kind that you know are coming by the foreshadowing of the story. The aforementioned characters lived a little bit too fast to survive for long, and their deaths don't tarnish the romantic way in which they lived.

"Wreck on the Highway," the chilling closing track on *The River*, is a different type of death song. Again, we can't know for sure whether or not the victim in the song survives after his ambulance ride since Spring-steen never specifies, but the narrator's somber tone tells us to expect no miracle ending. Anyway, this song has to be about a death to make sense.

The man who dies in the song is unknown to the narrator. His death represents no inevitable conclusion of a moral arc. There are no florid words to sum up his life, no spectacular thud when he hits the ground, no ghostly return. He is just dead.

Springsteen probably was aware of the similarly-themed country song of the same name by Roy Acuff. Acuff's "Wreck on the Highway," however, brings alcohol into the story to explain the crash and also calls for religion at the time of crisis. There is nothing in Springsteen's song to indicate the reason for the crash, and God is certainly nowhere to be found.

What can be found are the unflinching details of the crash, such as the ubiquitous blood and glass, the unmerciful rain, and the man's dying cries. These are the images and sounds that the narrator takes away from the situation. Springsteen refuses to embellish or extrapolate any further than that, allowing his audience to let it sink in and draw their own conclusions.

He leaves much of the heart-tugging up to his band, who do a stellar job on the country-folk arrangement. This is one of Danny Federici's finest moments on record. He bathes the entire song in a warm and hazy glow that bestows some ironic light on the dark and rainy night.

It's a fascinating choice by Springsteen and Federici to go this route. They could have easily played up the misery in the story, but that would have probably overdone it. Instead, the organ gives the narrator some semblance of solace, even as pianist Roy Bittan and bassist Garry Tallent play off each other and move the story along with somber efficiency.

The narrator's reaction to this random tragedy makes up the latter half of the song, and we can easily imagine Springsteen imagining himself in this role, the filter between songwriter and character pretty much dissolved at this point. His immediate thought is of those left behind, the ones sleeping happily at home as the state trooper delivering the news that will destroy their happiness bears down on them.

In the final verse, he explains how the accident has stayed with him, how he thinks of it in the wee hours. When he does so, he pulls his own "baby" tight, maybe unconsciously, to stave off the dread of finality if only for those fleeting moments.

"Wreck on the Highway" then seems to comes to a close, only to fool us with a false ending as the band picks up again to play a coda. Only now Federici is nowhere to be found, while Springsteen's acoustic guitar, playing unsettling arpeggios, rises in the mix. The solace is gone and the mysteries linger.

Putting the song at the end of an album full of wild mood swings might seem like an uncharacteristic choice, but it makes ruthless sense upon further reflection. If *The River* was the first album where Springsteen allowed the fun stuff to play alongside some of the more serious songs for which he had become known, "Wreck on the Highway" provides the reason why it's necessary to not dwell too long on the hard times. Plus, it accentuates the necessity of rising above the limitations and boundaries that bedevil some of the characters in the more intense songs. It can all end without a moment's notice, so, in either case, best to heed the unspoken lesson of these haunting final words without delay.

56. "Death to My Hometown" (From *Wrecking Ball*, 2012)

In 1984, Bruce Springsteen's monster hit album *Born in the U.S.A.* ended with the quiet, lilting strains of "My Hometown." It was a song in which a father takes his son on a ride around the town, just as Springsteen's own father had taken him, and comes to the devastating realization that his family may no longer be able to stay.

Cut to 2012 and the song "Death to My Hometown," a firebomb of an offering from *Wrecking Ball*. The plot is similar: A man talks to his son about the carnage that their hometown has suffered. Only this time there is no resignation or capitulation. The father tells his son to fight back.

Springsteen knows that his audience will likely make the connection between the two songs. You could even probably stretch it even further and say that it is the boy from "My Hometown" now all grown up and, in "Death to My Hometown," taking a different course of action than his Old Man once did.

The musical differences between the two songs are quite telling as well. "My Hometown" moves along at an ambling pace, as if to mimic the slow car ride. The song is awash in Roy Bittan's synthesizer and Danny Federici's organ, their duet at song's end the most memorable thing about the recording. (It's not one of Springsteen's best melodies and the lyrics, while important, are a bit strained in the way that they're jammed into the song in places, which is why the song doesn't quite make this humble list.)

By contrast, "Death to My Hometown" comes stomping out of the gate with a thumping drum beat, pennywhistles, violins, and banjos like a maniacal jig or a violent hoedown. The song also features an ingenious sample of musicologist Alan Lomax's 1959 recording of "The Last Days of Copernicus," an entrancing folk hymn performed by the Alabama Sacred Harp Singers.

Inventive recordings like "Death to My Hometown" are what made *Wrecking Ball* such a bolt of lightning upon its release in 2012. Yet Springsteen wasn't simply throwing genres together haphazardly for the sake of experimentation. The use of the antiquated sample and instruments drives home the point that the brazen crimes at the heart of the song have been perpetrated time and again throughout history.

Once again, this is a way that the newer song differs from its predecessor. "My Hometown" at times made it seem like the degradation of the town was happening in an almost passive manner; other than the line "They're closin' down the textile mills 'cross the railroad tracks," the downward trajectory seems to transpire as a matter of course.

There is a "They" causing trouble in "Death to My Hometown" as well, only this group is much more active, even if they're sneakier in their dealings. Their great skill is the way that they eradicated the town without leaving any evidence, no gunshots, bombs, or destructive fire in sight. "I never heard a sound," Springsteen sings. "The marauders raided in the night / And brought death to our hometown." Although they may have been clandestine, their ruthlessness is unquestioned: "They left our bodies on the plains / The vultures picked our bones."

In the final verse, the narrator looks his son in the eye and gives him fatherly advice that makes Polonius's stately words to Laertes in *Hamlet* sound awful meek. "Be ready when they come," he tells him. When they get here, "Send the robber barons straight to hell." Their time to pay is long overdue, these bandits and killers "whose crimes have gone unpunished now / Who walk the streets as free men now." Springsteen's voice echoes on the word "now," building up the drama before he relates their ultimate sin: "They brought death to our hometown, boys."

Again, the ability to connect different parts of Springsteen's career through common themes in his work gives this song extra resonance. That kid from "My Hometown" has spent his whole life watching his father's grisly predictions come true. That makes his fiery response understandable. How much can you put up with before you finally decide to match the oppressor's subtle violence with a more tangible response?

The time for measured reflection is long past in "Death to My Hometown." The town may be dead, but the boy, all grown up, has more than enough life in him for vengeance.

55. "Sherry Darling" (from *The River*, 1980)

The good-timey scamp version of Bruce Springsteen that showed up on *The River* didn't arrive on the scene out of thin air. He was available occasionally throughout Springsteen's first two albums, partying way too hard in "Spirit in the Night" and liberating damsels from their angry parents in "Rosalita (Come Out Tonight)."

That funny fellow did take a hiatus, however, during *Born to Run* and *Darkness on the Edge of Town*, two albums whose conceptual tightness left little room for screwing around. Those albums are unassailable, but those fans who first knew Springsteen from "Born to Run" might have thought he was a relatively humorless dude.

That misconception was quelled with hilarious magnificence two songs into *The River* with "Sherry Darling." The song is the perfect showcase for the cornball sense of humor that was such an integral part of Bruce's live shows but had been dormant for about seven years in the studio, at least on songs that actually made it to a finished album.

In actuality, "Sherry Darling" was written during the *Darkness* sessions. There's a wonderful scene in *The Promise*, the documentary about the making of that landmark 1978 album, where Springsteen plays the song on piano for Steven Van Zandt, who sings along. Clearly, Van Zandt hadn't yet heard all the words at that point, because there several occasions when he cracks up listening to the myriad ways Springsteen's narrator finds to insult his mother-in-law.

Once he got around to including it on *The River*, Springsteen filled up the recording with enough throwbacks to 1960s rock and pop to fill up an entire episode of *American Bandstand*. The raucous "natural sound" of folks yelling back and forth in the studio recalls the Beach Boys' "Barbara Ann," while the overall chaotic nature of the recording is a welcome reminder of that ultimate frat-party anthem, "Louie Louie" by the Kingsmen.

The vaguely Latin rhythm is driven by a Garry Tallent bass line that harkens back to some of the Drifters' biggest hits like "Under the Boardwalk" and "Save the Last Dance for Me," but Springsteen's surf-rock guitar solo could have soundtracked a Frankie and Annette beach party. Heck, the girl's name even brings to mind a big hit by the original Jersey Boys: "Sherry Baby" by the Four Seasons.

On top of all that, you get Danny Federici's organ soaring high above the tumult and some punchy sax work from Clarence Clemons. It's an embarrassment of riches, as Springsteen and the boys make some really skilled playing sound tossed-off and reckless. Such is the innate chemistry of the E Street Band, who truly seem liberated by the looseness of the song.

"Sherry Darling" tells the tale of a threesome, only not the fun kind: The narrator, the title character whom he loves, and her mother whom he loathes. It seems as though he can't get at Sherry without her tag-along mother: "Now Sherry my love for you is real / But I didn't count on no package deal."

Among his many humiliations, he's forced to drive this harpy on her weekly trips to the unemployment agency and deal with her big mouth and even bigger feet. He draws a line in the sand, or at least in his car upholstery: "And baby this car just ain't big enough for her and me." His

final ultimatum is a doozy: "So you can tell her there's a hot sun beatin'
on the blacktop / She keeps talkin' she'll be walkin' that last block."

Springsteen keeps the song from sliding too far down into novelty-
song territory by detailing the genuine emotions the guy has for Sherry.
He gets downright poetic toward song's end ("Let there be sunlight, let
there be rain / Let the brokenhearted love again") and sounds a bit like the
dreamer in "Born to Run" when he speaks of his future hopes: "Sherry we
can run with our arms open wide before the ride."

That bit of romanticism doesn't dampen his hatred for his nemesis,
whom he ultimately dismisses, even though it probably means an angry
Sherry: "She can take a subway back to the ghetto tonight." And all of
those flowery words pale in comparison to the touching bluntness of the
refrain: "Say hey hey hey what you say Sherry Darlin'."

Songs like these can't be dismissed, because they humanized Springsteen and made him more than just a composer of street anthems. He was
always more than that, of course, but "Sherry Darling," in uproarious
fashion, retrieved the jovial jokester lurking beneath the earnest song-
smith.

54. "If I Should Fall Behind" (from *Lucky Town*, 1992)

It's been said many different ways by various authors, poets, screenwrit-
ers, and so forth. But William Shakespeare, as he did with so many
subjects pertaining to human nature, pretty much provided the most efficient and definitive summation of the unavoidable trials and tribulations
of romantic relationships when he wrote, in his comedy *A Midsummer
Night's Dream*, "The course of true love never did run smooth."

That little quote has become a cliché for a reason. It comes in handy
because so often the path of love does indeed become fraught with obstacles. Yet the quote is so ubiquitous that you'd think people would heed
the wisdom in it and tread carefully when they embark upon a new
romance.

In much the same manner, the quote effectively serves as a reminder
to those in the midst of some romantic turmoil that complaining about
something that was cosmically predetermined to occur is folly, and the
only greater error is bailing out of a potentially good thing because of the
fear of a bumpy ride.

Shakespeare's eternal wisdom usually only sinks in with time and a few miserable experiences in the rear-view mirror. Whatever it took for Bruce Springsteen to get there, it was clear he had finally arrived by the time he wrote "If I Should Fall Behind" and recorded it on *Lucky Town* in 1992.

Springsteen's song doesn't try to argue the infallible truth of Shakespeare's maxim. It simply tries to make peace with it and adjust on the fly. Considering that he wrote the song at the time he was about to marry Patti Scialfa, a marriage that has defied the odds for rock-star unions by being both long-lasting and by all accounts happy, it's apparent that he was also ready to practice what the song preaches.

"If I Should Fall Behind" is the finest offering on *Lucky Town*, an album that outperforms its 1992 counterpart *Human Touch* based on the seeming lack of strain and effort of the recordings on the former. On *Human Touch*, even the songs that were meant to sound like fun romps instead seem labored. By contrast, *Lucky Town* feels unburdened and relatively off-the-cuff in terms of both its music and its lyrics. There aren't enough true gems to call it a masterpiece, but it probably deserves better than its overall reputation, a reputation that's a byproduct of being released alongside the letdown that was *Human Touch* and the fact that it has to compete with so many classic Springsteen albums.

Certainly, "If I Should Fall Behind" can stand with his very best love songs. Musically, it's subdued yet stirring. The subtle Latin accents in the rhythm are brought out by the Spanish twang of the acoustic guitar that comes to the fore as the song progresses. The song was a Springsteen solo effort with the exception of drummer Gary Mallaber, and it highlights Springsteen's underrated ability at crafting a track from scratch without having it come off like an unfinished demo.

The song is a literal and metaphorical walk down the aisle. In each verse, Springsteen describes idyllic wedding-night surroundings then quickly contrasts it with the hidden danger lurking behind the bliss. The twilight is picturesque, but it might cause the lovers' entwined hands to come apart if they're not careful. They walk in perfect tandem, but how long can they possibly keep up that synchronicity? Even the oak tree that serves as a natural wedding altar throws disconcerting shadows at the pair.

In the bridge, Springsteen puts it in more direct terms. "Now everyone dreams of a love lasting and true," he sings. "But you and I know what this world can do." The implication is that these two people have been with others and thought that those other relationships were pristine and untouchable as well before the world got in the way.

That's a nice way of saying that those couplings failed, and, no it wasn't entirely the world's fault. Yet even the roughest patches can be endured not only if the love is strong enough, but also, and this is what the refrain is trying to say, if the two people involved have an understanding that they will abide these unexpected pitfalls together. Springsteen sings, "I'll wait for you / And should I fall behind wait for me."

What a lovely sentiment, as simple as it is to say as it is difficult to do. "If I Should Fall Behind" doesn't deny the truth of Shakespeare's maxim. It just offers a way for two people to sustain when true love's road inevitably gets rocky.

53. "Johnny 99" (from *Nebraska*, 1982)

Nebraska is known as Bruce Springsteen's folk album, but calling it that limits it in a way. Springsteen understood that just because a record consists of one man performing on an acoustic guitar and little else, it need not be a dour affair all the way through. With a few splashes of humor and a little musical variety, you can hold an audience all the way through and still get your points across just fine.

"Johnny 99," based solely on the story it tells, could have easily been a rather somber affair in the manner of other songs on the album like "My Father's House" or "Highway Patrolman." Instead, it comes out of the gate firing, right from Springsteen's falsetto exhortations at the beginning of the song through the rapid tempo that never hesitates for a moment.

That gives the song a different feel from "Atlantic City," another *Nebraska* song that tells a similar story. Maybe the perspective makes a difference: Whereas "Atlantic City" is a first-person account of a desperate man, "Johnny 99" is told by a narrator with no stake in the game. Since he has an audience to entertain, he can afford to spice things up a little.

Springsteen puts a little rockabilly into his acoustic rhythm and subtly modulates his performance throughout the song so that it seems to rise in intensity as Johnny 99's story unfurls. On other *Nebraska* songs, Springsteen used extra recording tracks to achieve little mini-arrangements, but here it's just a full-steam-ahead, no-frills assault. It's no doubt one of the most memorable performances on the album.

It also proved impossible to repeat or embellish when he took it into the studio to introduce it to the band. He explained this in a 1984 interview with *Hot Press* magazine of Dublin, Ireland, and his words could also be extrapolated to represent the *Nebraska* album at large.

> The songs had a lot of detail so that, when the band started to wail away into it, the characters got lost. Like "Johnny 99"—I thought "Oh, that'd be great if we could do a rock version." But when you did that, the song disappeared. A lot of its content and style, in the treatment of it. It needed that really kinda austere, echoey sound, just one guitar— one guy telling his story. (144–45)[22]

Of course, it helps when the guy telling the story is as deft with his characterizations and details as Springsteen. "Johnny 99" is structured like a thousand other outlaw folk songs: A man goes on a crime spree, gets caught by the law, and serves his punishment, which is usually death. Yet the difference is that "Johnny 99" is no larger-than-life Robin Hood who has noble intentions and a heart of gold. He's just a normal guy pushed too far by his circumstances until he snaps.

Springsteen still manages to make him somewhat sympathetic by explaining just what brought him to this point. He lost his job in an auto plant in Mahwah, New Jersey, and his efforts to find a new job went for naught, putting him on the brink of financial collapse. As he explains in his closing statement before the unforgiving judge, "Now I ain't sayin' that makes me an innocent man / But it was more'n all this that put that gun in my hand."

It's a fine line that Springsteen walks here because giving this guy too much sympathy would negate the fact that he killed somebody. Over and over on *Nebraska*, his characters are put to the test by circumstances beyond their control, usually poverty and lack of work options, but ultimately their reactions are based on how they're wired. For example, the guy in "Mansion on the Hill" doesn't go on a killing spree because he can't get into that closed-off community he witnesses. In "Highway Patrolman," two brothers from identical backgrounds veer off onto wildly divergent paths.

Springsteen isn't judging any of these characters, least of all "Johnny 99," whose violent behavior earns him the ultimate punishment from the law. But it's important to remember that "Johnny 99" was once just a guy named Ralph who had a job and a home. How he got from those humble beginnings to his gun-wielding theatrics is the important part.

"Johnny 99," with its action-packed story-telling full of criminal exploits and courtroom histrionics, allows you to enjoy its thrilling surface. The almost nonchalant way in which Springsteen inserts the sociological subtext is where it leaves most other outlaw anthems way behind.

52. "The Wrestler" (from *Working on a Dream*, 2009)

They were both robbed.

That's the only rational takeaway from the fact that both Bruce Springsteen and Mickey Rourke came up short at the 2009 Academy Awards. At least Rourke was nominated for his searing performance in Darren Aronofsky's *The Wrestler*, only to come up short for Best Actor to Sean Penn. Still, it's hard to walk away from that film and not reach the conclusion that Rourke deserves every accolade possible.

Springsteen, meanwhile, didn't even get nominated for his song "The Wrestler," which was a huge head-scratcher considering that he'd won the Golden Globe Award for Best Song in a Motion Picture just prior to the Oscar nominations. Maybe the Academy, in their ever-bizarre collective thought process, surmised that, since Bruce had already won the award with "Streets of Philadelphia," it was time to spread the wealth a little bit. Or perhaps they had a collective brain cramp, which they've been known to suffer on occasion.

In any case, Springsteen's song undoubtedly stands high above most Oscar-winning songs in terms of integrity, truth, and raw power, so it will outlive any disappointment Springsteen fans might have had at that strange outcome. "The Wrestler" displays Springsteen's ability to get inside the head and heart of a specific character and expose something deep inside that's universally relevant.

In his acceptance speech for the Golden Globe win, Springsteen talked about how his old buddy Rourke had communicated to him what his role entailed. "He told me a little bit about the character," he said. "He said some people invest themselves in their pain and they turn away from love and the things that strengthen and nurture their lives."[23]

The two men had similar tasks. Rourke had to make this beast of a character relatable and sympathetic, even when he engages in recklessly self-destructive behavior with no regard for how it will affect the people who care about him. Springsteen had to take this very specific character and make him resonant to those who had never seen the film, because that's the hallmark of a truly great movie song. (That quality also serves the song well as an album-closer, a role it filled when Springsteen tacked it on to *Working on a Dream* at the last minute, making it seem like he planned it all along because the song beautifully tied into many of the album's themes.)

"The Wrestler" begins with a symphonic wash before Springsteen counts in and commences strumming his acoustic guitar. He also later adds some stray piano notes that veer off just enough from the main melody to evoke tender moments the narrator will likely spurn in the long run. The tune is workmanlike in the verses, but in the refrain it soars and reveals the hidden emotion that this guy has spent years attempting to bury.

In the verses, Springsteen's metaphors (men with one limb, dust-filled scarecrows) are testaments to futility and ineffectuality. The narrator, identifying with them, stubbornly presses on in spite of the self-made obstacles he endures. That resilience is what makes you root for the character even when he's at his worst.

If you know these hopeless creatures, the narrator sings, than you know what his life is like. His efforts are always in vain: "I always leave with less than I had before." And yet he takes comfort in knowing that his pain and suffering bring pleasure to others who can vicariously indulge in his self-immolation without getting their own hands dirty: "Bet I can make you smile when the blood it hits the floor."

As the refrain rolls on though, the humanity in this battered warrior comes to the fore, and the error of his ways briefly flashes through his bruised brain: "These things that have comforted me I drive away / This place that is my home I cannot stay."

All that remains is the pain, a pain that becomes both his reason for living and the thing that's killing him: "My only faith is in the broken bones and the bruises I display." That kind of statement can be appreciated not just by this specific character, but by anyone who has been beaten down by life for so long that the only thing that makes sense is the purity of the misery. If hope and friendship and love constantly let them down, people like that wallow in the pain, the one thing on which they can rely.

Springsteen does an amazing job with "The Wrestler." Not only does he cut to the heart of what Rourke's performance and the film are trying to say, he expands upon it to make it an object lesson for anyone else treading a similarly wayward path. If that's not award-worthy, nothing is.

51. "None But the Brave" (from *The Essential Bruce Springsteen*, 2003)

"None But the Brave" is a song that lingered in the Bruce Springsteen vaults, along with a million other false starts and fascinating might-have-beens, until finally seeing the light of day on the bonus disc of *The Essential Bruce Springsteen*. That extra disc certainly renders the title of that compilation accurate since Springsteen's songwriting story wouldn't quite be complete without this and some of the other lost gems unearthed at that time.

In the case of "None But the Brave," it was part of the mountain of material that Springsteen recorded for *Born in the U.S.A.* Although it has a much warier view on nostalgia, it's similar in sound and theme to "Bobby Jean," so Springsteen may have thought including it on the album would have been a bit of overkill.

If you could choose only one song out of the hundreds they've recorded to encapsulate the sound of the E Street Band, you could do a lot worse than "None But the Brave." All of the elements are there: the romanticism, the drama, the propulsion, and, of course, a whole lot of Clarence Clemons.

The Big Man's saxophone bookends the song with emotional flair, and Springsteen brings the proceedings to a whole other level with his elegiac guitar solo in the bridge that sounds like David Gilmour dropped in for a special guest appearance. If you took all the words from the song, you could still glean the emotional response Springsteen was seeking. That's how in tune this band is with their leader.

"None But the Brave" takes place "tonight," but the narrator is hopelessly lost in the past, specifically all the nights he would rendezvous at the local bars with the girl he's addressing in the song. Like "Bobby Jean," he has to imagine that she can hear him because she's no longer a part of his life. Yet unlike "Bobby Jean," who made the choice to move on to greener pastures, the girl in "None But the Brave" seems to have had her choices taken from her because the implication is that she never made it out of the local scene that the singer now sees for the prison it always was.

Although Springsteen never overtly says that she is dead, that's what we could imply based on the narrator's wishful thinking that "in my heart you still survive." Yet she is everywhere still to him, a kindly ghost that he hopes will continue to haunt him. About the words she once spoke to him, he sings, "From passing cars, their voices sing out / In empty bars where guitars ring out."

If she is still literally alive, her figurative death is undeniable. The essence of what she was lives no more "except for a moment in some stranger's eyes / Or the nameless girls in cars rushin' by." Over and over he remembers her former answer to his query about who could ever survive this dead-end life: "None baby but the brave / No one baby but the brave."

The ironic thing is that the girl, after a fashion, has escaped, leaving the guy still trapped both in memory and in a nightlife that no longer holds any illusions for him. Desperate to shut out the present, he returns to the scene of their former trysts and seeks out a substitute, pulling her in for a dance while Springsteen's guitar goes soaring off into the night. We can imagine him, eyes closed in an effort to remember his former love, even as we know that it's an empty pantomime.

"None But the Brave" resembles some of the tracks on *The River*, like "Point Blank" and "Jackson Cage," where the overarching malaise that hangs over the characters threatens to do them in if they're not careful to avoid it. Springsteen references this in the final verse as the narrator sees familiar faces "caught in a game they got no chance to win / Getting' beat and then playin' again / Till their strength gives out or their heart gives in." Finally fed up, he futilely lashes out at the fates for their cruelty: "Now who's the man who thinks he can decide / Whose dreams shall live and whose shall be pushed aside?"

As we've heard over and over in Springsteen's work, dreams are precious cargo, so to have them be so carelessly toyed with and destroyed is too much for anyone to bear. "None But the Brave" carries in its title the inherent promise that there is a way out for those with the fortitude and guts to make it. The song itself heartbreakingly suggests that sometimes even courage isn't enough.

50. "Streets of Philadelphia" (from *Greatest Hits*, 1995)

Here we are at another point in Bruce Springsteen's career where he rose to the occasion with a great song when he needed it most. When he released "Streets of Philadelphia" in 1994, he was coming off decidedly mixed reviews for his previous albums (1992's *Human Touch* and *Lucky Town*) and a tour that was successful at the gate but left many longtime fans somewhat at a loss as to why he had jettisoned the E Street Band. It seems strange now, but he was perilously close to "What's wrong with Bruce?" status. (Or, even worse, "What ever happened to Bruce Springsteen?" as *Entertainment Weekly* asked in a 1992 cover story.)

He ended up with a song that pulled off the rare Daily Double of winning Song of the Year and the Grammys and Best Song at the Academy Awards. Yet the importance of the song in Springsteen's career pales to its importance as a pioneer in terms of its sensitivity to the issue of AIDS at a time when much of America was still very much struggling with wrapping their collective heads around it.

The song was written for director Jonathan Demme's film *Philadelphia*, which also made a huge impact in bringing the issue to the mainstream in a thoughtful and forceful matter. Demme made a huge contribution to Springsteen's song as well by suggesting that he leave his homemade demo unchanged for inclusion in the film. That decision lent the song immediacy and rawness, elements that are largely responsible for the power that it displays and that easily could have been lost had the recording been beefed up.

As a result, "Streets of Philadelphia" largely consists of a hip-hop flavored drum beat and droning keyboards that lurch from chord to chord. Some ghostly backing voices add to the atmosphere, but mostly it's just Springsteen's voice coming intently through the speakers as if he's delivering a message to which attention must be paid.

For the lyrics, Springsteen drew on a recent experience with losing a friend to cancer. It's telling that he doesn't bring any references to the narrator's sexuality in the song. It was a wise choice, because "Streets of Philadelphia" isn't meant to be a treatise on the differences between gays and straights. It is a plea for mercy and sympathy, and it works astoundingly well at that basic level.

"There was a certain spiritual stillness I was trying capture," Springsteen told the *Advocate* in a 1996 interview. "Then I just tried to send in a human voice, as human a voice as I possibly could. I wanted you to be in somebody's head, hearing their thought—somebody who was on the cusp of death but still experiencing the feeling of being very alive" (237).[24]

Springsteen's descriptions of the narrator's state are beautifully observed. As his body betrays him, this man finds that his sense of self also starts to wane. But he is not dead yet, so there is constant conflict between his deteriorating exterior and the fire that still burns within him.

For what does that fire burn? The character is doubtful of receiving the grace of heaven ("Ain't no angel gonna greet me"). He yearns for the compassion and embrace of his fellow man. "Oh brother are you gonna leave me wastin' away / On the streets of Philadelphia?" he asks. It's a question that should easily be answered with a resounding "No," but the implication that Springsteen makes is that many of the folks dying with AIDS can't be sure they'll get a reassuring response.

As the song progresses, the narrator's condition gets worse, until in the final verse he sings, "I can feel myself fading away." One more time he asks for the love of his companion in the song: "So receive me brother with your faithless kiss." The way he phrases the alternative is telling. He doesn't say, "Will you leave me alone?" He says, "Or will we leave each other alone like this," which intimates that one man spurning another in his utmost time of need is a decision that ultimately isolates them both.

Maybe it took Demme's request to get Springsteen out of the solipsism that hampered much of those maligned 1992 albums and force him to look outward again. Whatever the case, the song helped him regain his footing. When he next appeared on record with *The Ghost of Tom Joad* in 1995, social concerns were once again on his front burner and his songwriting was much more assured.

In any case, the impact of "Streets of Philadelphia" spreads far beyond Bruce Springsteen's career, even beyond the specific issue of AIDS and the gay community that suffers the wrath of the disease. It is a song that spreads to the heart of humanity because it movingly demonstrates that we're all we've got.

49. "Shut Out the Light" (from *Tracks*, 1998)

The hangover from the end of the Vietnam War lasted a few years in the mid-1970s, but once people starting waking up and seeing the struggles that veterans were having assimilating to their lives back at home, depictions of these problems started to show up everywhere in the culture. Films like *Coming Home* and *The Deer Hunter* dealt with them, as did books like *Born on the Fourth of July* (a book that had a big influence on Bruce Springsteen).

Films and books have the advantage of the length afforded them to deal with issues like this in comprehensive fashion. To take on such a complex topic in a short song is not for the meek or timid of spirit, so it's a good thing that Bruce Springsteen is neither of those. His 1984 B-side "Shut Out the Light" does its job as well as any of its cultural brethren at depicting both the isolation and disorientation that veterans faced upon their returns home and how the horrors of the war stayed with them long after the final battles.

"Shut Out the Light" was one of a bevy of songs that drew strong consideration for inclusion on *Born in the U.S.A.* Throughout a good portion of the sessions, Springsteen had a more contemplative album in mind for the follow-up to *Nebraska*. That 1982 album had satisfied his artistic cravings in a way that surprised him, and he was more than willing to follow that path of musical simplicity coupled with lyrical depth for as long as it would take him.

So he had no problem with the thought of including a homemade recording like "Shut Out the Light" on a major release. As modest as it might be, there is no doubting the potency of this expertly modulated duet between Springsteen on guitar and Soozie Tyrell on violin. It haunts in a quiet way that a full-band recording would have great difficulty matching.

Springsteen was ultimately swayed back to making the big, rock record he had originally set out to make, and you can't quibble with the results or the success *Born in the U.S.A.* achieved. Add in the fact that the title track had a similar theme, and it's understandable how "Shut Out the Light" would be relegated to B-side status, eventually finding its way onto *Tracks* in 1998, where it closes out the second disc in mesmerizing fashion.

The song tells the story of a man named Johnson Leneir, who is first seen as a passenger on a plane about to touch down. The fact that "the runway rushed up at him" is a hint at the kind of shellshock he's enduring. So is the fact that his first stop is a bar where he finds a dark corner to hole up in.

In the next verse, a woman primps herself for a rendezvous, one that takes place without any elaboration from the songwriter. Only the aftermath are we allowed to witness, when Johnson lies awake in the wee hours and finds himself paralyzed: "He was staring at the ceiling / He couldn't move his hands."

Only in the second verse do we start to glean from the reaction of his proud family that this is a returning veteran. Reassuring symbols of the American Dream are on display: A doting family, a Ford, the promise of employment. Yet for all that, the chilling chorus makes clear that Johnson is wracked by terror.

That chorus is the only time that we get to hear Johnson speak, as he cries out in the night for the comfort of his mother like a child. "Throw your arms around me in the cold dark night," he pleads. "Hey now mama don't shut out the light." Springsteen repeats that line over and over again, but, for Johnson, he could say it forever and it would never bring him the inner peace he lacks.

For the final verse, Springsteen changes the setting to a dark forest with pine trees and steady rain. In a nearby river, Johnson stands in the icy water, and "he stares across the lights of the city and dreams of where he's been."

It's not a dream, of course. It has been transformed into a gruesome nightmare, one that will stay with him even in full consciousness. "Shut Out the Light" ends with another chorus and another round of Johnson begging for the light that will likely remain permanently doused for him, even with Springsteen shedding such insightful illumination on this dark subject matter.

48. "The Last Carnival" (from *Working on a Dream*, 2009)

And every night at 8 p.m., we walk out on that stage together and that, my friends, is a place where miracles can occur . . . old and new miracles. And those you are with, in the presence of miracles, you never forget. Life does not separate you. Time does not separate you. Animosities do not separate you. Those you are with who create miracles for you, like Danny did for me every night, you are honored to be amongst.[25]

The preceding quote was taken from Bruce Springsteen's eulogy for E Street Band keyboardist Danny Federici, who passed away in 2008 after a long battle with cancer. It is a far shorter list of the Springsteen songs on which Federici did not have a major impact with his intuitive feel and evocative touch than the ones on which he did. Although he did not play on "The Last Carnival," it did give him a chance to have a significant impact on one more E Street Band classic.

There is something comforting in knowing that Federici's son Jason is on board on this track off *Working on a Dream*, playing the accordion as his father did so memorably way back on 1973's "4th of July, Asbury Park (Sandy)." The instrument manages to be a good fit for the song because of the ingeniously apropos way that Springsteen conjures to memorialize his friend and bandmate.

On the same album that contains "4th of July," 1973's *The Wild, the Innocent & the E Street Shuffle*, there is an oddity of a song called "Wild Billy's Circus Story." The title pretty much says it all, as Springsteen describes in minute detail the various goings-on at a circus passing through town, one that enthralls a young boy named to Billy into coming aboard.

"Wild Billy's Circus Story" is a little bit too well told to be one of Springsteen's better songs. His descriptions are vivid and inventive, but he's so wrapped up in trying to portray the scene that the wonder of the carnival life gets a little bit lost in the shuffle. The music falls into the same trap as well; yes, the tuba indeed conjures a dancing elephant, but it's like the song does all our imagining for us.

In "The Last Carnival," Springsteen brings back Billy, making the song a sort of sequel. Only this time around it's time for Billy to get off while the caravan moves on without him. Suddenly, the metaphor that Springsteen maybe hinted at a bit too vaguely in the original song becomes achingly clear. The band is the circus, and Springsteen and the rest, devastated as they might be, now have to move on without their friend.

But they won't go without paying the proper tribute. After some calliope sounds rise out of the stillness, Springsteen's acoustic guitar comes into focus. His vocal on the song is truly wonderful. The man gets a lot of credit for the power of his voice, but in a song like this, his interpretive skills are pristine. In the verses, he tries to stay matter-of-fact about the reality of the situation, but as the melody rises, his emotions began to emerge. It's a fair assumption that Springsteen didn't have to dig too deep to find those emotions this time around.

The narrator bemoans the things that he'll miss about his time with his friend. "We won't be dancing together on the high wire," he sings. Their camaraderie and teamwork is referenced as well: "Hangin' from the trapeze my wrists waiting for your wrists." Notice also how Springsteen gently hints at the raw emotions such a close working relationship can engender: "You throwin' the knife that lands inches from my heart."

As the song progresses, Springsteen starts to drop the pretense of the circus metaphor and speaks directly from the heart. "The thing in you that made me ache has gone to stay," he sings. In his final lines, he imagines the entire cosmos rearranging itself to acknowledge the death of his friend: "A million stars shining above us like every soul livin' and dead / Has been gathered together by a God to sing a hymn over your bones."

With that he asks one more time, "Where are you now my handsome Billy?" At that point, the other members of the E Street Band step forward to belt out a wordless wail that's part loving benediction, part cry of pain. It is one of the most misty-eyed moments in the entire Springsteen catalog.

If *Working on a Dream* is Springsteen's album about aging and the resultant pleasures and heartbreaks that come with it, it makes sense that there be a song about the death of old friends. "The Last Carnival" is a fond farewell to Danny Federici, a man who was integral to making Springsteen's traveling circus a once-in-a-lifetime show.

47. "My Father's House" (from *Nebraska*, 1982)

The infinite mysteries of the father-son relationship have fueled many a great rock song by some of the most successful and influential songwriters of the genre. It's probably fair to say though that no one in the rock and pop music world has ever explored this subject matter with the thoroughness and emotional insight as Bruce Springsteen has over his long and storied career.

Without getting too far into specifics, Springsteen's relationship with his own dad traveled an arc that is similar to that of many fathers and sons, which is perhaps why his songs on the topic so resonate with listeners. Springsteen's father couldn't relate to his son's choice of career in the beginning, while Bruce in turn had a hard time understanding the way his father worked jobs that seemed to make him miserable, thus breeding distance and contempt between the two. As time passed, the younger Springsteen began to understand the sacrifices his father had made, and the relationship between the two men thawed and strengthened before the death of Douglas Springsteen in 1998.

Yet it's also clear that it wasn't an easy road getting to the point of understanding and reconciliation for Springsteen. In a revelatory 2012 article in the *New Yorker* by David Remnick, he opened up about the severe depression that hounded him throughout the most successful part of his career in the 1980s. And much of that depression was rooted in the struggle to understand his past with his father.

He eventually began seeing a psychotherapist who helped him root out where songs like "My Father's House" were emanating from, and the article quotes Springsteen's introduction of the song in a concert, which remembers the words of his psychotherapist, as proof. "He [the psychotherapist] said, 'What you're doing is that something bad happened, and you're going back, thinking that you can make it right again,'" Springsteen said. "And I sat there and I said, 'That is what I'm doing.' And he said, 'Well, you can't.'"[26]

Songs like "My Father's House" show that, on a subconscious level anyway, Springsteen realized this truism, even if his conscious self wasn't ready to accept it. The song is, in many ways, the emotional climax of *Nebraska*. Springsteen doesn't have to do any sort of character sketch or make his points by embodying another person in the song. As a result, the filter between himself and the song is pretty much eradicated.

There is also little blocking his listening audience from this revelation of his innermost feelings, and much of that is due to the stark nature of the acoustic backing. The melody is like a folk hymn, and Springsteen sings with the sonority of a preacher who has learned the lessons of his sermons the hard way.

In "My Father's House," you can tick off many of the features that have become hallmarks of Springsteen's music since the early days. There is a dream that spurs the narrator on to take charge of his destiny. There is road trip that, as in most Springsteen songs, leads to some sort of freedom, at least in a spiritual sense. And, of course, there is that difficult relationship with his father overhanging everything else.

With all of these archetypes in place, it's natural as a listener to secretly hope for some sort of deliverance from these hang-ups that have been hounding the narrator for years, which would maybe signal hope for anyone else in a similarly turbulent boat concerning their own complicated familial relationships. When the dream ends with the frightened child safe from his perilous journey in his father's arms, it only strengthens that feeling. Indeed, the narrator believes it too: "I awoke and I imagined the hard things that pulled us apart / Will never again sir tear us from each other's heart."

So he hits the highway to go back and share with his father these warm feelings. When he arrives, however, he finds a woman he's doesn't know, setting us up for a gut punch of an ending: "I told her my story and who I'd come for," he sings. "She said, 'I'm sorry son but no one by that name lives here anymore.'"

In the last verse, he can no longer kid himself with childish dreams of Hollywood reconciliations and happy endings. He can see that the house, even as it continues to call him in the night, offers no deliverance: "Calling and calling so cold and alone / Shining 'cross this dark highway where our sins lie unatoned for."

"My Father's House" is Springsteen's unrelentingly realistic depiction of how this scenario usually plays out, the way that we often desire to reconcile the most important relationships in our lives only when it's far too late to do so. And sometimes, even if we do, that old house still looms large in our mind's highway, calling us back to feel the pain that time can't erase.

46. "The Ghost of Tom Joad" (from *The Ghost of Tom Joad*, 1995)

Most casual fans know the connection between Woody Guthrie, the father of modern folk music, and Bob Dylan, who literally sat at the master's feet and carried on his tradition into the world of pop and rock and roll. Yet Dylan only carried that ball for a few years into his recording career before splintering off into flights of fancy that likely would have left even Guthrie dumbfounded had he survived to hear them.

Bruce Springsteen, on the other hand, gets labeled most broadly as a rocker, yet he has more in common with Guthrie than most people assume. Springsteen shares Guthrie's belief both in being a voice for those who might not have the opportunity or the means to speak up and in using that voice on behalf of opinions and beliefs that might fly in the face of the powers that be and even to stir up more than a little controversy.

Maybe that connection is most noticeable in "The Ghost of Tom Joad," a song that can be traced back to John Steinbeck's *The Grapes of Wrath* and the character he created as the mouthpiece for the unheard Everyman. The song also makes a pit stop at the movie of that book that featured Henry Fonda playing Joad and giving the stirring speech that is paraphrased in the closing verse of Springsteen's song. But Woody Guthrie's own song "Tom Joad" also was a clear influence on Springsteen, if not so much in structure or content, then certainly in its willingness to eloquently be that populist voice that needs to be heard.

Guthrie's "Tom Joad" is pretty much a blow-by-blow retelling of Joad's exploits in the movie, which fired him up when he saw it. In one of his columns for the magazine *People World*, Guthrie told his readers, "You was the star in that picture," and it "shows the damn bankers men that broke us and the dust that choked us, and comes right out in old plain English what to do about it."

Springsteen's song, the title track of a 1995 album of mostly topical material, accepts that mantle and runs with it. The music, with high lonesome harmonica by Springsteen and moaning pedal steel guitar by Marty Rifkin, evokes the bygone era of the Dust Bowl. But the lyrics describe scenes that were taking place at the moment Springsteen wrote the song, a time when the concerns that Steinbeck expressed in 1939 were somehow still a factor despite all of the technological advancements in the fifty-six years that had passed.

In "The Ghost of Tom Joad," there are folks in lines for shelter, others sleeping in cars or living in boxes, bathing in city irrigation systems, and hungry, all hungry. When they seek answers from politicians, all they get are hollow slogans that simply serve to mock their problems: "Welcome to the new world order."

Even their faith is tested by the religious promises that are taking their sweet time coming true. When Springsteen sings about these luckless characters "waiting for when the last shall be first and the first shall be last," he's not just calling the Bible into question, he's also referencing the prophecy Dylan himself quoted in "The Times They Are A-Changin'" ("And the first one now will later be last"). Dylan insinuated in that song that change was a constant; Springsteen suggests that the evidence shows otherwise.

And yet there is Tom Joad at the end of the song, a ghostly beacon of hope for the downtrodden and oppressed members of society whose flesh-and-blood role models have all deserted them for greener pastures. It's important to remember that, in the book and film, Joad ended up an outlaw for the violence that he perpetrated on those who dared to inflict their power trips in his vicinity. Springsteen's story doesn't so much condone that violence as it does come to the conclusion that it is inevitable when people are pushed too far: "Got a one-way ticket to the promised land / You got a hole in your belly and a gun in your hand."

In the chorus, Springsteen references the highway that, in so many of his songs, carries infinite possibility and promise, but here it's a harbinger of doom: "The highway is alive tonight / But nobody's kiddin' nobody about where it goes." Those lines seem to be a harsh recalibration of the youthful optimism that Springsteen evinced in the days of *Born to Run*. Consider that the only hope in the song comes from a dead guy who wasn't even real in the first place, and you might subtitle this song "Nowhere to Run."

It's not the kind of postcard scenario that grinning politicians and captains of industry would ever publicize. In the proud tradition of Woody Guthrie, Springsteen understands that's exactly the reason why the message he delivers in "The Ghost of Tom Joad" is so essential.

45. "You're Missing" (from *The Rising*, 2002)

The Rising is more admirable than effective. The 2002 album featuring many songs inspired by the 9/11 attacks on America was heavily praised upon its release, but objectivity was nearly impossible for a project so closely tied to that horrendous event. It was only natural for people to want Bruce Springsteen to rise to the occasion and deliver some semblance of a victory in a time of so many losses, so the album's lofty status became a kind of self-fulfilling prophecy.

In truth, the album is a bit of a grind. Maybe no songwriter, not even Springsteen, could possibly sum up the complexity of the nation's collective feelings in the aftermath. Maybe he was biting off more than he could chew in also trying to reintroduce the E Street Band to his sound for the first time on an album in nearly two decades on top of the already difficult task he was undertaking.

Whatever the case, *The Rising* is unnecessarily long at fifteen songs, a few of which are sore-thumb, good-timey numbers that don't fit with the dour material surrounding them. As for the songs Springsteen wrote in the wake of 9/11, he does a fine enough job of putting us in the midst of that tragic day, but everything feels a tad strained, from the chunky music that never gets off the ground to the lyrics that lurch a bit clumsily from detailed descriptions of the carnage to testaments to the hope and faith those in mourning needed to summon.

Ironically enough, a pair of songs written prior to the attacks ended up being the most moving testaments to the massive loss suffered, both on personal and national levels, in those terrorist attacks. "My City of Ruins" and "You're Missing" are the best things on the album by a long stretch, songs that glide effortlessly from Springsteen's impassioned pen to the eloquent and fresh recordings of them by Bruce and the band.

In the case of "You're Missing," its origin can be found in a moody soundtrack piece called "Missing" that Springsteen wrote for the 1995 film *The Crossing Guard*. Although some of the lyrical motifs are similar, "Missing" is more of an existential plea, while "You're Missing" hits home with heartrending immediacy.

Much of the song's success derives from the music, which isn't the type usually associated with Springsteen. The interplay between cello and violin brings out the melancholy of the melody without overplaying it and achieves the elegance of a Beatles ballad. At song's end, Danny Federici breaks into one of his distinctive organ solos that doesn't skimp on the sadness in the lyrics but also finds the kind of resilience that the forlorn protagonist desperately needs.

The lyrical focus of "You're Missing" is the jarring disconnect between the familiar and normally comforting sights and sounds of home and family and the way they are horribly skewed by the prolonged absence of one of the family members. In this case, it's the narrator's wife who is missing. While there is nothing in the song that says it specifically, the tenor of the music and the context of the album suggest that it is death that has separated her from her family, most likely a sudden one that doesn't allow for the kind of adjustment time necessary to ease the sting of the loss for those left behind.

There is something truly noble in the courage and persistence of the bereft husband, the way he tries to soldier on for the benefit of his children by keeping a hollow routine. Maybe part of his plan is to keep everything normal so a reunion that contradicts the laws of the universe can potentially occur. "Your house is waiting," he sings, "for you to walk in."

As the song weaves wearily on its path with those somber strings as its impetus, the stoic facade of the narrator begins inevitably to crack. His children tug at his heartstrings with their innocent pleas for their mother's return, and he gets fed up with all the well-wishers who can't possibly know how he feels. "How's everything, everything?" they ask, as if such a question could ever be answered without spilling his guts onto the floor in front of them.

Springsteen songs get described in a lot of ways, but "beautiful" isn't a word you would normally use. "You're Missing" is downright beautiful, not just for the delicacy and tenderness of the music, but also for the way it conjures up the broken heart of an entire nation in the single story of a grieving man.

44. "Girls in Their Summer Clothes" (from *Magic*, 2007)

"Girls in Their Summer Clothes" was released by Bruce Springsteen on his excellent 2007 album *Magic*, but it would have fit better with the follow-up, 2009's *Working on a Dream*. The song's tale of a past-his-prime lothario who can't shake the lack of impact that he makes on the idyllic scene he describes would have fit right in with the meditations on growing older that dot *Working on a Dream*.

That said, the song is such pop perfection that it would have found a welcome home no matter where it ended up. Maybe Springsteen realized that he had tapped into a rich vein with the themes he explores in the song, thus spurring him to go even deeper on the following album.

The music is lovingly retro, reaching back for some Wall of Sound lushness that the E Street Band hadn't fully indulged since the mid-1970s. Acoustic guitars play well off the surging string arrangement. Note the way the bridge releases back into the final verse like a lovely sigh, or the way the chord changes are slightly altered in the closing refrain to play up the drama. Touches like these are all over the song, propelling what could have been a sterile homage to a particular sound into pristine proof that the best music, when properly executed, never goes out of style.

Springsteen's underrated melodic flair also gets a showcase here, which forces him to break out of the monotone, desert-dry accent which was his standby throughout much of the 1990s and get back to the full-throated singing of his younger days. He embodies the character with ease, subtly evoking the false bravado and wounded pride that drives this guy.

In the lyrics, Springsteen creates a picturesque suburbia that's almost too good to be true. The business names ("Pop's Grill" and "Frankie's Diner") and the street titles ("Blessing Avenue" and "Magic Street") sound like they were created for a fictional television town where the neighbors all know each other and bake each other pies on a regular basis. The narrator encounters on his walk lovers holding hands, kids playing ball, beaming storefronts, the whole works.

Everything is so seemingly perfect that it's natural for the protagonist to feel hopeful, even if the realities of his life don't warrant such optimism. For all his confidence that "tonight I'm gonna burn this town down," he can't help but slip in clues to his true situation. "Things been a little tight," he says in the second verse. In the bridge, he describes the neon sign on the diner he frequents as "a cross over the lost and found." That line foreshadows his own lost status that will be revealed in the song's closing moments.

In the final verse, he gets to the point: "She went away, she cut me like a knife." His remedy for his loneliness is a cheesy pick-up line that only serves to betray his desperation: "Hello, beautiful thing, maybe you could save my life." It doesn't sound so bad backed by the soaring music, but it's still an offer that can easily be refused.

Still, his persistence is admirable in the face of his defeats. "Love's a fool's dance / I ain't got much sense, but I still got my feet." It's the first flash of self-awareness he has shown, and it makes clear the reason why he fixates on his little town. Focusing on his surroundings keeps him from dwelling on his mess of a life.

The chorus is brilliant in the way Springsteen sets us up one way and then resolves it another. "The girls in their summer clothes / In the cool of the evening light," he sings, the music rising to a lush crescendo behind him. But it quickly gets undercut by a plummet down the musical scale as he throws in a punch line so funny it hurts: "The girls in their summer clothes / Pass me by."

Back in "Out in the Street" from *The River*, Springsteen sang, "Pretty girls, they're all passing by." That character was a younger man, though, full of himself and his potency in his little world. It didn't take much to imagine one of those girls coming over and joining him in his escapades for the rest of the night.

Springsteen poses a scenario in this fascinating track where that same guy from "Out in the Street" ended up fetishizing his hometown nightlife to such an extent that he never saw the way it stifled his progress in the bigger world. So ineffectual has he become, those "Girls in Their Summer Clothes" passing him by are now certain to keep heading in the other direction.

43. "Glory Days" (from *Born in the U.S.A.*, 1984)

The way that Bruce Springsteen described this smash from *Born in the U.S.A.* in the liner notes to his 1995 *Greatest Hits* compilation tells you a lot about why it was so successful, reaching No. 5 on the Billboard charts when it was released as a single in 1985. Springsteen wrote, "The 1st verse actually happened, the 2nd verse mostly happened, the 3rd verse, of course, is happening now."[27]

It wasn't just that Springsteen was taking on earthy, heartland topics that most MTV rockers wouldn't have known the first thing about in the middle of the 1980s. It was that he was doing it with the authenticity of someone who knew whereof he spoke without shorting the artistic power that made him one of the greatest songwriters in the world.

The big mistake that could have been made with a song like "Glory Days" would have been to look down one's nose at these characters, to sneer at their relatively humble existences, or, at worst, to judge them for the seeming simplicity of their lives. Whereas fans from small towns and other relatively out-of-the-way locations looked to other rock and pop stars and saw an example of what their lives could be if they ever got out, in Springsteen they saw one of their own who didn't lose those inherent local values and, even more important, recognized the worth of those same values in characters who were strikingly similar to themselves.

So hearing that Springsteen definitely ran into an old Little League buddy in an experience that sparked the first verse, kind of flirted with a divorced ex-classmate to inspire the second verse, and struggled daily with his own fixation on the past and how it was always spiraling further away from him (the third verse in a nutshell) was reassuring in a way. But we could have guessed as much just from hearing how true his reminiscences sounded.

"Glory Days" was recorded as if the E Street Band were playing it live in a bar, which is critical to the song's party-rock atmosphere and makes perfect sense considering the lyrics. Every instrument is pitched to the rafters to be heard above a raucous crowd, from those chiming keyboards to the booming drums to the gritty guitars. Only Steven Van Zandt gets a little chance for commentary, playing a brief mandolin solo that hints at the nostalgia that the lyrics are trying to reconcile.

It's crucial to the song that the narrator is in the everyday trenches with the other characters in the song. Springsteen could easily have written the song without inserting himself into the narrative. Such an approach would have been practically anthropological in technique, viewing these characters as one would a strange species. While it can work when done right, it can also in lesser hands be a condescending mess.

Springsteen was actually in the bar with the speedball-thrower reminiscing, so maybe that made his choice for him. It's rare that a rock song references sports in any way without becoming a kind of novelty song, but it makes sense that Springsteen would be the one to pull it off, and it makes sense to the song. Since high-school sports mean so much to the prestige of small towns, the stars of those sports tend to enjoy high renown long after their playing days are over, renown that can skew reality for those folks.

That's in the subtext of Springsteen's song, the way that these two who haven't seen each other for years can only talk about the big games and triumphs from long ago and not what their lives are like now. But it's not something at which he scoffs. It's something he understands.

As for the part that "mostly happened," Springsteen sketches the trajectory of this woman's life in a few short strokes. She uses her stories of the past as a salve for the wounds of the present: a painful divorce and the pressures of single motherhood.

Those stories may be "boring," as the narrator suggests in the final verse, but they have great worth. For those who may be suffering through the doldrums of the present, they're a surefire way to buoy spirits and maybe even give some hope that things can be that good again. Springsteen realizes that even though the "Glory Days" are fleeting, they're never really gone if they're kept alive via some beer-addled, rose-colored stories or, better yet, through classic rock-and-roll songs with which you can shout along at the top of your lungs.

42. "The Line" (from *The Ghost of Tom Joad*, 1995)

The best issue-oriented songs are the ones that put human faces and relevant stories at the forefront and let the issues hover in the background underpinning it all. Anyone can get on a soapbox and rant, but getting people to listen to it is another thing entirely. When Bruce Springsteen began writing songs like these in earnest on *Nebraska*, although the issues may have been vaguely defined, he already understood this notion of putting stories and characters first.

By the time he got around to *The Ghost of Tom Joad*, the issues about which he was singing were much more specific and clear, thereby making his job even harder. In the case of "The Line," the most effective song on that 1995 album, Springsteen strikes the perfect balance between making his point and telling a story.

The issue hanging heavy over "The Line" is immigration, a hot-button political issue lately but not exactly on the front-burner in 1995. His moral compass generally pointing toward situations where individuals are being marginalized for reasons that are beyond their power to control, Springsteen had the problem in his sights well before it became a fashionable talking point, at least on a national level.

Springsteen was living in California at the time, having moved there from his native New Jersey. A lot of ill-advised criticism followed that move, as fans and critics somehow felt he was betraying his roots. He was booed at times in concerts when he mentioned his new home. Among the many reasons that such opinions were asinine is the fact that a song like "The Line" or, for that matter, much of the topical material that Springsteen wrote in the 1990s and beyond, probably wouldn't have happened without that move and a respective broadening of outlook, which would have eliminated a crucial component of his songwriting catalog.

In any case, Springsteen clearly did his research here, creating a song that is as thorough and detailed as it is emotionally compelling. The melody is borrowed from Bob Dylan's "Love Minus Zero/No Limit," although Springsteen slows down the tempo to create something less jaunty and more impassioned. Only gentle acoustic guitar and atmospheric keyboards accompany him on this journey.

"The Line" tells the tale of a pair of border patrol agents in California. The narrator, Carl, is fresh from the armed forces and reeling from the death of his wife. His partner Bobby Ramirez does his job even as he understands the desperation that forces the Mexican immigrants to take such a dangerous chance. As he sums it up to his partner, "Carl, hunger is a powerful thing."

These two men understand how blurry "The Line" really is, but they need the jobs and swallow their feelings to do them. That is until Carl begins a relationship with a Mexican woman with designs on getting across the border. His commitment to his job and its principles, which he never really could get behind anyway, quickly falters in the face of this burgeoning attraction: "We danced and I held her in my arms / I knew what I would do."

So Carl commits to bringing not just her across "The Line" but also her brother, and that's where the trouble at which those ominous keyboards have been hinting begins. Carl becomes aware as he's attempting to drive them across that the brother is smuggling drugs across the border.

In a showdown reminiscent of the one between the two biological brothers in Springsteen's "Highway Patrolman" from *Nebraska*, Carl and Bobby meet on that fateful night, the two friends facing off in a Jeep's headlights. Carl's judgment is now completely compromised, to the point where he considers the unthinkable: "I felt myself movin' / My gun restin' 'neath my hand." Instead, his lover darts out of his truck and into the night.

The song's title obviously references the border that's the source of deliverance and danger for the immigrants. Yet it also represents that imaginary line that rests within us all, the point where conscience and common sense put up their own borders against self-destructive actions of impulsive passion. Carl readily crosses that line, oblivious to the consequences. That choice humanizes the talking points and renders "The Line," written well before illegal immigration was a part of the zeitgeist, one of the most moving treatises on this complex subject ever composed.

41. "Blinded by the Light" (from *Greetings from Asbury Park, N.J.*, 1973)

Bruce Springsteen quickly realized that the wildly wordy, free-associating madness of "Blinded by the Light" was both a commercial dead end (the single, his first ever, didn't chart despite much hype from Columbia records) and an artistic point of diminishing returns.

For this one song though, he proved he could do verbose as well as anyone and create the kind of thrillingly reckless wordplay that somehow connects at song's end in a fashion that probably not even the songwriter saw coming. And for all of Springsteen's modesty about the song coming out of a rhyming dictionary, the truth is that it is the rare talent that could string together those rhymes into something both wildly off-the-cuff and surprisingly coherent.

Of course, the obvious influence here is Bob Dylan, and it's not for nothing that Springsteen often quotes *Highway 61 Revisited* as the album that turned him on to Bob. If it weren't so subtly hopeful, you might easily imagine "Blinded by the Light" alongside songs like "Highway 61 Revisited" and "Tombstone Blues" from that Dylan album. The barrelhouse thrust of the music is similar, as is the way the lyrics take seemingly unconnected characters and events and place them under the same surreal umbrella.

If anything, Springsteen crams even more into his charmingly chaotic song. Dylan at least took a few lines each to tell us about manic characters like Gypsy Davey and Mack the Finger in those classic songs. On "Blinded by the Light," Springsteen generally gives each of his cats and kittens just a line or two to make an impression, but he stuffs those lines so far past the breaking point that it's like he's devoted a novella to each.

The music of "Blinded by the Light" tumbles along with the same sort of forward momentum as those Dylan classics. There is, as is the case on several of the songs on Springsteen's 1973 debut album, *Greetings from Asbury Park, N.J.*, the issue of sound quality. In the sections where the entire band is rumbling all together, the instruments blend into a kind of muddle. Still, Clarence Clemons's saxophone pokes out of the mix to provide some necessary personality, and the words were always going to be the star here anyway, so it's forgivable.

Springsteen's cavalcade of misfits and malcontents all futilely try to make their mark on the overarching scene, only to be lumped in with the rest of their motley crew in the songwriter's estimation, each one just "another runner in the night." Yet there is never any animosity directed toward these folks by Springsteen. He may be able from his vantage point to see the error of their ways, but he doesn't begrudge them the right to make those errors.

Which is why "Blinded by the Light" might be one of the best snapshots of the glorious folly of youth ever laid down on disc. And Springsteen, himself around twenty-three when he wrote the song in late 1972, nails it from the perspective of one who's in the midst of it and can see the allure of the daring nature of these folks even as they crash and burn.

Again, this is one of those songs where Springsteen tells a lot of stories about a lot of people but also includes some moments where a first-person "I" interacts with them. The narrator is the one with the "boulder on my shoulder." He's the one who encounters the "silicone sister" and her lustful promises. And he's the one who checks the "kidnapped handicap" out and gives him a clean bill of health only after discovering the kid's lack of brains.

So it makes sense then that Springsteen eventually declares that these crazily romantic characters will "make it all right." Since he's in the trenches with them, it would be kind of a downer to declare that the whole scene is on a fast train to oblivion. When Dylan stood looking over an entire avenue of outcasts and ne'er-do-wells, he called it "Desolation Row." In "Blinded by the Light," Springsteen's societal oddballs may be individually messed up, but at least they can hold on to each other while they flail.

"Blinded by the Light" gained enduring popularity through the No. 1 cover version of it by Manfred Mann's Earth Band, who made a cottage industry out of bizarre, prog-rock renditions of Springsteen songs. Maybe the song needed music as insane as many of its characters to truly reach a mass audience. Whatever the case, it stands as Springsteen's one true entry into the New Dylan arena, which only served to prove how different from Bob he really was, not in terms of talent, but in terms of temperament.

40. "Kingdom of Days" (from *Working on a Dream*, 2009)

"Kingdom of Days" has the kind of regal music that befits a kingdom. Bruce Springsteen's love of Roy Orbison is clear in that soaring melody, which tests Springsteen's upper register as a singer. (He passes with flying colors.) The strings bring back warm vibes from rock's Golden Era, while Springsteen adds a guitar solo that arches into the forgiving heavens. The walled backing vocals show that there is nothing lonely to be found in the four minutes of the song.

That kind of foundation deserves lyrics that are equally inspiring, and Springsteen rises to the occasion with one of the best love songs of his career. *Working on a Dream* deals with many of the harder aspects of getting older, but Springsteen has never been one to settle on giving just one side of the story. So "Kingdom of Days" shows the benefits of the autumn years, especially if you're blessed enough to find the right person to share them with.

Springsteen's attempts to write upbeat romantic songs over the years haven't always produced the expected results. Most notably, his 1992 album *Human Touch* was almost too adamant about love's healing power, making it preachy in ways that Springsteen's topical material never has been. *Lucky Town*, the album released at the same time as *Human Touch*, got things right more often, with songs like "If I Should Fall Behind," "Book of Dreams," and "My Beautiful Reward" opining realistically about the difficulties inherent in relationships while still basking in the rewards awaiting those who persist through those issues.

Prior to that, Springsteen's songs about love tended to skew toward the dark side, especially on 1987's pitch-black album of tortured romance, *Tunnel of Love*. But again, it all goes back to how tracing the music of Springsteen is similar to tracing the arc of a life. The man on *Tunnel of Love* learns from his mistakes on *Human Touch*, even if he overshares about the depth of his emotion. By the time we roll around to *Working on a Dream*, that guy is settled and comfortable in his emotions, even as the spark is as strong as it ever was.

The title of "Kingdom of Days" hints at the way the song deals with the concept of time. Instead of dreading the changing seasons and slowly eroding years, the narrator flips the script and sees the bright side of a routine day in all its simplicity and perfection. Building these days one on top of another, he sees just how fortunate his life is.

That's because of the transcendent love that he enjoys, one that has both withstood the harder times that no doubt popped up in the past and has proven strong enough to handle what's to come. In the midst of this love, time becomes irrelevant, as the first verse makes clear with its eschewing of the meddling minutes and hours and the threatening seasons. The narrator only notes it in the way the light reflects off his love's face.

"I watch the moon trace its arc with no regrets," Springsteen sings in the second verse. We should all be so lucky as to reach a point in our lives when we can look skyward without the burden of things that we've done or, sometimes even worse, things we haven't done clouding the benevolence of the heavens. Note how Springsteen casually sets the scene in a picturesque autumn of falling leaves and gentle breezes, a symbol of an advanced time of life that holds an abundance of happiness.

In the bridge, he professes his love in the most direct way possible, and she ups the ante by asking him to prove it. The final verse presents a couplet as lovely as any that Springsteen has ever written: "And I count my blessings that you're mine for always / We laugh beneath the covers and count the wrinkles and the grays." Again, it's a depiction of time as a benign transformer, not a ruthless ravager.

When that final chorus—with its strings and horns saluting this couple so deeply smitten that they probably don't even hear it—comes around, it's clear the song is celebrating a love as sound as it is passionate. "Kingdom of Days" is a love song that was many, many years in the making for Bruce Springsteen, but that's okay because the lyrics insist that when love is just right, you've got all the time in the world.

39. "Cautious Man" (from *Tunnel of Love*, 1987)

One of the traps to which lesser songwriters often succumb is that they feel the need to wrap each of their songs up in a bow. There has to be a beginning, an ending, and some sort of moral, when, in reality, life is usually messier than that. Things often end by degrees, and, though we may yearn for one to make sense of some random misfortune, there is rarely a ready moral to attach.

Bruce Springsteen is obviously not a lesser songwriter. On *Tunnel of Love*, ambiguity and uncertainty hang in the air like clouds stubbornly refusing to allow the light of clarity. Sad songs like "One Step Up" or (tentatively) happy songs like "Valentine's Day" don't feature any decisive actions by their protagonists, only an inner struggle that is never ending.

The poster child for this kind of murkiness is "Cautious Man," a song where nothing all that out of the ordinary happens yet the atmosphere is thick with ominous portent. Part of that comes from the performance of it, as Springsteen rises from a dejected croak in the verses to exhibit extreme anguish in the connection portions. Other than quiet acoustic guitar, the only instrument that comes to the fore is a synthesizer that whips up briefly like a thick fog, as if these characters needed anything more to confuse them.

"Cautious Man" tells the story of Bill Horton, who comes on like a stoic gunfighter in the first verse. He's quiet, spends his life on the road, abides by the code of that road, and only moves forward once he's judged the opportunity from all angles. With his knuckle tattoos straight out of some pulpy movie, he seems more like the kind of guy to clean out a town's worth of outlaws than get swept up in an unlikely love story.

But that's exactly what transpires; whether he's caught up in the hopeful signs of spring or not, Billy finds himself in the last place he ever expected to be: "It was there in her arms he let his cautiousness slip away." While he initially tries to laugh off this strange turn of events, his old suspicious ways start to take hold of him once again, even after marrying this girl and building her a home.

As the facade of happiness starts to wears thin, Billy attempts to pray himself into being the kind of husband she needs. "For he knew in a restless heart the seed of betrayal lay," Springsteen sings. It's the kind of motto that's easier said than done, especially by someone whose whole previous life was based on solitude and isolation. When faced with commitment, his immediate fear is that he'll mess things up.

Billy's moment of truth comes, as it does for so many of Springsteen's morally conflicted protagonists, as the result of a dream. In this case it's a nightmare in which he desperately calls for his wife, only to wake and find her "in a peaceful sleep, a thousand miles away." Whether that sense of distance is something that this girl has helped to foster or whether it's just the paranoia of this guy's addled brain, the chasm forces him out into the night to look for answers.

In an attempt to make sense of his roiling emotions, he heads out onto the highway that once was his home, the highway that gave a sense of purpose and a meaning to his life. Only on this night, "when he got there he didn't find nothing but road." Again, this is an example of Springsteen subverting his own archetypes, turning the road into just a road after it had symbolized so much else in past songs.

So Billy returns to his wife's side, hoping that there might be more comfort there, but it is to no avail: "Billy felt a coldness rise up inside him that he couldn't name / Just as the words tattooed 'cross his knuckles he knew would always remain." The road lets him down and his marriage lets him down, so he is now a man utterly rudderless in a suffocating world.

In the closing moments, an ironic scene of peacefulness plays out. "At their bedside he brushed the hair from his wife's face as the moon shone on her skin so white," Springsteen sings, "filling their room in the beauty of God's fallen light." God's light may be shining down in that bedroom, but Bill is immune to it, couched as he is in the coldness and darkness that are destined to be his lot in life no matter how many unlikely love affairs come along.

At no point in the song is there any mention of his wife doing anything to cause these suspicions. In fact, she really doesn't do anything at all, and all Billy does is go for a late-night ride and then come back home. Yet the fissure between the two is about to rip open irreparably wide, which makes "Cautious Man," all subtle hints and clandestine clues, as decisive a song about relationship misery as Springsteen has ever delivered.

38. "I Wish I Were Blind" (from *Human Touch*, 1992)

For whatever faults 1992's "Other Band" album *Human Touch* might have had, it did include one of the finest love-gone-wrong ballads Bruce Springsteen has ever produced. This is not to compare "I Wish I Were Blind" to some of the darker meditations on crumbling trust and growing disillusionment that made up the core of *Tunnel of Love*. The song doesn't go that deep into the psyche, nor does it attempt to do so.

"I Wish I Were Blind" is best appreciated as one of a long, long line of songs devoted to replaying the awful emotions that go along with seeing your old love with someone new. The reasons why it all fell apart are not the concern of this particular track. All it wants to do is wallow, allowing the listener to hop on board if he or she is in the same boat or ever has been in the past. And haven't we all been in that boat at some point?

It's a bit of a change of pace for Springsteen to write in this way, without delving into the whys and wherefores of the situation. Yet pulling off a song like "I Wish I Were Blind" is no less difficult than writing more in-depth excavations of relationship squabbles and broken love affairs. That's because there is a long tradition of great weepers throughout rock and pop history, so it's a daunting group to try and join.

In that way, "I Wish I Were Blind" might be the closest that Springsteen has ever come to mimicking Roy Orbison. There have been many songs—a few of these we've already tackled in this countdown with one or two left to come—where Springsteen used the musical template of Orbison, the soaring melodies, the stately pace, the timpani, as a foundation. But never before had he tried to tap into that well of deep, deep sorrow to which Orbison pretty much owned the deed throughout his career.

Think in terms of songs like "Crying," "It's Over," or "Running Scared" and you can get on the wavelength of what Springsteen is trying to accomplish with "I Wish I Were Blind." The trick to it is finding a different way to communicate what it feels like in that woeful situation without unconsciously repeating something that Orbison or any other songwriter has said before.

Springsteen's approach is to point out the disorienting contrast someone in that situation experiences between the benign feelings brought about by viewing the wondrous world around him and the total torment that occurs when he sees his ex out on the town with his replacement for her affections. As he said about the song in a 1992 interview with *Q* magazine, "It's about that sinking feeling. There's a world of love, a world of beauty, a world of fear, and a world of loss and they are the same world and that person is wending his way through that maze and at that moment he's very much in touch with both of those things" (172).[28]

Springsteen's achievement with "I Wish I Were Blind" is the way he translates the accurate but clinical observation from the quote above into lyrics that can be sung and appreciated by the heartbroken everywhere. It helps that he gets Bobby Hatfield of the Righteous Brothers to help him out on backing vocals. Who better to assist on a song of torturous longing than the man who showed the world how it's done with his performance on "Unchained Melody?"

The narrator can still appreciate the natural beauty of the trees and birds and stars, the stuff of love songs since someone first put words to music. He even still finds himself agape at the way his former love's hair shines in the sun. But his eyes are his enemy when a certain sight comes into focus: "I wish I were blind / When I see you with your man."

That's when the contradictions of the above quote start to become painfully clear to this guy. "Oh these eyes that once filled me with your beauty / Now fill me with pain," he laments. Soon the good things are blotted out by the bad: "And the light that once entered here is banished from me / And this darkness is all baby that my heart sees."

Springsteen gets in a howling, elongated guitar solo that conjures every last morsel of pain pulsating within his protagonist. The harmonies with Hatfield are lovely in the saddest possible way. Everything really comes together on this track, one which, if Springsteen had to do it all over again, he might have pushed as a single since it is radio perfection.

In any case, "I Wish I Were Blind" is one of the most underrated songs in Springsteen's canon, perhaps because it is unknown by casual fans. That's too bad because any song that can stand with the best of Roy Orbison in the department of heartbreak dissertations deserves the widest possible audience.

37. "The Promised Land" (from *Darkness on the Edge of Town,* 1978)

Over and over in these pages there have been examples of how those trying to limit a certain piece of work by Bruce Springsteen ultimately underestimate the complexity and multifaceted nature of that work, whether it's an album or a single song. That applies certainly to *Darkness on the Edge of Town*, an album that many critics pegged as Springsteen's darkest album, an antidote to the hopefulness and optimism of previous efforts.

That view is true only to a point because it omits what might be Springsteen's ultimate message on the album, one of individual empowerment and the need to take control of life instead of having life take control of you. Even as bleak as things may get on the album, they are never hopeless.

"The Promised Land" is an excellent example of a song where the crushing pressures and devastating circumstances of life are no match for the human spirit. Starting off the second side of the album with a blast of defiant energy, Springsteen was clearly urging his listeners, and maybe himself, to stand up in the face of the negative and demand the control that others would try to take away.

One of the most distinguishing characteristics of *Darkness on the Edge of Town* was how the arrangements were tightened up for maximum impact. Gone were the multiple musical motifs and tonal shifts that could be found in some of the epic endeavors on *Born to Run*. As fruitful as that previous approach was on that landmark album, the best songs on *Dark-*

ness are the ones that trim away the excess and try to put across the same amount of power in a shorter amount of time.

In "The Promised Land," every instrumentalist gets time in the spotlight but each focuses on what's best for the song rather than individual showiness. After Springsteen's harmonica leads the way, the verses star the limber bass of Garry Tallent and Roy Bittan's tinkling piano. In the lead-up to the chorus, it's time for Danny Federici's chirping organ to meet up with the thumping drums of Max Weinberg. That leads to a full-band assault in the chorus with a multi-tracked Springsteen harmonizing with himself.

In the instrumental break, Springsteen steps up for an electric guitar solo that doesn't go completely for the gusto. It sounds as if he's just setting us up for something bigger, and that something comes crashing through in the form of Clarence Clemons's potent sax solo. In the closing verse, Springsteen adds some moaning backing vocals to build up the drama. The harmonica comes back in at the end for a little bit of symmetry in this flawless recording.

Springsteen was also in the process of streamlining his lyrical assault. His attention to meter in "The Promised Land" fits well with the precision of the music. Yet he keeps his street-poet sensibilities about him. Check out this unlikely but effective rhyme that nails his protagonist's existence: "Working all day in my daddy's garage / Driving all night chasing some mirage."

The narrator feels marginalized by the doldrums of his life, to the point where he fears he might lash out. "Sometimes I feel so weak I just want to explode," he sings, as if that burst would somehow shake off the figurative shackles. Yet his is a spirit that can't be contained even if physically restrained, which is why he finds kindred spirits in wild animals: "The dogs on Main Street howl 'cause they understand."

In the final verse, he feels oncoming turbulence, but he refuses to run: "I packed my bags and I'm headed straight into the storm." After all, he sees this storm as a turning point, something that will separate the weak-willed from the indestructible. "Gonna be a twister to blow everything down / That ain't got the strength to stand its ground." Included among the things he sees as fodder for the storm are the foolish dreams to which people cling, dreams he equates with lies (a notion that would come up again famously in "The River").

In the chorus, Springsteen lays it all on the line for those who would try to keep him down. "Mister, I ain't a boy, no I'm a man." This is one of the great lines of his career, one that could pertain to the personal turmoil he endured around the making of *Darkness* with lawsuits and whatnot, but one that can also be understood by anyone who has ever felt mitigated as if they were a helpless child.

The title of the song is "The Promised Land," but Springsteens sings, "I believe in *a* promised land." The indefinite article is crucial to understanding what he's after here. It's not some specific biblical promise or an American Dream long-tarnished. It's a sense of personal freedom that's out there for anyone with the guts to reach for it. As long as that's available, there's hope to be found even in the darkness.

36. "No Surrender" (from *Born in the U.S.A.*, 1984)

Whether it's booming over a sports arena's public address system in an effort to conjure a rally from the home team, blasting out of car speakers and inadvertently causing speeding tickets, or just rattling the windows of a home via the stereo system, "No Surrender" comes in handy. If *Born in the U.S.A.* was indeed going to be the ultimate crowd-pleasing Bruce Springsteen album, it needed this song as an unabashed, regretless paean to the merits of staying young at heart and the power of rock and roll.

It's nigh impossible to listen to "No Surrender" without the blood running a little faster in the veins or the heart pumping with a little more purpose in the chest. Those who would criticize the song as being naive are missing the point. Springsteen is saying that only the prevalence of cynicism makes such a song naive and that our hearts are naturally inclined to believe before the world starts telling us otherwise.

The song features as energetic a performance as the E Street Band has ever delivered. Spurred on by Max Weinberg's relentless drumbeat, everybody charges ahead without regard for their own personal safety. Roy Bittan glissandos wildly while Springsteen underpins it all with pumping electric guitar. It's probably a good thing that Clarence Clemons takes five for this performance. That kind of pleasure overkill might have started exploding the heads of those in the listening audience.

Springsteen also makes sure to include as many "whoa-oh" and "lye-lye-lye" refrains to reaffirm the primal power of rock. We understand those nonsense syllables as the sound of burdenless youth and unfettered freedom, and no amount of articulation can make that any clearer.

Once Springsteen gets around to giving us some actual words, his narrator begins to compare halcyon younger days with the staid pull of his current life. It's as if he's trying to find out what happened to those kids. How did they turn out like this? It's a good thing that the message of the song is that it's never too late to reclaim the passion and fire that's been lost.

A good place to start is with the redemptive power of music. Springsteen's assertion that "we learned more from a three-minute record than we ever learned in school" gets a lot of attention from those who would analyze this song. Yet just as important is the way that he doesn't back down from that schoolboy view as he ages. When the world closes in on him, he finds a familiar way out: "Well maybe we'll cut someplace of our own with these drums and guitars." Might as well make use of that old 45 RPM knowledge.

The narrator is disgusted at the petrification of the wild hearts and free spirits he once knew, and he won't abide a similar attitude-change befalling his longtime friend whom he addresses in the song. "There's a war outside still raging / You say it ain't ours anymore to win," he sings, portraying the situation as an eternal conflict that's slowly tipping to the wrong side.

Should this friend decide to give in and "follow your dreams down," the implication is that it's not just a personal choice, but a betrayal of what these two companions once represented, and ultimately, it'll be a betrayal of their friendship as well. "We made a promise we swore we'd always remember," he recalls. In fact, it was a most solemn oath: "Blood brothers in the stormy night with a vow to defend."

Using these exaggerated terms is the only way that the narrator can convey the desperation he feels at the state of his generation. And the only possible setting in which to place those momentous words to properly express his feelings is full-throated rock and roll, the kind that provided his buddy and him an outlet as young boys and still can sustain them against all odds even now.

Is it overdramatic and unsubtle? Yes and yes. But there are times when you need a jolt of unbridled naiveté, and what better time than when you're listening to the radio trying to forget about worries and woes. "No retreat, no surrender," Springsteen implores, if only for the duration of the

song, to get us back to that place when it seemed possible to beat the
world simply by refusing to be beaten.

35. "State Trooper" (from *Nebraska*, 1982)

"State Trooper" is another example of a song whose original spot on an
LP was chosen for the utmost impact by Bruce Springsteen. On CD, it sits
in the middle as track six out of ten, threatening to kill all the other tracks
around it. But on the original album, it sat at the end of side one, meaning
that listeners were sent into the silence of the record's end in the most
unsettling way possible.

Speaking of placement, there was a reason David Chase chose the
song as the song to play over the closing credits of the final episode of
season one of *The Sopranos*. After the episode closed out on a relatively
calm note with the family eating dinner together and Tony Soprano ex-
horting his kids to remember the good moments, Springsteen's ominous
guitar comes in as if to remind the audience that those good moments are
fleeting at best and illusory at worst.

No song in the Springsteen canon builds up as much tension as "State
Trooper." The title refers to the one person that the narrator doesn't want
to see on his frenzied, late-night journey, for both their sakes. That
monotonous guitar rumble gives the song the feel of a Hitchcock thriller.
At some point, you know something is going to jump up at you out of the
dark. You're just not sure where or when.

Springsteen uses the stark but evocative music to show us the dangerous state of mind of this character. Unlike some of the other songs on
Nebraska, there is no underlying context within the song that tells us how
this guy came to be such a live wire. That makes it more frightening
somehow, knowing that there's no real motive driving him to be out on
that road looking for trouble that seems destined to find him.

The narrator sets the scene on the New Jersey Turnpike on a dark
night in wet conditions, and that foreboding guitar lets us know that this
cat isn't going at a legal rate of speed. Before he even describes the acts
that he has committed, he's already defending himself: "License, registra-
tion, I ain't got none / But I got a clear conscience 'bout the things that I
done." We can only imagine what those "things" were.

In the second verse, the situation gets even more threatening, as he
addresses either the person who has made the foolish act of stopping him

on this rainy night or the audience at large that would dare to judge his conduct. "Maybe you got a kid, maybe you got a pretty wife / The only thing that I got's been botherin' me my whole life," Springsteen sings, drawing a line between the blissfully unaware domestics and this unpredictably, wild element that is just outside the house walls.

Springsteen then goes back to words that are similar to ones he used on "Open All Night," another song on *Nebraska* that is also about a night rider but is looser and more happy-go-lucky in tone. Whereas the narrator in "Open All Night" gets amusingly frustrated with the bad music and the approaching sunrise that accompany him on his journey, the killer in "State Trooper" is pushed to the edge by them. Although there are subtle divergences in the words of the two songs as written on the page, you can tell the difference clearly in the way Springsteen adapts his performance.

As "State Trooper" progresses, the narrator's coiled energy, so palpable that you can practically feel it buzzing if you touch the speaker, begins to uncork beyond his control. At one point, Springsteen lets out a quick whoop, then cools it down slightly with a less aggressive falsetto wail. It's as if the narrator is attempting to calm himself down so as not to unleash the rage and violence welling up inside him.

Those efforts soon become futile. He begs, "Hey somebody out there, listen to my last prayer / Hi ho silver-o deliver me from nowhere," but it's too late. He's already in the void, and the only proof of his existence is the carnage he leaves behind.

After that final verse, the guitar gets louder and louder until Springsteen explodes with a shout that sends the needles frantically into the red. It's a chilling moment that releases the tension by implying that the protagonist has finally lost his fragile sense of control. The unlucky "State Trooper" has met the wrong man at the wrong time, as Springsteen's most harrowing song comes to a close with neither a lesson to be learned nor any mercy shown.

34. "Jack of All Trades" (from *Wrecking Ball*, 2012)

Most great albums have a centerpiece. It's the song around which all the others revolve, one that sums up the main themes of the album. In most cases, such a song should also have an aura about it that lets you feel its import the first time you hear it and every time thereafter. It can be the first song, the last song, the first single—doesn't really matter. It's just important to have a good one somewhere if you're going to make an album that will stand up as a classic somewhere down the road.

In the case of 2012's *Wrecking Ball* by Bruce Springsteen, that song is, without a doubt, "Jack of All Trades." From the opening moments, with the atmospheric fade-in and the glacial tempo, there is an immediate sense that you get while listening that it's crucial to hear exactly what Springsteen is trying to say. Once he gets your attention, he keeps it with a powerful statement on the deterioration of the American Dream and the havoc such a vast phenomenon can engender in a single life.

One of the reasons that *Wrecking Ball* was such an artistic success was that it was as cohesive in its messaging as anything Springsteen had released since *Tunnel of Love*. That's not to say that there's no merit in a catch-as-catch-can collection of songs like *The River*. But *Wrecking Ball* was an album that you could hear from start to finish (with the exception of oddball "You've Got It") and understand how the pieces connected to each other and then to the whole. In an era when album-making has become a bit of a lost art, it's a thrill to hear Springsteen going for broke and making a record that demands full attention for its entirety. "Jack of All Trades" is essential to tying it all together.

The song falls into the category of first-person character sketch. This was a type of song that Springsteen didn't really do much in the early part of his career. When he sang in the first person on albums like *Born to Run* or *The River*, that person was either a minor part of the narrative or was mainly used as a cipher to get to bigger themes. It was on *Nebraska* that Springsteen found that he had a knack for this technique of getting inside the mind of a character and seeing the world through his eyes. Through such a character, he could still explore the bigger issues via the very personal perspective of one who is affected by them.

The character at the heart of "Jack of All Trades" sums up one of the great dichotomies in Springsteen's ongoing work: the necessity of hope in a world that pushes people to despair. In the case of this guy, he starts out the song calmly reassuring his family that his skill set will allow them to get by in the hard economic times implied in the narrative. There may not be many jobs out there to do, but this guy is pretty sure that he's capable of handling whatever jobs come his way.

Therein lies his hope, which he expresses in a verse that connects the break of a new day with the religious promise of brotherhood and togetherness given by Jesus. All along, the music is telling us to believe otherwise; with the funereal horns and dirge-like pace, it seems like it's commenting on the death of something. And indeed, the narrator's attitude gets significantly more jaded in the song's second half.

He sees a pattern of economic oppression repeating itself ("The banker man grows fat / Working man grows thin"). When he reasserts his faith in the final verse, there's an ominous tinge to it this time around. How can he suddenly believe in a new world after the evidence he's given us unless he plans to take action?

In the final verse, as the music all but drops away, he lets us know just how much rage he is hoarding, the lengths to which he will go now that all his other options have been stripped away. "If I had me a gun," he sings, "I'd find the bastards and shoot 'em on sight." Including that line gives the song an edge that might be uncomfortable for some folks to hear, but Springsteen has never been one to sacrifice a character's inherent truth for the sake of easing tension.

Special guest Tom Morello comes in at that point and clears the air with a guitar solo that helps to relieve some of that tension, but it's still clearly lingering as the song ends and we ponder the fate of this guy and the ones he loves. "Jack of All Trades" is the song that defines *Wrecking Ball* in one elegiac package, a treatise on what happens when a man stops believing in what the world should be and deals with the harshness of what it is.

33. "Zero and Blind Terry" (from *Tracks*, 1998)

This seems like the perfect song to comment about one of Bruce Springsteen's great contributions to music: his ingenious and inexhaustible supply of character names. His songwriting may have originally contained many influences, but these crazy, evocative names and nicknames were a calling card right from the start (his very first song on his very first album, "Blinded by the Light," has a bunch of them). As years passed, Springsteen eventually had to tame the wildness of the names in order to be consistent with the tone of his songs and the age of the characters within them, but those early appellations are still missed.

Bob Dylan used a lot of names as well to concoct his rich tableaus, but those were often borrowed from historical men and women, fictional characters, biblical folks, and the protagonists of old blues songs. At least when he gently ribbed Bruce on a song with the Traveling Wilburys,

Dylan's title characters, Tweeter and the Monkey Man, had appropriately Springsteenian monikers.

In the case of "Zero and Blind Terry," the names add a bit of a fairy-tale aspect to a song that's already larger than life. Springsteen wrote and recorded the song during the making of 1973's *The Wild, the Innocent & the E Street Shuffle* but didn't include it on the album, possibly because "Incident on 57th Street" detailed a similar gangland story albeit in a bit more realistic fashion. "Zero and Blind Terry" made it to *Tracks* in 1998, where it stands as a prime example of the thrilling theatrics of Springsteen's early career.

The story told in the song is pretty much as old as literature (imagine Blind Terry calling out "Wherefore art thou Zero?" and you've got the drift). Springsteen's innovation is to give the star-crossed couple and the warring gangs surrounding them a superhuman aura, the better to play up just how momentous young love can feel to those in the midst of it.

"Zero and Blind Terry" also goes back to a time when Springsteen favored ambitious musical arrangements that played out like Broadway scores in miniature. The song keeps rising to emotional crescendos and then crashing back down to intimate proportions. Clarence Clemons's saxophone bursts through in the middle of the gang fights, but early E Street Band drummer Vini Lopez deserves a lot of credit for keeping this saga moving through all of its distinct passages, deftly dusting his hi-hat in the quieter middle section and bashing away in the battles.

Springsteen frames the song as if the narrator were an old codger relating an urban legend to some unbeliever in a bar late one night. He captures the personalities of these young men who fight hard and love even harder: "These boys live off the milk of a silver jet / And the love of sweet young women." His descriptions of the fighting in this West Side of Jersey Story range from sci-fi–tinged (George Lucas had to have heard the lines "The Pythons fought with buzz guns / And the troopers with swords like light") to flat-out spectacular ("Now snow-white troopers from the council of crime / Rode silver foxes through Terry's field"). Who wrote like that? Nobody but Springsteen.

As the "whoa-whoa-whoa" backing vocals evoke the rallying cry of these charismatic brawlers, the music drops away toward the end so the veteran can reveal the ambiguous fate of our hero and heroine. "Well now some folks say Zero and Terry ran away / Others say they were caught and brought back," he sings in a conspiratorial hush.

But this isn't some Shakespearean tragedy that ends with a heap of dead bodies. The supernatural power of romance is Springsteen's main focus, which is why the narrator tells his captive audience to make a pilgrimage to the sight of that memorable battle. "If you look hard enough, if you try," he promises, "you'll catch Zero and Terry and all the Pythons / Oh just hikin' the streets of the sky."

That's probably as close to happily ever after as these two crazy kids will ever get, so those of us who were rooting for them can take comfort in that. "Zero and Blind Terry" proves that a song about the power of romance, by any other name, wouldn't be as sweet. Nor would it be Springsteen.

32. "Prove It All Night" (from *Darkness on the Edge of Town*, 1978)

"Prove It All Night" became one of Bruce Springsteen's most durable concert warhorses pretty much from the moment it was released on *Darkness on the Edge of Town*. It's not hard to hard to see why. That memorable piano riff from Roy Bittan is not only a killer intro but a kind of reset button for the band, allowing them to veer off from the main structure of the song in instrumental breaks for a while before those eleven notes call them back home and invariably bring the crowds to their feet roaring.

What is difficult to understand is why the song wasn't a bigger hit than it was. Predicting the vagaries of the pop charts is a fool's errand, but it's still a mystery how a song so tight, so melodic, and so hook-filled could get lost in the shuffle (No. 33 was its peak on *Billboard*). Not only that, the guy-girl subject matter is usually the stuff of pop hits, as is the easily remembered refrain.

The song's lack of success probably says more about Springsteen's overall difficulties cracking the pop charts at that time than anything else. Even though he had made a national splash with *Born to Run* in terms of media exposure, it didn't translate to anything resembling a smash single. Yet once he finally did break down that dam with *Born in the U.S.A.*, everything he released for a prolonged stretch of time was a hit.

Regardless of its status as a single, "Prove It All Night" definitely provided an accessible track among the tougher, grittier stuff on *Darkness on the Edge of Town*, making *Darkness* a more well-rounded disc than it otherwise might have been. It's fine to explore the less desirable aspects of life, but too much of that without any sliver of hope can easily become a burden for listeners. Springsteen understood that the need for balance on an album extended beyond just musical motifs; it was important that listeners could find uplifting or inspiring material alongside the downers.

"Prove It All Night" has that balance embedded in it. The narrator wants to prove to his girl that he is worthy of her love, even as he demands a little reciprocation. Only he's not asking her for the material things that he's working to provide to her. He's looking for signs that she's not going to give in to the unrelenting pressure of life. If she can give that back to him, he'll at least have a partner in defiance.

In essence, he's telling her to toughen up a little bit. He acknowledges the million little defeats that life presents: "Everybody's got a hunger, a hunger they can't resist / There's so much that you want, you deserve much more than this." Note how he equates her problems with everybody else's, thereby implying that she's not alone in her suffering. He sarcastically chides those who would be defeated by unrealistic expectations. "But if dreams came true, oh, wouldn't that be nice," Springsteen sings, thereby adding another page to his ever-complicated Book of Dreams.

The antidote to waiting for some unrealized dream is to go out and grab hold of something, whether it's the romance he's offering or something else that won't be easy but will be worth it: "Girl, you want it, you take it, you pay your price." It's a forceful reiteration of one of the most common themes of the *Darkness* and *River* era, the idea that those who passively wait for desires to be fulfilled essentially ensure that those desires won't ever be, while those who actively pursue what's important to them at least give themselves a fighting chance.

All along, the E Street Band seconds the lyrics with aggression and power. Even though this is rock music, the band adds the kind of rhythmic sway that few rock bands at the time could produce, making it more of an all-around pleasure. In the bridge, a little of that genre-mixing comes through in the soulful smoothness of Clarence Clemons's solo as opposed to Springsteen's subsequent screaming guitar heroics.

In the final verse, the narrator contrasts the vivid existence he envisions for them with the stale imitation of life that the naysayers would propose: "They made their choices and they'll never know / What it means to steal, to cheat, to lie / What it's like to live and die." Again, he equates acts that most would consider negative with the essence of living.

"Prove It All Night" was about as close as Springsteen got to a love song on *Darkness*, but it ultimately is less about the romance between two people and more about the romance of life. That's what the narrator wants for the girl in the song more than anything else, and it's something Springsteen clearly wants for his listeners.

31. "The Promise" (from *18 Tracks*, 1999)

The Great White Whale of all Bruce Springsteen unreleased tracks, "The Promise" gained its massive reputation based on live performances of it during the period after *Born to Run* and before *Darkness on the Edge of Town*. It finally got the grand stage it deserved when it was used as the title track to Springsteen's collection of *Darkness* outtakes from 2010.

Yet the track information listed above shows the album *18 Tracks*, which was a 1999 single CD–sampler of the best songs from 1998's *Tracks* (along with four unreleased fan favorites). "The Promise" was included in that relatively unheralded collection, and it is that recording that earns the song this hallowed ranking in the Springsteen countdown.

Before we get to the reason for that, there is some important information about the song's history that will help to explain. Since it was written around the time Springsteen first became embroiled in a lawsuit with former manager and producer Mike Appel, most people assume that the legal imbroglio was the impetus for the song. While he has never come out and said that was exactly the case, Springsteen has hinted that the personal nature of the song is what kept it from being deployed on *Darkness*. Concerning the song, he told actor Edward Norton in a 2010 interview to promote *The Promise* documentary at the Toronto Film Festival, "I left ['The Promise'] out because it felt too self-referential and I was uncomfortable with it. Maybe it was too close to the story I was actually living at the moment" (354).[29]

That may have been the case, but it's also clear from the evidence on *The Promise* that the studio version done by the band in 1978 robbed the song of some of its power. The slow tempo seemed plodding with the backing of the full band, and the arrangement lacked any real distinguishing characteristic to make it special.

That's why, when it was time to put it on *18 Tracks*, Springsteen went into a studio to record the song anew in a solo piano version. That version is bittersweet magic. Springsteen's husky vocal fits the narrative better, since it better represents the passage of time that has separated the narrator from his ideals, now in tatters. The simple piano chords also project an achingly elegiac tone. Do yourself a favor and search out this take if all you've heard is the full-band take and compare and contrast them yourself.

In any case, "The Promise" is fascinating for the way that Springsteen, just a few years removed from the heights of *Born to Run*, negates the irrepressible spirit of that album. When he invokes "Thunder Road" here, that famed highway that once promised to take him out of a "town full of losers" is now despoiled: "There's something dyin' down on the highway tonight."

It's fascinating that Springsteen inhabits one of the working stiffs in the song instead of the guy working in a "rock-and-roll band lookin' for that million-dollar sound." Maybe that was the byproduct of a guy a bit jaded about the rock establishment. Or perhaps Springsteen was acknowledging how, but for the grace of his incredible talent and a little luck, he could easily have been struggling in his own work life.

In any case, "The Promise" calls into question all of the archetypes on which "Thunder Road" and many of the hopeful songs on *Born to Run* were built. Not only is the highway cast in a shadowy light in this update, but the cherry car, in this case a Challenger, goes from the narrator's pride and joy to just another piece of ephemera to be sold. And when this guy does make it out of town and gets a chance to fulfill the hope expressed at the end of "Thunder Road," the end result hardly seems worth the effort: "Well I won big once I hit the coast, hey but I paid the big cost."

The self-awareness of this guy is a far cry from the beat-the-world naiveté found on *Born to Run*, which is why it sounds better when the more mature version of Springsteen sings the song. That voice evokes every mile traveled and every deep wound suffered, especially in this powerful, summarizing couplet: "When the promise is broken you go on living, but it steals something from down in your soul / Like when the truth is spoken and it don't make no difference, something in your heart runs cold."

Springsteen implies that this character represents everyone who has ever become disenchanted with life as their innermost longings are proven to be counterfeit. He ends up all alone and far from home, but in the song's final moments, he still exhibits a loving nostalgia for those old friends who lived and loved hard and flamed out even harder. Maybe "The Promise" hit way too close to home for Springsteen at the time he wrote it, but the betrayals and defeats it eloquently catalogs are universal experiences in a world so hard on fragile dreams.

30. "My City of Ruins" (from *The Rising*, 2002)

When Bruce Springsteen opened *America: A Tribute to Heroes*, a telethon held just ten days after the 9/11 attacks on the United States, with "My City of Ruins," it seemed inconceivable that the song could have been anything other than Springsteen's touching, powerful reflection on that awful tragedy. With the title suggesting the literal debris of New York City and Washington, D.C., and the stirring refrains calling the listeners to "rise up," it seemed as though Springsteen had made the perfect statement at a time when we needed it most.

"My City of Ruins" may indeed have been that perfect statement, but it was an accidental one. Springsteen had already written and performed the song live in December 2000 in wistful honor of his former hometown of Asbury Park, N.J., the seaside burg that lent its name to the title of his first album. Years of blight and decay had left the town a shell of its former self, and the song was intended as Springsteen's combination of incisive commentary on this sad degradation and uplifting message to its residents.

When Springsteen placed the song at the end of *The Rising*, he probably confused casual fans even further about the true meaning behind it since that album featured a bevy of songs that were indeed inspired by 9/11 and its aftermath. The funny thing is that "My City of Ruins" is so well-written and beautifully performed that it works as a 9/11 tribute better than all the songs Springsteen wrote specifically for the occasion and, for that matter, better than the vast majority of tributes or laments about that horrible day that any artist could muster.

Gospel-inflected rock is a tricky bit of business that has tripped up many a would-be inspirational rocker. Springsteen gets it right here by tempering the arrangement so that it isn't overblown. The triumph at song's end is earned lyrically only after the denizens of the town suffer great tribulation, so the music should reflect that by exposing the pain before the deliverance from it arrives.

"My City of Ruins" borrows its descending bass line from "The Weight" by The Band, which is apropos because of the onerous burden that is toted around by the inhabitants of the wasted city. The playing is wonderful throughout, with Max Weinberg's soulful beat and Danny Federici's soothing organ solo deserving of special mention.

In the opening verses, Springsteen paints a none-too-pretty picture of a ghost town full of cold rain, boarded windows, and churches where organs play for no one. In the midst of this, the citizenry are literally adrift: "Young men on the corner like scattered leaves." The "sweet bells of mercy" that ring go largely unheard, both by the downtrodden folks below and by any higher power that would deign to offer some help.

When Springsteen sings, "While my brother's down on his knees," it calls to mind Sam Cooke's epic cry for brotherhood, "A Change Is Gonna Come," a song that insisted that a transformation was in the offing even with no evidence of one available. Springsteen takes a more proactive approach. When he starts singing, "With these hands," we expect him to say that he will physically rebuild the debris and carnage and make the city whole again.

Instead, he puts those hands together to pray for strength, faith, and love, the spiritual building blocks that have to precede any construction. As he makes these prayers, the backing vocalists steadily get louder, before Weinberg's drums come pounding in to take us all to the "Rise up" refrain.

This point in the song is one of those signature Springsteen moments that can induce chills even through the filter of stereo speakers. His singing here is some of his best on record, resilient and fiery even as the anguish and pain are evident. This is not just any city; it is "My City of Ruins," meaning Springsteen's city. With such a stake in the game, it's one that he won't take lightly.

Considering that a lot of folks post-9/11 were hurting and hoping that their own cities could rise from the ashes, "My City of Ruins" struck unexpected chords. Maybe the song's meaning even cosmically changed by the force of tragic circumstance, but only because Springsteen's original construction was movingly malleable enough to allow it to happen.

29. "Racing in the Street" (from *Darkness on the Edge of Town,* 1978)

When Bruce Springsteen's adoring fans finally picked up their long-awaited copy of *Darkness on the Edge of Town* after the interminable three-year wait following *Born to Run* and saw in the track listing a song at the end of side one named "Racing in the Street," expectations of a souped-up anthem with pumping music and cathartic lyrics likely started dancing in their heads.

Springsteen knew all that, and he also knew that *Darkness* was the delivery system for a much more ambivalent message than the one that *Born to Run* promoted. As a result, "Racing in the Street" is one of the most dejected, defeated odes to street racing you're ever going to hear. The only subversive thing about the song turns out to be the title because, once you hear the music, the lyrics are never going to fool you into thinking there is any triumph hidden beneath them.

The first clue is the somber piano of Roy Bittan that sounds like Springsteen had Jackson Browne's *Late for the Sky* on heavy rotation when he wrote the song. Musically, "Racing in the Street" never speeds; it idles, it putters, and finally it stumbles forward as if its time in the fast lane has long since passed. Other members of the band come quietly in, but only Danny Federici's organ surges to the forefront to join Bittan's piano, and that's mostly in an evocative coda that's like a pair of Sunday drivers ambling around seeking a hopeful view instead of hot-rodders jockeying for position at breakneck speed.

The first verse-and-a-half is clinical in its description of the narrator's vehicle and the various roads and races he encounters on it. By keeping up the steady diet of shop talk, he can hold the gnawing feeling in his stomach temporarily at bay. But the haunting music always knows his inner malaise, even when he brags about his seemingly endless winning streak on the road.

At the end of the second verse, this guy suddenly feels the need to defend himself and the reckless hobby he keeps. "Some guys they just give up living and start dying, little by little, piece by piece," Springsteen sings. "Some guys come home from work and wash up and go racing in the street." Throughout *Darkness*, Springsteen often posits these impossible choices between bad alternatives. In the case of "Racing in the Street," he wonders if it's better to die by degrees or die before your time.

Pete Townsend may have thought he had the answer, but Springsteen complicates the question.

In the refrains, Springsteen cannily paraphrases Martha and the Vandellas' "Dancing in the Street" to make clear the contrast between the joyous abandon of that 1960s Motown smash and the crushing sense of hopelessness that lurks in his song. By the time the final verse rolls around, the narrator can no longer pretend that his daredevil racing is a way to seize the day. What we find out is that it is his method of escaping the truth.

That truth lies in the bottomless depression suffered by the girl he loves, a girl whom he once carried away as a kind of prize for one of his racing victories. "She stares off alone into the night / With the eyes of one who hates for just bein' born," Springsteen sings. Having witnessed her slow but steady transformation from a young, vibrant girl to a wrinkled, tormented woman, the narrator can't sustain any illusion that his street racing has delivered him any win that's lasting and real. It's just a source of cheap thrills, even if it is preferable to the slow death of his home life.

Springsteen is joined by some ghostly backing vocals as the last verse staggers to the finish line. The narrator makes a futile attempt to outrun his problems: "For all the shut down strangers and hot rod angels rumbling through this promised land / Tonight my baby and me we're gonna ride to the sea and wash these sins off our hands."

In those lines, the florid eloquence of *Born to Run* returns to try and save the day, but that's not going to happen. All that we've heard, from the funereal pace and tenor of the music to the suffocating depictions of the couple's ennui, indicates that "Racing in the Street" may get this guy some victories in the dashes. In the long run, however, he was lapped by the field long ago, and there's no hope for any late rally.

28. "Spirit in the Night" (from *Greetings from Asbury Park, N.J.*, 1973)

Bruce Springsteen's desire to get a full-band sound on what was essentially singer-songwriter material is part of the reason that his debut album, 1973's *Greetings from Asbury Park, N.J.*, is a bit of a bumpy ride, consisting of a few glorious peaks and several could-have-been-great near-misses. Maybe the pressure from record executives and management about what he should sound like was too great for a guy making his debut album to ignore, and the mixed messages ended up hampering the finished product. If nothing else, the album helped prove to Springsteen that his songwriting spark was too volatile for the whole sensitive-troubadour thing.

The ironic thing is that the best full-band recording on the album was accomplished with a makeshift trio. "Spirit in the Night" was one of the last songs written and recorded for the debut album when it was decided by Columbia Records that Springsteen didn't have any hit single material among what was in the can. As a result, Springsteen played most of the instruments on the song himself since other session players, with the exception of Vini Lopez on drums and Clarence Clemons on saxophone, were no longer available,

They ended up with a single that didn't make any dent on the charts but a song that turned out to be more durable and impactful than some temporary flash-in-the pan hit. "Spirit in the Night" is a piece of unlikely studio magic, which is only fitting for a track about the supernatural power of reckless youth.

Springsteen may have been working with a small crew, but the two players who did show up turned in stellar performances. Clemons's opening riff is full of sexy mystery, inviting listeners to go along with this wild ride if they dare. Most saxophone parts in rock songs are solos that come in and go out and are never heard from again. The Big Man manages to saunter along with pretty much the entire tune here, but he never gets in the way. If anything, his commentary on the proceedings is as essential as Springsteen's lyrics.

Lopez provides some hepcat attitude with his drumming, giving the song a jazzy patter and soulful swing all at once. Springsteen does the rest on piano and bass and acquits himself quite well. The sound certainly owes a debt to Van Morrison, but it's more grounded in its way, even with the lines about spirits and gypsy angels.

That's because Springsteen, even as the song indulges in flights of fancy in terms of the magical nature of Greasy Lake, creates characters you can believe. And if there's any doubt about the veracity of the night in question, the call-and-response vocals make it seem like Lopez and Clemons are seconding Springsteen's story.

You can easily picture these seven or eight (it's easy to lose track) ragamuffins all crammed into Wild Billy's car in pursuit of all kinds of raucous entertainment. Springsteen has always been known as that rare rock star who does not overindulge in drugs, alcohol, and the like, but he manages to sound pretty convincing describing the antics of characters who happily partake of those extracurricular substances in this shaggy-dog tale of a song.

It's also fun to hear Springsteen winking at us with some innovative innuendo as he describes the backseat fumblings of the narrator and Crazy Janey. But there's a hint of melancholy surrounding all these characters that makes them seem much more tolerable than another bunch of mindless hedonists on a Saturday night. The narrator tells Janey, "I'm hurt," while he in turn describes her as a "lonely angel."

In the final verse, most of the music drops away except for Springsteen's sad little piano. It's one of the first examples of a ploy that Springsteen would use to great effect throughout his career. The quieter accompaniment heightens the drama as the night ends with various outcomes for our merry band: Killer Joe unconscious, Hazy Davey making a kamikaze charge into the water, the narrator and Crazy Janey consummating their star-crossed romance. When the other instruments subtly return and then explode back into the last refrain, it's a rush.

And what of these magical spirits? Maybe they're the hallucinations brought about by the mystery stuff that Wild Billy provides his passengers. Or maybe they're actually ghosts, benevolent yet mischievous ghosts that lure partiers into the water so that they can add them to their army of dancing apparitions. Most likely, the "Spirit in the Night" is the unspoken camaraderie between boys and girls celebrating their fleeting youth with random acts of self-destruction. In any case, may we all be so haunted to have a night as fun as this.

27. "Dancing in the Dark" (from *Born in the U.S.A.*, 1984)

One of the hardest things to do in the field of Bruce Springsteen analysis is to properly assess the worth of "Dancing in the Dark." Accurate judgment of the song is clouded by its mega-hit status, something that no other Springsteen song has ever enjoyed at that level. Then there is the sound of the song, chiming synthesizers and robotic syncopation, which was anathema to Springsteen's normal way of doing things even if it was very apropos for the era in which the song was released.

It's first important to understand some of the history behind the track before we can get to where it belongs in the hierarchy of Springsteen songs. After three years' worth of sessions for *Born in the U.S.A.* produced approximately seventy songs for the album, Springsteen thought he had it whittled down to a final track list, only to be told by producer Jon Landau that the album was still lacking something. An argument ensued, but Springsteen went home that night and dashed off "Dancing in the Dark."

After several attempts to capture it in a typically meaty rock arrangement, Springsteen and company settled on the modern, danceable sound that made it a natural choice as the first single on *Born in the U.S.A.* Accompanied by a video that gave hope to rhythmically challenged dancers at wedding receptions everywhere, "Dancing in the Dark" rocketed to No. 2 on the charts, denied the top position for a few weeks by one of the few artists at the time who could hang with Springsteen in the superstardom department: Prince, whose sublime single "When Doves Cry" held firm at No. 1.

Much of the critical reaction about the song has focused on the contradiction between the bouncy music and supposedly downbeat lyrics. This is the first of many misconceptions about the song. Saying that the music somehow masks or distorts the lyrics isn't true, because the words don't appear in a vacuum.

If you were just reading them on the page, the lyrics to "Dancing in the Dark" might seem dark and brooding. But in the context of the propulsive beat and optimistic keyboards, they become what they are meant to be: a statement of purpose for a man who is frustrated and bored with being so frustrated and bored all the time.

There are those who would dump on the song simply because of the supposed artificiality of the recording techniques, but that's just a bias against accessibility that's hounded pop music forever. Part of that bias has probably been exacerbated by Springsteen's own ambivalent comments about how far he went to court a mass audience.

The 1980s as a decade usually get labeled as having produced fun but frivolous music. So that also works against the song in terms of its critical reception since it embraces many of the stylistic strategies of that time. Yet "Dancing in the Dark" doesn't sound dated even today, as unusual as the approach may have been for Springsteen. If anything, the music coaxes out of him one of his most dynamic vocal performances.

All preconceived notions aside, "Dancing in the Dark" is of crucial importance in Springsteen's career, and not just for the obvious reason.

Yes, the song's success brought the chart popularity that had somewhat eluded him to that point and brought him to levels of rock and pop eminence that few have ever reached. Even for all that, the song's ultimate contribution might just be the way it sounds, even amid the dance beats and synth washes, like it is about Bruce Springsteen.

One of Landau's directions on that fateful night when the song was written was that it should give fans an idea of where Springsteen was at that point in his life. Instead of looking outward at social ills or masking any personal hopes or fears in a character sketch, Springsteen reveals himself in the song like never before. Insecurity, frustration, self-deprecation, hunger: all of these were characteristics that he might have ascribed to others in his catalog, but here, in this first-person account of a lonely night, they were his alone.

So it is reassuring that Springsteen, who constantly advised the characters in his songs to reach for their moment and attack the world even when it seems unforgiving or cruel, would solve his problem in a similar manner. In "Dancing in the Dark," he finally gets fed up with the sedentary life of the mind and sets about healing his heart.

That's not to say he leaves his audience out. When he gets to the refrain, he notably switches to the second person, telling the listeners that "you" shouldn't be dwelling on a broken heart or the crumbling of your world. That little touch, and the unconquerable spirit that Springsteen displays in the midst of his crisis, makes the song one of his most inspirational.

"Dancing in the Dark" manages to be autobiographical without oversharing or navel-gazing—an affecting, humanizing portrait of the artist. It's also the springboard in many ways for *Tunnel of Love* and albums that would follow in which Bruce Springsteen became as big a part of his songs as his beloved cast of characters. All of that makes it an indispensable and impressive part of the Springsteen body of work; everything else is trivia.

26. "4th of July, Asbury Park (Sandy)" (from *The Wild, the Innocent & the E Street Shuffle*, 1973)

The improvement Bruce Springsteen made in songwriting and recording skills from his first to second album was quite remarkable considering that they were released in the same year. Although there are some undeniably wonderful songs from his debut, *Greetings from Asbury Park, N.J.*, you just get the sense that there was a firmer hand on the tiller on *The Wild, the Innocent & the E Street Shuffle*. That hand was not the hand of the record company or of management; it was Springsteen's, and he was quickly proving that his musical instincts were rarely off the mark.

"4th of July, Asbury Park (Sandy)" is a wonderful example of Springsteen's growing prowess as a songwriter and record-maker. He creates a vivid tableau of the Jersey Shore that is instantly recognizable to anyone who's ever been there and instantly imaginable for those who haven't. What makes the song so successful is that, unlike some of the songs on the first album, he does that as much with the music as he does with the lyrics.

The sound on "Sandy" still isn't as sharp as it could have been, and that probably costs it a few notches on these rankings. The arrangement, on the other hand, is thoughtful and serves the song faithfully. Most people immediately note the accordion part of Danny Federici, for good reason, since Federici beautifully conjures the romance of shore life.

Yet Springsteen plays a big part in the musical success of the song with some dreamy guitar that at times sounds like the call of the shore birds soaring above the beach. David Sancious steps forward on keyboard in the final verse when the rest of the instrumentalists recede, tripping along behind Springsteen's words in melancholy fashion. Instead of just focusing on a single instrument, Springsteen was making the most of everything he had at his disposal, and the recording is much better for this strategy.

"Sandy" is a one-sided conversation between the narrator and the title character, his would-be romantic partner, in which the former tries to impress upon the latter that the "boardwalk life" they are living is more of a dead end than the beautiful scenery and fascinating nightlife would suggest. Yet it's obvious that he's also trying to convince himself because, for all his protestations, this place definitely has a hold on him that's just as strong as any faulty Tilt-a-Whirl.

The song takes place on Independence Day, but the narrator is sticking around long enough to see the fireworks and, hopefully, coax some romantic fireworks from Sandy before declaring his own freedom. For all of his florid promises to Sandy in the choruses, she's not the only girl on his dance card, as evidenced by his escapades under the boardwalk.

Springsteen's descriptions go beyond simply pinpointing the sights and the sounds; he captures the attitudes and emotions that make the scene a kind of life form, one that can be as warmly embracing as a lover and as coldly dismissive as your worst enemy. The narrator sees a kind of transformation in this scene; even Madame Marie, a real-life Boardwalk denizen whom Springsteen actually befriended, gets rousted out by the cops, so whom can you trust?

The final verse is a tour de force, as Springsteen overstuffs the lines seemingly well past the breaking point and nimbly sings them as if he were rapping with one of his buddies. He comes on like just as much of a player in this section as any of the lotharios and temptresses he describes, yet the undercurrent of sadness really comes to the fore here, exacerbated by Sancious's lovely work.

The narrator anticipates the new day's promise will deliver him from the boredom in which he is trapped, but he's a little bit scared to go it alone. That's why he is pleading with Sandy in the chorus. You never believe for a second that he's actually going to hold on to Sandy for the rest of his life, and it's likely that she won't believe it either, making his decision to leave something he'll have to follow through on his own.

In the end, "4th of July, Asbury Park (Sandy)" is more about growing up and the unsettling doubts and fears that go along with it than it is about romance. The narrator seems to have made his choice, but we leave him on the precipice of his departure wondering if he'll actually ever leave. Springsteen doesn't skimp on the allure of this place, of what was essentially his home at the time. But he also shows how it can be as much a prison as a postcard.

25. "The Price You Pay" (from *The River*, 1980)

Since Bruce Springsteen has rarely played this song live, it is part underrated and part legendary. "The Price You Pay" is probably unknown to casual fans who don't own the entire Springsteen collection and only know the radio songs and concert staples. Yet the fact that Springsteen, for whatever reason, allowed decades to pass between live takes of "The Price You Pay" meant that diehard fans debated and discussed it maybe more than they otherwise might have in an effort to figure out the reasons for the cold shoulder toward it.

Perhaps Springsteen viewed the song as one that would have resisted improvement or variation had he played it in concert more often. The truth is that the song is just about perfect in studio form as heard on *The River*. The performance by the E Street Band is forceful and conveys an epic sweep but doesn't stampede the complex, emotional tenor of the lyrics. There is both brooding portent and unrelenting potency in the song's instrumental makeup, a tricky balance that is likely difficult to transmit on stage.

"The Price You Pay" is also one of Springsteen's most existential epics. For the most part, Springsteen takes on big themes and weighty topics through the eyes and hearts of the everyday people affected by them. In this case, there is a vagueness and mystery to the proceedings that represents a relatively unique songwriting approach for Springsteen.

Put it this way: Attentive, insightful listeners should be able to tell what the vast majority of Springsteen songs are about after, at most, a few listens. That is part of the reason he is songwriter of the people; he doesn't make you work for it. What he manages to do is to present these themes and topics in captivating and persuasive fashion without hiding them behind inscrutability.

By contrast, "The Price You Pay" has more than a little bit of that head-scratching inscrutability in its DNA. The evidence here shows that Springsteen, had he chosen this method of songwriting more often, probably would have been a ringing success anyway, even if he probably wouldn't have come near the popularity he eventually achieved. As a fascinating change of pace, this song really stands out.

Springsteen never puts any faces or names to the "they" whose exploits are described in the song. One guess is that it's a generation of people who once acted based on their ideals and the intuition of their best selves, only to find those well-intentioned actions squelched. That's the price that's been paid, and, as a result, they end up compromising those beliefs just to eke out their existence, making the song a corollary of sorts to Jackson Browne's "Before the Deluge."

As painful as it might be, Springsteen insinuates that life requires some sort of acceptance of and reconciliation with this price. Running from it, he sings over and over again, is impossible; best to brace yourself and take it on with eyes wide open. Note how Springsteen's self-harmonies add emotional depth to the song. His lower register represents steadfastness and courage, but an octave above, the harmony vocals he sings project great frustration and torment about the harshness of the world.

Using biblical allusions, Springsteen tries to teach a final lesson to the girl holding a baby in the final verse (making it one of many songs on *The River* where Springsteen gives advice to women in hard-luck situations). He tells her to go for broke while she can, for the time is limited ("So let the game start, you better run you little wild heart").

Lest you think that this entire song sticks to such a downcast message, something unlike Springsteen, the closing lines represent a kind of acting out against the order of the universe as the song sees it. The narrator speaks of a sign put up by a stranger that acts as a cosmic scoreboard tallying up all the defeated souls. That's when the pragmatic, sensible approach of acceptance and capitulation explodes into an act of defiance. Speaking of that horrible sign, Springsteen sings, "And girl before the end of the day, I'm gonna tear it down and throw it away."

When he sings these lines, Springsteen's voice breaks out of the composed moan that he has sustained throughout the song and he wails, a release of the tension that has been steadily mounting. It may be an act of futility, but it's an act nonetheless, one that flies in the face of all his previous gloomy exhortations. It brings a song that was desperately trying to keep at arm's length flying into our faces with touching urgency. "The Price You Pay" may have become the stuff of Springsteen legend inadvertently, but once you hear it, you'll know that it earns that legendary status all on its own.

24. "Loose Ends" (from *Tracks*, 1998)

Over and over during this countdown we've seen examples of excellent songs that were tossed to the side by Bruce Springsteen instead of being included on studio albums. In many cases, his decision-making process was understandable. It usually boiled down to these songs, excellent on their own, not quite matching up with the message Springsteen was trying to convey on a specific album.

In the case of "Loose Ends," what was going on in Springsteen's head when he decided to leave it on the cutting-room floor until its eventual release with the treasure trove of goodies on *Tracks* in 1998 has never quite been explained. The song was recorded in 1979, which would have put it in line for inclusion on *The River*. As it turns out, the song was briefly marked for inclusion on a Springsteen album around that point, but that album wasn't *The River.*

According to Dave Marsh's *Two Hearts: The Definitive Bruce Springsteen Biography,* Springsteen had originally intended a single album as a follow-up to 1978's *Darkness on the Edge of Town.* "Loose Ends" was slated to be the closing song on the album, a pretty important spot, so it's clear its creator had a high opinion of it. But Springsteen had second thoughts about the project and shelved it, eventually taking seven of the ten songs with him for *The River* but not "Loose Ends," rendering its title a bit too literal.

The funny thing is that the song would have easily fit *The River* since the whole point of that project was to include a wide variety of songs and styles under one big umbrella of a double-album. As a matter of fact, "Loose Ends," with its pristinely powerful music, would have made a killer single, something that the album could have used considering "Fade Away," the follow-up to hit "Hungry Heart," faltered at the charts.

This is what you would call an uptown problem, having so many available songs that a surefire classic like this one can fall by the wayside. The whys and wherefores are why God made message boards; anyway, we can all enjoy "Loose Ends" now whenever we want.

Considering when it was recorded, it's interesting to think that "Loose Ends" could have been one of the first songs primarily about relationships on a Springsteen album. There are no tangential bigger themes at play; it's simply a narrator speaking to his on-again, off-again paramour and trying to make sense of why they continually hurt each other.

Springsteen comes at it from a perspective that he uses to tackle much of his other subject matter. He contrasts the nostalgia for the good times of the past with the pain being suffered in the present. "How could something so bad, darling, come from something that was so good?" he asks, and the song doesn't provide any easy answers.

Maybe the reluctance to put the song on an album comes from the fact that Springsteen is unsparing in his descriptions of how bad things have gotten between these two. In the first verse, he sings, "Then little by little we choked out all the life that our love could hold." The refrains are similarly blunt: "It's like we had a noose, and baby without check / We pulled 'til it grew tighter around our necks."

This is not docile stuff. These are violent metaphors that the narrator conjures, and the leap can easily be made that such harsh words are borne out of actual events between the two. Yet the two stick with each other simply because neither is willing to make the first move: "Each one waiting for the other, darlin', to say when."

Despite all of the negativity brewing between the two and the sad comparison between what was and what is in their relationship, the narrator's ultimate impulse is to go back to her. "Well baby you can meet me tonight on the loose ends," Springsteen sings, suggesting that these two are ready to continue their destructive cycle.

Another pop song might have backed off from such a downbeat denouement, preferring instead that the couple separate or promise not to hurt each other anymore. "Loose Ends" prefers realism to safety. For all the gleaming surfaces of the music, which practically begs to be heard on a radio at as loud a volume as possible, that's a dark message at the core, and perhaps one that Springsteen wasn't ready to embrace or promote. That would explain why it took so long for this pitch-perfect, pitch-black power bomb of a song to reach us.

23. "Your Own Worst Enemy" (from *Magic*, 2007)

It's the hallmark of great artists that they can still find a way to surprise fans many, many years into their career. For those who might have had a preconceived notion of what Bruce Springsteen was supposed to sound like, this unjustly forgotten gem on 2007's *Magic* was likely a shocker.

In these days when albums are less valued than they once were, it's easy for songs like this, an album cut by a veteran rocker with many high-profile triumphs in his past, to get lost in the shuffle. That's too bad in the case of "Your Own Worst Enemy" because it's more than just surprising. It's stunningly great.

Imagine a song with music by the Left Banke, mid-1960s melders of classical and pop, and lyrics by Warren Zevon, he of the acerbic piano ballads, and you kind of get the drift of what the little ditty is going for. The music takes you one way and the words pull you the other, and it's a thrilling, shadowy ride.

Magic was the second post-reunion album for Springsteen and the E Street Band. The first, 2002's *The Rising*, found them straining to sound modern and forceful, draining much of the band's charm in the process. *Magic* was on much firmer ground simply because the band and Springsteen both seemed to be more at ease with their place in the musical world. As a result, a left-field departure like this song sounds right in their wheelhouse.

It should be noted that the band gets ample help from a string section that brings Victorian pomp to the song and underlines the somber tone of the lyrics. But the E Street Band keeps its personality among the violas and cellos, primarily though the steady hand of Max Weinberg on drums and Danny Federici's expressive organ chirps.

One pleasant development that has accompanied late-period Springsteen's willingness to embrace classic sounds, which in this case also includes a few connecting passages that harken back to the Beach Boys' *Pet Sounds*, is his return to a more natural, full-bodied vocal style reminiscent of his earlier years. While the bone-dry Southern accent he affected in the 1990s suited some of the material from that period, the kind of singing he does on "Your Own Worst Enemy" is more expressive and aesthetically pleasing.

The "you" Springsteen addresses in the song might as well be the same guy from "Darkness on the Edge of Town" or "Brilliant Disguise" still scuffling along and unable to get out of his own way. There are hints of a more all-encompassing sorrow in the song, but it works best as a searing character sketch of the kind of personality that sabotages itself at the moment it is closest to bliss.

After all, the title is a play on the cliché that says, "You're your own worst enemy." In this case, Springsteen imagines this enemy as a second self, one that arrives to wreak havoc in times of peace and comfort. These more benign moments are now in the past: "You closed your eyes and saw her / You knew who you were."

As things get progressively worse, the identity of the person he's addressing starts to come into question. "There's a face you know / Staring back from the shop window," Springsteen sings, intimating that the reflection that the person would expect to see is somehow skewed and unfamiliar. "Your Own Worst Enemy" is a kind of dark parable without lesson or moral because Springsteen posits the situation as one that's unavoidable for a certain kind of individual who continually snatches misery from the jaws of happiness.

In an effort to hide the evidence of his Jekyll/Hyde transformation, the protagonist takes futile action: "The times they got too clear / So you removed all the mirrors." Of course, none of this happens in a vacuum, so he's bringing his loved ones down with him into his pit of confusion and uncertainty. "Once the family felt secure / Now no one's very sure," Springsteen sings.

The thing that sticks with you from "Your Own Worst Enemy" is the matter-of-fact way that this all takes place, as if one night this guy was a well-adjusted, loving, unselfish fellow only to have his dark side erupt like an inward-flowing volcano. "Everything is falling down," Springsteen intones in the chorus, and no amount of gliding stringed instruments can reverse that process. Still, psychological deterioration has never sounded so lovely.

22. "Hungry Heart" (from *The River*, 1980)

As contemporaries like Billy Joel, Bob Seger, and Tom Petty peppered the pop charts with hits in the late 1970s and early 1980s, Bruce Springsteen was probably wondering just what he had to do to break through with a big hit single. "Born to Run" may have been too big for easy digestion on the radio, and "Prove It All Night" was maybe a shade too dark. Wonderful songs both, the relatively lukewarm response they received from pop radio might have even had Springsteen believing in the mistaken maxim that says that a hit is a hit, a great song is a great song, and never the twain shall meet.

It took a song that he was all ready to give away for him to finally rock AM radio with his unique brand of crowd-pleasing profundity. Springsteen famously had the Ramones in mind for the song, which is kind of funny considering that the elegant sheen the E Street Band eventually put on the song was likely a far cry from the thrashing the punk legends likely would have given it. Producer Jon Landau, with his well-trained ear for what works on the radio, stepped in and made the save.

"Hungry Heart" cried out for the gleaming production spin that Springsteen and Landau worked up for the song, a throwback to golden hits of the early 1960s that still managed to stay current enough so as not to sound like the oldies circuit. The snap and crackle of Max Weinberg's drums immediately grabs your attention and Roy Bittan's chiming piano chords keep it. Along the way, Danny Federici pipes in with a soulful organ solo that, as is typical with Federici's contributions, is exactly what the song needs.

One other notable characteristic of "Hungry Heart" are the skyscraping backing vocals. On previous albums, Springsteen tended to handle most of the vocals himself. If a song required harmonies, he would often do the honors by multi-tracking his voice. This was an effective enough technique, especially on the inward-looking monologues on *Darkness on the Edge of Town*. (It also would come in handy on *Nebraska*, when those yelping harmonies were like ghosts trapped within those haunted songs.)

Yet for a song like "Hungry Heart," which, despite the tinges of sadness that dogged the narrative, was essentially an uplifting sort of track, a different strategy was in order. As a result, Springsteen called upon Mark Volman and Howard Kaylan of 1960s hitmakers the Turtles to join the session. As they soar above Springsteen wordlessly in the verses before joining him in belting out the refrains, they provide a dreaminess and sense of togetherness that makes the song instantly endearing.

Indeed, much of the song's success has to do with the community that the lyrics imply is united by the yearning and longing of their collective heart. There's a reason that this is the song, when played in concert, that engenders a massive crowd-wide sing-along, allowing Springsteen to simply hold out the mike and take a much-needed breather. It's because the people in the audience easily identify with the simplicity and truth of the refrain: "Everybody's got a hungry heart."

The first two verses are examples of the narrator's own inner restlessness, told succinctly by Springsteen as if the relationship catastrophes were matter-of-fact and unavoidable. In the opening verse, the wife just up and leaves without any word of why or any warning to her imminent departure. The second verse presents a barroom hookup doomed to failure. "We fell in love I knew it had to end," Springsteen sings, insinuating that a long-lasting relationship is not in the cards for those whose hearts have insatiable appetites.

And yet the final verse insists that it's in everyone's nature to desire something lasting and real, even as we tend to fumble it away once it's within our grasp. The unifying message of the refrain isn't really a celebratory one, but there is comfort for someone in the audience or listening to a car radio in knowing that there is an infinite chorus of folks hurting just as bad belting out those cathartic words in unison.

Standout performances and lean production aside, the real reason that "Hungry Heart" broke so big is how it brought the lovelorn together in a massive support group. That's a pretty ironic outcome for a song that insists our hearts tend to invariably push us toward loneliness.

21. "Wrecking Ball" (from *Wrecking Ball*, 2012)

You hear it all the time from artists of every stripe, be they painters, poets, filmmakers, songwriters, or whatever. They'll say about their latest work, "This is a metaphor for . . ." If they have to explain the metaphor and you can't glean the meaning just from experiencing the work they've created, they've probably missed the boat. The best metaphors are the ones that reveal themselves almost by accident, even if the artist in question always intended them to eventually sneak out.

"Wrecking Ball," on the surface, is one last tribute to Giants Stadium, the New Jersey sports complex that was demolished in 2010. On the E Street Band's last stand there in 2009, Springsteen opened the first show with the song, one he had written specifically for the occasion. With its references to the football team, the Meadowlands, and Springsteen's own Jersey upbringing, it seemed like a simple, ad hoc homage to the stadium, at least if you didn't listen closely enough.

Springsteen then made the interesting decision to not just include the song on his new album in 2012, but also make it the title track. It seemed like an odd choice, considering the specificity of its origin. Would it be able to transcend its reason for existence and fit in with all these new songs?

The answer is a resounding and thrilling yes because "Wrecking Ball" was never just about some creaky old stadium. That stadium represents anyone and everyone who has ever been mitigated or marginalized in their own lives, folks who once stood young and proud only to find themselves seemingly shunted aside as the years pass. When Springsteen sings in the chorus, "Bring on your wrecking ball," he is singing with the collective voices of these people.

Wrecking Ball is an album that was recorded by a cast of rotating guest players, and it contains hardly any contributions from the E Street Band. The title track is an exception, however, since it features Max Weinberg, Steven Van Zandt, and, in one of his last appearances with the band before his death, Clarence Clemons. Who better to conjure the ghosts within those hallowed grounds than those who had encountered them with Springsteen over the years? The recording is elegiac in parts due to Soozie Tyrell's mournful violin, but it gets rollicking in the instrumental passages, the blaring horns turning this funeral procession into a defiant celebration.

That defiance is the main calling card of "Wrecking Ball." In the very first verse, after throwing a knowing shout-out to "the swamps of Jersey" as if Rosalita herself were listening, Springsteen dares the unnamed enemy, "If you think it's your time / Then step to the line." In the second verse, he warns these would-be demolishers that he's got a whole army ready to defend this place: "'Cause tonight all the dead are here."

In the bridge, Springsteen turns toward those on his side, the ones most affected by the passing of a landmark, to give an inspirational speech. He urges them to gird their loins for the tough days ahead: "Hold tight to your anger / And don't fall to your fears."

The final verse, with the music falling away to a low rumble behind him, shows Springsteen accepting the changes that inevitably will come. He is one with those whom he addresses in the song, just another one-time warrior who had some big wins but is destined to come up short against Father Time. "And all our little victories and glories," Springsteen sings, "are turned into parking lots."

His ultimate message is that we're all going to go down, but it's best to go down swinging. "Hard times come and hard times go," he repeats over and over leading to the final refrain, yet with each chord change, another demon is exercised and the will grows stronger. It is a breathtaking moment that will get you misty-eyed and fired up all at once, the kind of moment that Springsteen does better than anyone.

The amazing thing is that "Wrecking Ball," written at a different time and for a different purpose than the other songs on the album that bears its name, manages to work perfectly as a summation of the kind of resilience and fortitude necessary to bear the heartbreaks endured by the hard-luck characters in those other songs. That's the kind of serendipity that only the finest songwriters can conjure. In this stirring anthem, Springsteen shows just how powerful a metaphor can be, using one to implore his entire army of listeners to face down their own personal wrecking balls and send them flying back from whence they came.

20. "Stolen Car" (from *The River*, 1980)

"Stolen Car" is one of the first songs about relationships to ever appear on a Bruce Springsteen album. It remains one of his finest. Hollow and haunting in a disconcerting way, it is that rare song about a deteriorating relationship that honors psychological truth over clichés and platitudes that sound good with a melody attached but have little relevance in the real world.

Springsteen wrangled with the right tone and lyrical approach for the song when it came time to record it. On *Tracks* in 1998, he released an earlier version of the song that had more of a fleshed-out arrangement with a slight country attitude and lyrics that embellished upon the story of the man and the woman in the song.

His instinct to cut the excess lyrics away and render the song in the muted, atmospheric version that appeared on *The River* was dead-on. Sometimes less is more, and suggesting certain things can be more effective than spelling them out. It's a lesson that many songwriters fail to get but that Springsteen demonstrates brilliantly here.

For the audience members who want the reassurance of easy answers and clear motivations, a song like "Stolen Car" is never going to be their bag. Springsteen writes like the character living through this situation would speak. This guy wouldn't be able to pinpoint why things have turned out so badly, even when the reasons are probably emanating from somewhere deep inside him.

The music is in tune with this minimalist approach. For most of the song, all that's heard is a low guitar rumble and Roy Bittan's piano pecking away at the edges, fading in and out like the protagonist's conscience. Some timpani by Max Weinberg calls to mind Roy Orbison's classic criers, but this resemblance is only on the surface; Orbison's melancholy grandeur at least offered catharsis, but Springsteen's story is too ruthlessly accurate for any kind of release to be gained. Danny Federici washes over everything with his keyboards in the closing moments, the song fading out even as the narrator's tormented journey continues.

The fact that he's riding a "Stolen Car" as he attempts to collect his thoughts and retrace the steps that left him at this precarious point is telling. Just as the car is a counterfeit of sorts, so is the romance that haunts him. It's important to note that the narrator never says that he has actually separated from his wife. In many ways, thinking of the two of them grinding their way through life in a shell of a marriage is more painful than if Springsteen gave us evidence of a clear break. But again, he's not out to make it easy on us so much. He's telling it like it is.

Even the narrator desperately wants to define the problems that enveloped his marriage, but he continually comes up empty. His initial notion that it was just simple restlessness that would be overcome with time is proven incorrect when the situation only gets worse. "In the end it was something more I guess," he ponders, "that pulled us apart and made us weep." "Something more" is the telling phrase; how can you rectify a problem when you can't even say for sure what it is?

The woman gets her chance to speak up in the last verse, and with one anecdote, she evokes just how damaging a broken relationship can be. She asks him if he recalls his old habit of writing her love letters, letters that she sentimentally kept. "She said last night she read those letters," the narrator wearily recounts. "And they made her feel one hundred years old."

Unable to deal with her pain and loss of zest for her life, the narrator hits the road. He sees his symbolic stolen car as a way to get out, but he can't get that lucky. "Each night I wait to get caught," he sings, "but I never do." It's a pretty sad state of affairs when someone would prefer incarceration to a normal home life, but it's clear that his prison follows him around no matter where he travels.

Still he rides. He pretends that he's just imagining it all, that all of the problems will simply blow over. But in the black of the night, his deepest dread is revealed: "I ride by night and I travel in fear / That in this darkness I will disappear."

Springsteen ends the song without any final blowout by the pair, no emotional climax to at least let us have the peace of knowing that this spoiled love has run its course. "Stolen Car" just keeps riding deeper and darker into the night, carrying its despairing passengers to the oblivion for which they were destined from the moment they met.

19. "Tenth Avenue Freeze Out" (from *Born to Run*, 1975)

Every superhero worth a damn needs a great origin story. Spiderman was bitten by a radioactive insect. Superman crash landed from another planet and gained inhuman strength from Earth's sun. Bruce Springsteen was hit by a saxophone blast from Clarence Clemons and made it his mission to save rock and roll.

That's the story told by "Tenth Avenue Freeze Out," a song that's larger than life and too much fun for words. Springsteen somehow intuited, even at an early part in his career, that building a hokey mythology around his music career would pay off in the long run. He started it with a few of the self-referential comments on *The Wild, the Innocent & the E Street Shuffle*. This exhilarating song takes it to another level.

In retrospect, the story isn't all that embellished. After all, Springsteen's classic sound truly didn't coalesce until Clemons came aboard at the tail end of the recording of *Greetings from Asbury Park, N.J.*, Springsteen's 1973 debut album. *The Wild, the Innocent, & the E Street Shuffle* improved by leaps and bounds from there with Clarence onboard full time. And as for *Born to Run*, the 1975 album that contains "Tenth Avenue Freeze Out," the fact that its songs dominate the Top 20 of our humble countdown should tell you all need to know about its quality.

Yet Clemons wasn't the only E Street Band member to play a part in the success of this irresistible number. Steven Van Zandt wasn't even a member of the band yet when he marched into the studio and told the shocked horn pros just how the main riff should be played. And Roy Bittan, whose piano work on *Born to Run* tended toward the stately and somber, shows his versatility here by ladling on the funky attitude.

That contrast between Bittan's styles also brings up an important point about the role "Tenth Avenue Freeze Out" played on *Born to Run*. The album is full of stunning set pieces, but all the epic songs could have rendered it a bit too grand and stuffy. "Tenth Avenue Freeze Out" provides just the right amount of levity for balance.

Springsteen certainly seems to be enjoying himself in the song, just as he has in its countless live performances over the years. The story sets him up in the beginning as the underdog, playing the role of Bad Scooter (note the initials), woeful and "searching for his groove." The copious street life seems to mock him, berating him on all sides and taking advantage of his lack of backup.

The song could easily have come off as too much of a lark, but there are real emotions in there that prevent that from happening. In the bridge, Springsteen sings about being "alone" and "on my own" and that he "can't go home." While Dylan might have asked him at that point, "How does it feel?" Clemons pipes in and tries to get him to open his eyes: "And kid you better get the picture."

It's a good thing that the final verse comes along to allow our heroes the chance to save the day. "When the change was made uptown and the Big Man joined the band," Springsteen sings, followed immediately by Clemons's saxophone clearing out the entire neighborhood with a few notes. At that point, comeuppance is due for all those who tried to keep this kid down. "I'm gonna sit back right easy and laugh," Springsteen promises, "when Scooter and the Big Man bust this city in half."

No one, not even Springsteen himself, has ever been able to properly explain what the title phrase means. Suffice it to say that its import is tied to the fortunes of the main character. In the first two refrains, it seems like a harbinger of doom. With Clemons at his side, Springsteen wields the threat of a freeze-out as if it's an unstoppable weapon.

"Tenth Avenue Freeze Out" took on special meaning in the wake of Clemons's death in 2011. When Springsteen toured again with the E Street Band, he didn't avoid the song. Instead, he would reach the point where he sang that triumphant line about Scooter and the Big Man and quickly go silent, the band following suit. The crowds cheered wildly during these moments of silence, allowing them to pay the proper tribute to this inimitable musician, without whom, Springsteen's career would not have been the same.

Not for nothing does Clemons appear on the cover of *Born to Run*, Springsteen literally leaning on him. Where "Tenth Avenue Freeze Out" once saluted that relationship, it now memorializes it. And ultimately, as long as there are ears to hear the song, it makes it as indestructible as a superhero and as eternal as love.

18. "Independence Day" (from *The River*, 1980)

"Now my dad, he passed away this year, but I've gotta thank him because what would I have conceivably written about without him? I mean, you can imagine that if everything had gone great between us, we would have had disaster" (284).[30]

Bruce Springsteen spoke the lines above as part of his Rock and Roll Hall of Fame acceptance speech on March 15, 1999. It's a bit of a comic exaggeration, but it's probably true that he would have had to dig a little deeper into a songwriting fault to fill out 1978's *Darkness on the Edge of Town* and 1980's *The River* if he didn't have plenty of material that emanated from his complicated relationship with his dad.

One of the reasons that Springsteen is probably rock's foremost chronicler of the father-son relationship is that he embraced that complexity in the songs. Rock and roll was built in part on the idea that it was a way for children to rebel against their parents, but that eventually grew, as represented in early rock songs, into a kind of clichéd rancor between the generations that could provide a little fun for the teens listening in but really didn't provide long-lasting answers.

Some of the more forward-thinking songwriters tried to rectify that problem. The Beatles' "She's Leaving Home" told the story of a runaway through the perspective of her grieving parents whose love for their daughter was never in doubt even as their insensitivity to her problems led to her departure. Bob Dylan went 180 degrees away from the norm, as he tended to do, with "Tears of Rage," a *Basement Tapes* track in which the daughter is the one doing the hurting and the parents are the oppressed pair.

Springsteen's songs about his dad generally don't so much mess with the perspective as they strive to keep from being one-sided. "Independence Day," which is the pinnacle of those dad songs, manages to see both sides of the story when the son is leaving home. Considering that fateful day is when the relationship is likely at its most strained, his willingness to try and understand his father at this point is positively enlightened.

"Independence Day," one of the emotional turning points on *The River*, benefits from one of the most elegantly understated performances ever by the E Street Band. Danny Federici's organ that starts the song has a pipe-like sound to it, leading into Springsteen's acoustic guitar foundation and some poignant piano touches by Roy Bittan. Clarence Clemons's saxophone, so often used to give a song a jolt of energy, is restrained here yet hits all the right emotional notes.

The song begins with the narrator putting his father to bed, the flipside of the traditional father-son ritual that lets us know that the old order is changing. He admits to the same stubbornness that he sees in his dad ("I guess that we were just too much of the same kind") and writes their estrangement off as something beyond both of their control, a "darkness" that infects both their town and their house. Understanding and conciliatory though he may be, he's still getting out: "But they can't touch me now and you can't touch me now / They ain't gonna do to me what I watched them to do to you."

The idea of someone's adult life veering far from the ideals and dreams of their youth is one Springsteen first explored in depth on 1978's *Darkness on the Edge of Town,* which makes sense because "Independence Day" was originally slated for that album before being held over for *The River*. The narrator is quick to accept that he was part of that problem for his father, but he's at a loss as to how to correct it.

Springsteen hints in the final verse at a kind of toxic, overhanging cloud that infects not just the narrator and his family but everyone surrounding them, causing instability in the normally safe havens of home and family. "And soon everything we've known will just be swept away," he predicts. The implication here is that the narrator isn't going to wait around for that to happen, even as the father will. That the son feels sorrow at this fact rather than some sort of vindication shows that there is genuine love between the two men buried beneath the years of conflict.

That love fuels the heartfelt regret that emanates from the narrator in the final chorus. "Papa now I know the things you wanted that you could not say," Springsteen sings, admitting an inner life for the older man that most rock songs would not grant him. That leads up to the heart-wrenching final couplet, the narrator begging his father to pay him back with the same understanding that he has shown for the entire song: "But won't you just say goodbye it's Independence Day / I swear I never meant to take those things away."

With those final lines, Springsteen spoke by proxy for countless others who either didn't have the words or never got the chance to express those same feelings to their own parents. The song is called "Independence Day," but although Springsteen might have left, he hadn't quite broken free. He kept writing about his dad, ending up with an insightful, nuanced, and powerful collection of songs in the process.

17. "Thunder Road" (from *Born to Run*, 1975)

Let's first dispense with why this song, generally regarded as one of the best and most stirring rock songs of all time, only ranks No. 17 in this Bruce Springsteen–centric list. The explanation is that these songs are ranked based on official studio recordings, and the rocking version of "Thunder Road" that opens up *Born to Run* doesn't serve the song as well as a more restrained approach might have.

The problem, and it's really a small quibble in the grand scheme of things but it costs the song in such a competitive list, arises when the song shifts into the full-band portion of the track. Up to then, "Thunder Road" is a ballad, and that's probably what it always was at heart. When it starts to rev up its engines, Springsteen has to really steamroll through the lyrics, every one of which deserves full attention. The band also seems to be rushing a bit to keep pace, making it seem like they're in a hurry to get through the thing, when it really should be savored.

By contrast, the opening section, with Springsteen's harmonica rising like the dawn and Roy Bittan's piano scurrying along beside him, is sheer perfection as the opening to the song and to a landmark album. There are live versions of the song, including the one on *Live/1975–85*, Bruce's mammoth concert compilation from 1986, in which this solo piano arrangement is carried all the way through. Not only does this approach allow us to really feel the full potency of the amazing lyrics, it also highlights the melody in all its swooping, soaring glory.

Again, this is all splitting hairs because no matter which way you choose to arrange and perform it, it's pretty near impossible for "Thunder Road" to be anything but brilliant. Anybody thinking that the "Born to Run" single was a once-in-a-lifetime kind of songwriting achievement found out as soon as they put the album on the turntable that Springsteen had another epic just as vast and invigorating in him. (And there would be more to come as the record continued to spin.)

The song begins with two immortal lines ("Screen door slams / Mary's dress waves") that seem like stage directions, which makes sense because Springsteen is indeed setting the scene for us. That scene is a kind of redux of Romeo calling out below Juliet's window, only this time only a porch separates Mary from her would-be romantic abductor beckoning from his car.

Springsteen immediately makes these characters real by refusing to idealize them. "You ain't a beauty, but hey you're all right," the narrator sings out to her before cataloging all of her doubts and fears that paralyze her on that porch. Not that he's got it all figured out: "All the redemption I can offer girl is beneath this dirty hood." But he insists that they should make their escape, suggesting the alternative is to just let these problems and hang-ups crush them: "Hey what else can we do now?"

In the chorus, the narrator makes his best case. "Oh come take my hand / We're riding out tonight to case the promised land." "Case" is the key word, suggesting they can only sneak into paradise via some sort of subterfuge. That doesn't matter to the narrator, who believes that his only true escape can come with her by his side.

He can't promise her much: "I know you're lonely for words that I ain't spoken," he admits. But he also tells her that the boys who once rivaled him for her affections, the ones who "haunt this dusty beach road in the skeleton frames of burned-out Chevrolets" (what a line), are all falling by the wayside: "You hear their engine roaring on / But when you get to the porch they're gone on the wind."

It's at this point that the narrator makes his final pitch: "So Mary climb in / It's a town full of losers and I'm pulling out of here to win." With those two lines, Springsteen makes the case in succinct fashion, even as we're glad as listeners that he elaborated so eloquently in the previous sections of the song.

This is one of those rare rock songs where every line is shot through with deep meaning and striking emotion. It's also a decisive argument against all those who would say that rock lyrics don't or shouldn't mean anything. "Thunder Road," as presented on *Born to Run*, is daringly wide-screen, but what lingers is the desperate intimacy of a conversation between two people on the precipice of their lives' defining moment.

16. "Meeting across the River" (from *Born to Run*, 1975)

For all its sweeping grandeur and epic scope, *Born to Run* is essentially an album of small stories. "Thunder Road" is a guy talking to a girl on a porch. "Backstreets" is just someone reminiscing on a youthful friendship now spent. For all the operatic drama on "Jungleland," no one even watches the ambulance departing with the body of the Magic Rat. That Springsteen renders them with urgency and import shows just how much he cares about these characters, how their lives, which others might not think are worthy of glorification, resonate far past their little corners of the world.

In "Meeting across the River," Springsteen scales down the tenor of the recording but still dignifies the exploits of two small-time thugs who just might be headed to their demise. In stunningly economical fashion, he manages to flesh out the motivations and inner workings of these two guys, one of whom never says a word during the course of the song.

The fact that "Meeting across the River" immediately precedes "Jungleland" on *Born to Run* has led some to consider it a kind of prologue. That view mitigates the singular accomplishment that Springsteen manages with the song. It is a complete story because the lyrics do all the setup work while the music subtly reveals the outcome.

In many ways, the song is a predecessor to some of the story songs on *Nebraska*. Songs like "Johnny 99" and "Atlantic City" featured characters who decide on shady dealings to try and solve their financial problems. The difference with the latter songs is that Springsteen made more explicit the sociological conditions that forced these characters into such desperate measures, not so much excusing them as explaining them.

He doesn't offer any such context in "Meeting across the River," yet he still manages to portray these guys sympathetically. The narrator, who does all the talking, posits a scenario to his buddy Eddie whereby the two can make some easy money by doing a little work in the city. Cajoling, bullying, and pleading with Eddie to step up, help him out, and be professional about it, the narrator seems to be trying to convince himself about the positive outcome he envisions as much as he is trying to sway his silent partner.

The narrator tells Eddie to stay quiet when they meet the man on the other side, "'Cause this guy don't dance / And the word's been passed this is our last chance." That line intimates both that this isn't the first time these two knuckleheads have tried something like this and that they may have screwed it up in the past. "And if we blow this one / They ain't gonna be looking for just me this time," he warns.

Even though these two are definitely bumbling-henchmen material, the danger factor is upped considerably when firearms enter into the equation: "Here stuff this in your pocket / It'll look like you're carrying a friend." Although they may be in over their heads, the narrator sees them as big-timers about to put their past errors right: "Change your shirt 'cause tonight we got style."

We might believe in the success of their mission were it not for the moody music accompanying their conversation. Musical adventurousness is no good if it's an end in itself; artists should only try something different if it fits the song. Springsteen gets it right here, employing special guests trumpeter Randy Brecker and stand-up bassist Richard Davis to join pianist Roy Bittan in conveying a jazzy, film-noir feel that suggests that this will be the last score these two ever try to pull off.

Had Springsteen simply kept the pair scheming and plotting, that sense of doom hanging over the song might not have been as affecting. But in the final verse, we find out just why this night is so important to the narrator. He wants the money to make things better for his girl Cherry, who's angry with him for hocking her radio. "But, Eddie man, she don't understand / That two grand's practically sitting here in my pocket," he sings, his seeming assuredness now overcompensating for his creeping fear.

He plans to show her the money and revive their stagnant love affair. "She'll see this time I wasn't just talking," he promises Eddie. But Brecker, Bittan, and Davis are realists; they play these deluded fools off on their journey and refuse to grant them a happy ending. "Meeting across the River" may be a small-time story, but it lingers long after the light at the end of these two characters' tunnel is snuffed out.

15. "Badlands" (from *Darkness on the Edge of Town*, 1978)

"Badlands" is the first thing you hear on *Darkness on the Edge of Town*. Since that album was released three years after Bruce Springsteen's previous masterwork *Born to Run*, it meant that the anticipation of those first sounds for hungry fans was intense. Suffice it to say that a few bars of the song were all they probably needed to know that Springsteen was still at the top of his game.

There is a noticeable edge to the song that immediately separates it from all that had come before in the Springsteen catalog. *Born to Run* had moments, like in the title track or "Backstreets," where the music surges to a point of joyous inspiration. "Badlands" takes that uplift to a fiercer, more primal level. It's as if it forces you to feel alive so you can't possibly consider the alternative.

It's easy to point to Springsteen's legal battle with former manager Mike Appel as the springboard for the more confrontational tone of *Darkness*. That may have been part of it, but it's likely that there would have been a natural progression for Springsteen away from the generally optimistic tone of *Born to Run* anyway. After all, much of the darkness on *Darkness* comes from Springsteen's growing awareness of the limitations of life, something that seems largely independent of any concerns about the status of his recording career.

The tone of *Darkness*, and of "Badlands" specifically with its unrelenting musical thrust and defiant attitude, often gets linked to the rise of punk music. That's a bit of a stretch as well, since the songs on the album have a lot more nuance and depth, lyrically and musically, than punk could or even wanted to capture. The punks and Springsteen simply had different agendas.

What tends to happen with "Badlands" is that people hear the anger and the edge, but they miss the fact that it holds a stronger connection to earlier Springsteen songs than might be audible on the surface. While Springsteen is more readily admitting some of the negative elements of life into his forecast, he's ultimately advocating, through the guise of his put-upon yet resilient narrator, for the afflicted to find whatever they spirit they have within them to rise above it all.

With music this forceful, overcoming long odds and numerous obstacles certainly seems possible. Springsteen has admitted to nicking the riff from the Animals' "Don't Let Me Be Misunderstood" for "Badlands." But while the notes are similar, the tone is different. In the Animals song, the riff, played on an organ that sounds like it's on loan from a horror-movie soundtrack, has an ominous vibe. With Roy Bittan banging away beside the martial beat of Max Weinberg on Springsteen's track, those same notes seem triumphant.

In the break, Springsteen plays a precise yet vigorous solo before ceding the stage to Clarence Clemons and his all-knowing saxophone. There have been numerous examples on this list of Springsteen using the last verse of a song to build up the drama by dropping the music away before ratcheting back up to the chorus. Never has this strategy been employed as effectively as it is in "Badlands," especially with Bruce capping it off with the unforgettable rallying cry, "I wanna spit in the face of these badlands."

Before he reaches that point, Springsteen precedes the final verse with some wordless, harmonized humming which seems to blow across the unforgiving landscape he describes like a redemptive wind. That brings up one way in which "Badlands" and the album that contains it differ from their forbears in the Springsteen canon, and that is their scope.

On *Born to Run*, the characters, sights, and sounds Springsteen described seemed to be localized to the New York/New Jersey area, which he knew inside and out. The "Badlands" don't seem to be based on any specific area, even as the title does give off the vibe of some desolate rural area. Instead, these lands seem more like the representation of unforgiving, depressing, suffocating situations that can befall anyone anywhere.

As such, Springsteen's call to arms against just such a soul-deadening outpost is somehow more universal than before, even as the hope and faith that sustain the narrator through such rough terrain are the same hope and faith that got all those gang members and highway riders through their predicaments on his previous work. Springsteen's message had toughened and thickened its musical skin to the point where denizens of "Badlands" everywhere could hear that message loud and clear and recognize its wisdom and worth.

14. "The River" (from *The River*, 1980)

You can usually judge the mood of a Bruce Springsteen song by its protagonist's relationship with his or her dreams. These are not so much the actual dreams that one has while asleep; although those come into play quite often as well, dreams are used in Springsteen's songs more as plot drivers, harbingers of things to come, or deceivers that lead characters down false paths.

More relevant to his work are the conscious dreams that mirror hopes and desires. At times they are treated as beneficial forces that should be cherished or nurtured. He had an unreleased 1980s song called "Follow That Dream" and as of 2009 was still "Working on a Dream." In "No Surrender," he sounds ready to die fighting for the right to dream.

Yet in many songs, dreams are to be regarded with extreme suspicion and sometimes even actively avoided since their propensity for not coming true is too great a disappointment for the human soul to constantly bear without cracking. Think of the "dark heart of a dream" in "Adam Raised a Cain" or "None But the Brave," which imagines some unseen being tossing aside dreams at random. Heck, there are so many shattered dreams on *Nebraska* that you'd swear Freddy Krueger was the cowriter.

The pivotal line in Springsteen's brilliant 1980 song "The River" finds Springsteen, with his struggling young father as his mouthpiece, questioning the very nature of dreams and the damage they are capable of doing. "Is a dream a life if it don't come true," he ponders, "or is it something worse?" It may be the single-most trenchant distillation of Springsteen's fascination, maybe even obsession, with dreams and their place in our lives.

The story for the song comes right out of Springsteen's own life since his sister and brother-in-law had a baby together and married at a young age with all the attendant pressures and stresses such a situation brings. In "The River," Springsteen doesn't judge or condescend to this predicament as much as probe it. Is it selfish for this guy to want his old life back? Why doesn't there seem to be any celebration at what should be the joyous rites of passage in their lives? And, most crucially, is it possible to reboot a life after the dreams that sustained it are rendered moot?

Certainly Springsteen has other irons in the fire with "The River," including the socioeconomic pressures that dog so many of his characters in that period of his songwriting. "Lately there ain't been much work on account of the economy," the guy complains, and he hints at having no opportunities in "the valley." But those issues are tangential at best, a way for Springsteen to set the scene for the closing part of the song, which takes a more existential view of the situation.

In this section, his former dreams become entangled with memories, which hint that he may not have realized how close to his ideal life he once was. This is too painful for him to conceptualize, which is why he and his new bride shun it: "Now I just act like I don't remember / Mary acts like she don't care."

Still, those memories persist, memories that Springsteen renders in idyllic fashion. The couple, now distant, were once inseparably close. Their lives were filled with carefree revelry; now they can barely smile. Maybe the memories were dreams after all, since it seems impossible to him, in his current sour state of mind, that such good times could really have ever transpired on an earthly plane.

"Now those memories come back to haunt me," he sings, "they haunt me like a curse." Those lines bring up the extremely depressing notion that since the halcyon days of youth invariably set us up for disappointment, it might be preferable to live a dreary existence right from the womb in order to spare ourselves the letdown. That's when Springsteen unleashes his association between dreams and lies, driving his point even further home.

Set in a tender folk-rock background distinguished by Springsteen's evocative harmonica, the song goes out on a refrain that once again plays up the contradiction between the then and the now. Whereas the river was once the symbol of their innocence and happiness, it is now a stark reminder of all that can no longer be. The song might have been inspired by true life, and it features plenty of grounding details, but "The River" ultimately digs much deeper than that and asks how we should react when the seemingly infinite wellspring of youthful dreams suddenly comes up dry.

13. "Atlantic City" (from *Nebraska*, 1982)

It's hard to imagine it now because it has become synonymous with Atlantic City, New Jersey, but when Bruce Springsteen released "Atlantic City" in 1982, casino gambling in the state was only about four years old. At the time it was the second state in America to legalize casinos, joining Nevada, so it was still a novelty of sorts.

Springsteen's narrative doesn't overtly take sides on the gambling issue, even as it captures the chaotic opening years when bettors flowed in with organized crime tumbling at their heels. He uses the city as the setting for a personal story of a struggling guy desperate to improve his fortunes. And where better to improve one's fortunes than in a place that promotes the ability to get rich quick with a little luck, even as the dark flip side of that luck is always lurking?

"Atlantic City" is found on Springsteen's acoustic album *Nebraska*, where it proves that songs with just guitar and harmonica can be every bit as stinging as full-band electric offerings. Part of the reason for that is that Springsteen clearly put a lot of thought into these demos, probably because he envisioned them making the transition to E Street Band recordings and wanted to get them in good shape.

That transition never happened, of course, so Springsteen's one-man band performances are for the ages. Using overdubs efficiently because he only had four tracks with which to work, he builds the song around his insistent guitar strumming and high-lonesome harmonica. To this he adds some mandolin, which evokes a simpler bygone era that the gambling swept away, and yelping backing vocals that complement the urgency of the lead.

The first verse of "Atlantic City" provides the context. The "Chicken Man" who, along with his house, meets his end in the opening moments was a real-life mobster (Phil Testa), giving Springsteen's tale some verisimilitude. Springsteen also mentions the warring elements at play: a hopelessly overmatched gambling commission and district attorney trying to keep some semblance of sanity while gangsters come pouring into the city from all corners.

The narrator really doesn't appear until the second verse, where it's quickly established that he is far removed from this world of big money and daring criminals. He doesn't even have a fancy nickname like Johnny 99, who shares his problem of "debt that no honest man can pay." So his answer is to take all of the money that he and his girl have saved and bus it down to Atlantic City.

At this point, it's still possible to assume that he's going to take this money and try to exponentially increase it by trying to ride a hot blackjack streak or putting it all on a single number on the roulette wheel. In the bridge, he sees the city as the answer to all of his problems, which go far beyond his economic concerns. "Now our luck may have died and our love may be cold," he admits. In that context, his speculation in the refrain that "maybe everything that dies someday comes back" seems to refer to the possible rejuvenation of that luck and love.

In the final verse, he once again bemoans his circumstances, and in the spirit of this sudden gambling mecca, he sees life as a zero-sum game: "Down here it's just winners and losers and don't get caught on the wrong side of that line." That's when Springsteen unleashes the big reveal at which he'd only been feinting to this point as the narrator uncovers his big plan: "Well I'm tired of comin' out on the losin' end / So honey last night I met this guy and I'm gonna do a little favor for him."

We've seen this kind of thing before in Springsteen songs. "Incident on 57th Street" climaxed with Spanish Johnny heading into the night in search of some easy money. The Magic Rat from "Jungleland" is embroiled in gang warfare. And "Meeting across the River" was one small-time thug giving a pep talk to another in advance of some shady deal. Not one of these characters even hints at the danger inherent in their exploits.

The difference with the guy at the heart of "Atlantic City" is that he is self-aware enough to intuit his possible fate. Those closing lines make it clear that when he talks about the inevitability of death in the refrain, it is his way of admitting that he is gambling with far more than his money and his love.

Therein lies the subtle shift in Springsteen's attitude toward these types of characters. In the early days, crime seemed like a romantic choice. In the chillingly brilliant "Atlantic City," it's a forced gamble in a rigged game with your life at stake.

12. "Highway Patrolman" (from *Nebraska*, 1982)

We hear the scenario several times on Bruce Springsteen's 1982 album *Nebraska*. The characters and their particulars vary, but it's essentially the same set-up in "Nebraska," "Atlantic City," "Johnny 99," and, to a lesser extent, even "State Trooper" and "Open All Night." You've got a character telling a first-person account of either getting into some sort of trouble or at least preparing to do so.

The context in which these characters operate is the key component that unites them and the album and makes it so coherent. Springsteen's point, often unspoken in the songs but always lurking in the background, is that these characters have an underlying reason for becoming so unmoored. That reason varies from song to song, but there's always something that pushes them to the brink.

"Highway Patrolman" might be the most important song on the whole album because it presents an interesting flip side to those hot-headed, unstable reactions. Joe Roberts runs into many of the same issues that the others do. He faces financial pressures just like "Johnny 99" and the protagonist of "Atlantic City." The Midwestern town in which he resides sounds like it's probably the same kind of quiet place where Charles Starkweather harvested the "meanness in this world." And it's fair to say that, coming from such a place, he feels at times the same types of suffocating stress that puts the narrator of "State Trooper" out on the highway in a dangerous mood.

Yet Roberts doesn't react in any way like the guys in those other songs. When faced with the colossal calamity of losing his farm, he shrugs his shoulders and finds other work. His small-town life doesn't send him off half-cocked into the night; he instead finds comfort in the reassuring pleasures of home and family. Here is a guy who stands up tall against all of those underlying factors and, as Springsteen has advocated in so many of his songs, rises above them.

Yet Joe Roberts is cursed by loyalty to a brother who does indeed resemble some of the aforementioned outlaws and hair-triggers. Franky Roberts seems to have been in trouble since the day he was born, which puts him in direct contrast to Joe's reliably upright nature. One of Joe's many redeeming qualities, however, is his loyalty, and that loyalty blinds him to what ultimately needs to be done with his brother.

Springsteen, singing in a slow, measured moan, does a wonderful job of embodying Joe. One of the ways that songwriters mess up a song like this is by putting words into the mouth or the interior monologue of a character that just don't fit. Yet there is nothing that Joe says or thinks that sounds even remotely strained or false. You can easily forget it is

Springsteen telling the story and start to believe you're hearing the confession of this officer of the law.

Listen to the way Springsteen sets up the conflict with just two simple lines at the beginning of the song: "I always done an honest job as honest as I could / I got a brother named Franky and Franky ain't no good." He then goes on to relate Franky's never-ending struggles with impulse control, but he also reveals his own decision to abide it: "Well if it was any other man, I'd put him straight away / But when it's your brother sometimes you look the other way."

In the refrain, Joe clings to the good times, hoping that these brief ports in the storm can someday be the rule and not the exception. He rationalizes his decisions to get Franky off the hook as the byproduct of a familial bond that supersedes everything, including his commitment to his job and simple common sense: "I catch him when he's strayin' like any brother would / Man turns his back on his family well he just ain't no good."

Note how Joe describes a disloyal person in exactly the same manner in which he described Franky earlier in the song. In his mind, his refusal to uphold the law and the recklessness of that decision in terms of how it could affect his job security and his beloved wife are the necessary sacrifices he must make to distinguish himself from his malcontent of a brother, who ends up being the ironic beneficiary of these choices.

Springsteen is showing us the impossible choices that folks like Franky create for the people in their wake. When Franky ultimately commits an act of violence that can't be swept under the rug, Joe finally decides to cut him free after an intensely rendered chase scene. Even as he essentially cuts all ties with Franky in this moment, he still pardons his crime by allowing him to cross the border.

And so it is that this guy with integrity and courage gets swept away by the foul tide that carries all the album's morally compromised antiheros. A masterpiece of storytelling, "Highway Patrolman" shows the devastating consequences that a good man can pay for being too close to the world's meanness.

11. "Bobby Jean" (from *Born in the U.S.A.*, 1984)

Songs about romance are a dime a dozen, but songs about friendship are relatively rare in the world of rock and roll. The ones that exist tend to focus on the positives of having a buddy on whom you can rely. There aren't too many that tackle the relationship from a realistic perspective in terms of changing lives and priorities over time that can put even the staunchest friendship to the test.

That's why "Bobby Jean" is not only a treasured component of Bruce Springsteen's catalog, but it also stands very high on any list of friendship songs that one might choose to amass. Springsteen had written on the subject before, most notably in "Backstreets," when the wounds of a severed friendship were still raw. In "Bobby Jean," though the hurt is evident at times in the narrator's shout-out to his friend, it is ultimately overwhelmed by wonderful memories and undying love than no amount of distance or time can harm.

It's interesting that "Bobby Jean" was one of the few songs on *Born in the U.S.A.* not chosen to be a single, because it is an absolute sure shot and probably would have added to the stunning number of hits the album produced. Maybe Springsteen wanted to save a little something special for those who bought the album, or the cassette as the case may have been in 1984, by keeping this one off the airwaves.

Nonetheless, "Bobby Jean" presents the E Street Band at their most evocative. Roy Bittan's piano chords veer from hopeful to heartbroken to wistfully resigned in perfect tune with Springsteen's narrative. Garry Tallent, ever the quiet contributor, does a wonderful job giving an already tuneful song a melodic boost at the bottom with his bass, while Clarence Clemons's sax solo at the end is one of his most heartfelt. When Springsteen wonders at song's end if his old pal will be able to hear this message, Clemons's closing word is a force of nature that demands it will be so.

By naming the title character "Bobby Jean," Springsteen ensures that the song will be a catch-all for the listeners who can imagine that the gender-unspecific name applies to whatever long-lost friend they might have. In Springsteen's case, most people have pointed to Steven Van Zandt—who left the E Street Band briefly in the 80s to pursue a solo career—as the inspiration. While this may have been true, Springsteen's song is too vast in its wisdom about friendship's ups and downs to be contained by a single incident.

When the narrator arrives at the home of his companion at the beginning of the song, just as he has done a million times before, he is greeted with the news that Bobby Jean is gone. This is when a complex cycle of emotions begins for the narrator. His first thought is of the times that they've spent together and how those times should have earned him, at the very least, the right to confront her (we'll go with her from this point, acknowledging that the gender is vague and unimportant) about her decision.

The second verse and the bridge contain numerous examples of how unique and special the friendship has been to the narrator. The foundation of it is built on more than just similar likes and dislikes and mutual admiration, although those are definitely important. What ultimately set it apart was the sense of belonging that it engendered in this pair, the kind of two-against-the-world notion it bred: "Now we went walking in the rain talking about the pain that from the world we hid / Now there ain't nobody, nowhere no how gonna ever understand me the way you did."

At some point, there has to be some form of acceptance that things are changing, that the past is no longer and that this girl is about to embark upon a life that will no longer include him. He makes that leap in the final verse, imagining her on her travels getting this cosmic epistle over the radio waves. Springsteen brings lumps into the throats of listeners everywhere by having the narrator put aside his hurt feelings and sorrow to muster the kind of well wishes that anyone would want from a beloved friend: "I'm just calling you one last time / Not to change your mind, but just to say I miss you baby, good luck, goodbye Bobby Jean."

In "Bobby Jean," we witness the subtle transformation of the narrator, from confusion at why youthful camaraderie is so hard to sustain, to understanding that this relationship won't ever really expire no matter how many miles separate the two. It's pretty amazing when a four-minute rock song can so accurately and movingly reflect something as vital in our lives as the pull that friendships from our formative years exert on us even into old age, but that's just the kind of magic that Springsteen performs here.

10. "For You" (from *Greetings from Asbury Park, N.J.*, 1973)

There is a relatively common misconception about Bruce Springsteen that he didn't start writing songs about romantic relationships until *Tunnel of Love*. While that 1987 LP might have been his first album-long dissertation on the subject and its infinite complexity, Springsteen dabbled in the area in specific songs throughout his early career.

As a matter of fact, one of the best songs on the topic he has ever written dates all the way back to his debut album, 1973's *Greetings from Asbury Park, N.J.* Written at a time when Springsteen seemed to be getting paid by the word, "For You" actually benefits from the excess verbiage simply because the relationship being highlighted seems to be so frenzied and tumultuous that simplifying it wouldn't have been doing it any justice.

On that debut album, some of Springsteen's better songwriting efforts were mitigated by ill-advised arrangements and murky production, but "For You" largely avoids that problem. David Sancious propels the song with his breathless piano patter and adds some organ just below the surface that comes burbling up at times to provide color.

For the most part, however, the arrangement of the song works because it largely stays out of Springsteen's way, allowing him to take his bully pulpit and make his case to the reticent, frustrating, yet captivating girl at the heart of the narrative. This narrative is exaggerated way past the point of coherence, which is only fitting because the guy can no longer understand her actions and motivations. His surreal mode of storytelling is the only way he can make even a little sense of it all.

It's probably a mistake, therefore, to take Springsteen's line about suicide too literally. The song just doesn't sustain a tone that's somber enough to jibe with such a drastic event. What Springsteen is doing is embellishing on the narrator's statement that her "life was one long emergency." In keeping with that, what bigger emergency could there be than a kind of symbolic suicide, which comes replete with the narrator's valiant attempts to revive her?

If there is a death in the song, it's the expiration of the narrator's ability to get through to her and connect with her on the level they once shared. The first line ("Princess cards she sends me with her regards") suggests a kind of formality and distance one wouldn't normally associate with lovers. In response, the narrator promises unyielding fidelity: "Wounded deep in battle, I stand stuffed like some soldier undaunted / To her Cheshire smile, I'll stand on file, she's all I ever wanted."

He is no match for her "blue walls" though. When the so-called suicide occurs in the second verse, it symbolizes a growing distance between them he can longer breach. "Reveal yourself all now to me girl while you've got the strength to speak," he begs. Instead of the hospital's promises of cure, he offers to save her: "But I could give it all to you now if only you could ask."

Frustrated by his present inability to get through to her, he flashes back to a time when she needed his strength and support. All he has left is the persistent memory of the homecoming theme that played when they were truly together, a song that now stings: "That ragged jagged melody she still clings to me like a leech."

For all of the pain that she has clearly caused him, for all the "vacancy" he sees in her eyes, for all her fickleness and unpredictability ("You could laugh and cry in a single sound"), his love endures and he musters up one more desperate charge on her defenses, an attempt to reach that "alien distant shore" to which she has decamped. Springsteen's voice keeps rising as the narrator senselessly blasts away at her windows and doors to recapture her heart.

As powerful as those climbing moments are, it is ultimately a futile gesture. The refrain returns, bringing with it his resignation to defeat: "I came for you, for you, I came for you, but you did not need my urgency / I came for you, for you, I came for you, but your life was one long emergency." "For You" is full of that urgency the narrator references, the kind that you feel when the person you most want to save loses the desire to be saved. For anybody who's ever been in the midst of that phenomenon, it's clear that Springsteen's equating it with suicide doesn't seem like all that much of a stretch.

9. "Born in the U.S.A." (from *Born in the U.S.A.*, 1984)

Anybody who was around at the time or has since become a fan of Bruce Springsteen is likely aware of the kerfuffle that arose in 1984 when President Ronald Reagan attempted to use Springsteen and "Born in the U.S.A" specifically in his reelection campaign. Springsteen rebuffed with extreme prejudice, which led to a lot more media attention than the story probably deserved.

That attention still sticks to the song somewhat, which is unfortunate because, all politics aside, "Born in the U.S.A." is a fantastic song. It's a shining example of how the right music can add all sorts of layers to the songwriter's original creation. And those layers are there, even after everyone has taken their respective sides, making this one of the most honest and malleable anthems ever created.

Springsteen originally performed the song in a moody, acoustic version along with the tracks that would make up 1982's *Nebraska*. He decided not to include it on that album, preferring to take a shot at it with the E Street Band. (You can hear the original acoustic demo on *Tracks*.)

The full-band take is a juggernaut. Roy Bittan provided the keyboard hook that is as memorable a riff as anything else in the Springsteen catalog this side of "Born to Run." Meanwhile, Max Weinberg, who had always subordinated any pyrotechnics for the sake of doing what's best for Springsteen's songs, was given full rein by the Boss to unleash his most feral drumming ever. The instrumental breakdown, featuring an improvised rolling solo by Weinberg, is an instance where the live energy and power of the band is perfectly captured in the studio.

With this kind of setting, the lyrics, as sung in a wild-eyed shout by Springsteen, take on an extra added sense of desperation. The tale is told by a Vietnam veteran who recounts his life story in sparse yet scorching terms. "Born down in a dead man's town / The first kick I took was when I hit the ground," he sings, setting the stage for the lifetime of abuse and violence he is about to lead.

He yields no details of his time in Vietnam, for that's the part of the tale that most already know. Instead, he lists the series of disappointments he receives upon his return home. Potential employers offer clichés but not work, while his pleas for assistance from his country go unheard. That's a hard pill to swallow considering what he has lost: "Had a brother at Khe Sanh fighting off them Viet Cong / They're still there he's all gone."

In the final verse, the narrator looks around at his skeletal hometown and takes stock of his progress since leaving the war: "I'm ten years burning down the road / Nowhere to run ain't got nowhere to go." It's a backbreaker of a statement, one that makes the refrain all the more wrenching. For if he was "Born in the U.S.A.," with all of its inherent promises and inalienable rights, how has this possibly transpired?

About thirty years have passed now since the song came out and the whole Reagan affair went down, and still "Born in the U.S.A." is a staple at patriotic fireworks displays across America. So what gives? Is everybody still mishearing the song?

Springsteen is not a naive guy. He had to know when he released the song in that version, with a riff that practically begs to be saluted and an overall sound that can't help but rouse even the most docile listener, that some people would only hear the chorus. And if they did, and beamed with pride, they haven't completely missed the intent.

Springsteen clearly intended, if not pride exactly, at least a kind of collective acceptance among his listeners when they heard the song. This is who we are as a country, the song seems to say, in all our glories and flaws. We live in a nation that does as much bad as it does good, but that doesn't separate us from it or absolve us of the responsibility to set the wrong right.

That's why those who say the song is subversive are the ones who are misinterpreting it. Springsteen wasn't trying to sneak the Vietnam angle past us. He was trying to move his audience to acknowledge this injustice as an integral part of the country as a complex whole and perhaps, in the spirit of the defiance that helped create America in the first place, to sing that refrain even louder to remind those who may have forgotten that our birthright not only entitles but also demands.

Ultimately, it's hard to deny that "Born in the U.S.A." is one of the most stirring songs in rock-music history. It's up to the listeners to decide what exactly it will stir them to do.

8. "Backstreets" (from *Born to Run*, 1975)

Much breath, ink, and computer data has been spent among Bruce Springsteen enthusiasts debating the gender of Terry, the person whom the narrator addresses in "Backstreets," Bruce Springsteen's tortured memory play that sends side one of *Born to Run* out in a blaze of broken-hearted glory. Springsteen has never seemed too worried about the debate, perhaps because he knows that's not where the focus should be anyway.

In concert, he would often extend the run-out to the song and use feminine pronouns to describe Terry, answering the question for some. But as it is on the record, you could easily make the case that "Backstreets" is about a friendship between two boys or two men that ran its course much to the enduring angst of the narrator.

While the gender isn't that important in the long run, what is important is the intensity of the relationship, be it platonic or romantic, and the majestic way in which it is rendered by Springsteen and his band. That performance bestows importance and dignity on this relationship, which is in turn worthy of such loftiness. Why else would the narrator be still so distraught about its implosion seemingly years after the fact?

It is impossible to overstate the importance of Roy Bittan to the overall sound of *Born to Run*. Springsteen began writing songs on the piano for the album, but he needed a technically adroit player to bring it across, one who also understood the emotional content of the song when he played. Bittan's work throughout the album is outstanding, but he takes it up several notches for "Backstreets."

His intro is a thing of beauty, coming on at times like a call to arms before diminishing to the wounded cry of one lone soldier. His hook also drives the main sections of the song along with the thunderous toms of Max Weinberg. Only four players are in the song (Springsteen on guitar and Garry Tallent on bass join Bittan, who doubles on organ, and Weinberg), yet their parts interlock to wring every last bit of meaning from the words and every last bit of emotion from between the lines.

Springsteen starts out his tale with two scene-setting lines that are pitch-perfect in both their ingenuity and their evocative potency: "One soft infested summer me and Terry became friends / Trying in vain to breathe the fire we was born in." Theirs is a friendship born out of desperation, and the way Springsteen describes their exploits, there seems to be little of the wild fun that once pervaded songs like "Blinded by the Light" and "Spirit in the Night." These two are holding on to each other for dear life.

Few songwriters have ever operated at a higher degree of difficulty than *Born to run*–era Springsteen. A song like "Backstreets" carries line after line that makes you stand up and take notice, as he veers from vivid details of their time together to metaphorical musings on what it felt like to be there within those moments. Springsteen would later streamline his approach, and there is surely something to be said for less-is-more. But songs like this one prove that when it's done right, more can be more as well.

In the bridge, we start to hear about the deterioration of this relationship that seemed to be indestructibly forged in the fires of adolescent frustration and futile rebellion. For all of the narrator's ponderings on grand lies and tear-stained streets that seem to make it impossible for this friendship to sustain, what ultimately breaks them down is a third party: "But I hated him / And I hated you when you went away."

Those lines are crucial because the raw emotions on display ground the airy proclamations about their relationship. In the final verse, they seem to be back together, as the narrator describes Terry "like an angel on my chest." But it's more likely that he or she is with him only in spirit, the memory still so real that it transcends his thoughts and takes human form again. He recalls their idealization of their heroes up on the silver screen and compares it to the painful realization that growing up engendered: "And after all this time to find we're just like all the rest / Stranded in the park and forced to confess / To hiding on the backstreets."

The most all-consuming relationships can easily devolve into rancor when they turn sour. Instead of just fading away like casual connections tend to do, they burn out and leave behind the ashes of youthful idealism. Springsteen conveys this with fierce brilliance in this song, honoring the oversized feelings with words and music intense enough to match them. Even with the bitter ending, there is a sliver of comfort in knowing that those "Backstreets" briefly gave this star-crossed pair a home.

7. "Lost in the Flood" (from *Greetings from Asbury Park, N.J.*)

With monikers like Jimmy the Saint, the Bronx's best apostle, and ragamuffin gunner populating the song, it might be easy for those who haven't heard "Lost in the Flood" to imagine it being one of Bruce Springsteen's loping, light-hearted tales of youthful spirits in the night. One listen to the song quickly quells that, as the young songwriter proved early on in the game that he could get serious with mesmerizing results.

What Springsteen accomplishes in "Lost in the Flood" goes beyond impressive to genius level. Not only does he create a rich tableau of memorable characters in short, sharp strokes, he also makes a trenchant, unifying point about a kind of inane fatalism that seems to linger in the hearts of an entire generation. These characters all seem to confuse the desire to feel with the need to hurt themselves.

By calling it a flood, Springsteen is referencing the biblical proportions of the ever-growing malignancy that the narrator witnesses but is helpless to stop. In many ways, the song is a second cousin to Bob Dylan's "Desolation Row." Dylan, always wary of scolding, simply put his cast of characters under the microscope and then joined them on their damned avenue at song's end in an act of kinship. By contrast, Springsteen tells the story in "Lost in the Flood" like the last sane man, poking holes in any perceived romance about the way these characters squander their existences.

In that respect, "Lost in the Flood" carries some of the jaded, post–*Born to Run* Springsteen in its DNA, even if the verbally acrobatic way in which this is displayed is par for the course for the songwriter circa 1973. It shows that Springsteen's eyes were always wide open, but he could alter the way those eyes saw the world based on the message he wanted to send at any particular time.

The first sound heard in "Lost in the Flood" is thunder (courtesy of special effects conjured in the studio by a pre–E Street Band member Steven Van Zandt), signaling the storm to come. That storm approaches, borne on the somber piano chords of David Sancious, who also later delivers the lightning with his wild organ squalls in the song's climax. Vini Lopez's drums are similarly paced, starting off sparse and menacing before erupting as the action intensifies. For much of the *Greetings from Asbury Park, N.J.* album, the music lags behind the lyrics, but this crackerjack track is a thrilling exception.

Springsteen begins the tale with the ragamuffin gunner, a Vietnam vet who returns to generalized chaos in a hometown that he can no longer recognize or comprehend. Although he wasn't yet making a statement about the poor treatment of veterans upon their return as he would on future albums, Springsteen captures the disorientation of those men in the character of the gunner.

And why wouldn't he be disoriented, what with his town overrun by wolfman fairies and crazed nuns? The delirious turns of phrase that Springsteen employs in the opening verse convey just what madness has descended upon the streets. That madness comes upon the racing-legend-in-his-own-mind Jimmy the Saint in his kamikaze final heat that leaves him a worthless heap. The narrator meticulously describes it all, occasionally interacting with the bystanders to correct any misconceptions: It's not mud, it's quicksand; it's not oil, it's blood. There is nothing benign to be seen here; it's all damaging and destructive.

The final verse quiets down only for a moment, long enough for the narrator to notice "some storefront incarnation of Maria" suspiciously watching him as if he embodies the antidote to peace and common sense. A battle quickly whips up, and Springsteen describes it as if he were a cross between a war correspondent and a play-by-play announcer. After one body falls, a voice can be heard glorifying the violence: "And someone said, 'Hey man, did you see that? His body hit the street with such a beautiful thud.'" Those sound like the words of another future victim.

The song is a ruthless indictment of reckless behavior, and it punctures holes in the live-fast-die-young ethos that fueled a lot of the more hedonistic fringes of rock and roll. One of the ideals that Bruce Springsteen has come to embody is the notion that the music can grow up and have a conscience without losing any of its effervescence or spark, that rock doesn't have to believe or indulge in its own self-destructive myths. Flickers of those ideas can be found in "Lost in the Flood" and its depiction of a senseless urban battlefield where few survive and even fewer emerge unscathed.

6. "Rosalita (Come Out Tonight)" (from *The Wild, the Innocent & the E Street Shuffle*, 1973)

Equal parts genius and daring bravado, "Rosalita (Come Out Tonight)" is the sound of Bruce Springsteen running a victory lap for a race he hadn't yet won. At a time when the future of his career was by no means a sure thing, it was as if he were trying to force his ultimate conquering of the rock world into existence through sheer will and moxie. Damned if he didn't pull it off.

Springsteen must have had a pretty good vision of his forthcoming career because he somehow foresaw the need for a showstopping live number that would bring the fans to fits of exultation by the time it was complete. "Rosalita" proved to be exactly that enduring concert staple, but it could only graduate to that point once it was rendered in the studio with undying passion.

His lyrics got most of the attention in the early part of his career, but Springsteen's innovative musical construction of "Rosalita" carries it most of the way. As tempos change and different instruments come to the fore and then recede, the band tries on several different genres. There is the soul rave-up in the middle section, a little bit of flamenco in the final verse, and breathless rock and roll propelled by Springsteen's reckless electric guitar just about everywhere else. The rhythm section of Vini Lopez and Garry Tallent never falters through all of these variations, while Clarence Clemons is at the forefront just about the whole way, right alongside his buddy in their indefatigable quest to rescue Rosie from her reservations and her parents.

Even as the music bounces around from style to style, its forward momentum is never in doubt. That makes it the perfect fit for Springsteen's narrator, who at times saunters up to Rosalita like a suave lover, and at other times charges at her like a raging bull, but never, ever stops coming. The vocal performance that Springsteen delivers is one of the best of his career, always finding the inherent humor in the situation even as he makes dead serious his intentions and desires for Rosalita.

The narrator can be quite the sweet-talker, which is a good thing considering Rosie's apparent reticence. You can imagine her laughing as he drops some ten-cent words in an exaggerated accent ("I'm coming to liberate you, confiscate you, I want to be your man") and blushing as he gets a tad risqué ("The only lover I'm ever gonna need's your soft sweet little girl's tongue"). Most of all, he is unwavering in his persistence, so much so that the National Guard wouldn't dare stand in his way, especially with Clarence at his side.

Now her parents, on the other hand, well, that's another story. Papa and Mama are the biggest obstacles, objecting to the rock-and-roll life that this cat has carved out for himself. Of course, there is some autobiography in there, but Springsteen still makes it relevant to all those would-be suitors out there who don't have a big record-advance in their pocket. The song, in humorous fashion, portrays that frustration of knowing you're the best thing for someone when the whole world, including the other person, doubts that to be the case.

Do you just give in, or do you give it your best shot? Well, we know what Springsteen's choice is: full speed ahead. And that reflects what he was doing with his career, even as the record company may have doubted the wisdom of that "big advance" as sales of his first two albums sputtered. Had Springsteen's career not proceeded to *Born to Run* and beyond, "Rosalita" would have sounded like hubris. Now, it sounds prophetic.

Even as his confidence never wanes in the song, Springsteen still comes off like the lovable underdog. Amazingly, he still comes off that way today, even after years upon years of huge artistic and commercial triumphs.

So maybe "Rosalita (Come Out Tonight)" was a case of mind over matter. Or maybe it was the sound of a guy whose belief in himself overwhelmed everything else, even the commonsense view at the time that his career was more "stuck in the mud somewhere in the swamps of

Jersey" than "coming on strong." What we do know is that, by song's
end, Springsteen may or may not have won the hand of Rosalita, but he
definitely captured our hearts.

5. "Brilliant Disguise" (from *Tunnel of Love*, 1987)

The same darkness that invaded Bruce Springsteen's depiction of jobs
and small-town life eventually seeped into his first full-length exploration
of adult romance on 1987's *Tunnel of Love*. There is probably no song on
that album more shadowy, in its way, than "Brilliant Disguise," which
may be why Springsteen coated it in such an elegant musical sheen. After
all, it is a song about hiding in plain sight.

He did such a good job creating a catchy ode to relationship misery
that the song reached No. 5 on the pop charts in 1987. That may have had
something to do with the intense anticipation for the first studio single
released by Springsteen in the wake of the monster success of *Born in the
U.S.A.*'s hits in 1984 and 1985. Still, this song is constructed in such a
way for maximum sing-along capability so long as the bile lurking under-
neath those words doesn't choke you.

Springsteen enlisted the help of E Streeters Max Weinberg, Roy Bittan, and Danny Federici on the track, with Weinberg's crisp drumming
being a standout. Everything, right down to the timpani in the outro, is
placed just so in the song's arrangement, creating a kind of tense perfection. You get the feeling that a single note out of place would have caused
the whole thing to crumble. As such, it mirrors the relationship on the
edge of meltdown that the lyrics depict.

Vocally, Springsteen does a little Elvis in the verses and a little Orbison in the choruses, but the cold preciseness of his phrasing is what sticks
and stings. If you don't parse those words too closely, you might assume
that "Brilliant Disguise" is meant as a putdown of the narrator's deceptive
significant other. After all, the chorus, at least until the final refrain,
places the burden of proof solely on the woman to verify she is who she
claims to be.

A closer reading reveals that the blame can easily be shared, since the
narrator's hang-ups are manifesting themselves in mistrust and insinua-
tion. Even the seemingly idyllic opening dance between the two is spoiled
by doubt: "What are those words whispered baby / Just as you turn
away?" When he sees her "out on the edge of town," Springsteen fans are

immediately conditioned to expect the darkness he once promised was out there.

Words that might otherwise seem like a compliment to her specialness ("But I just can't see / What a woman like you / Is doing with me"), in this context of suspicion, come off sounding accusatory. As the song progresses, it becomes clear that the weakness he perceives in his own fidelity is fueling his attack on her: "I want to know if it's you I don't trust / 'Cause I damn sure don't trust myself."

When it gets to the unbearable point where he can't even believe the fortuneteller who once proclaimed good tidings for their relationship, he asks his love to play along with the facade of their relationship, as if facing the truth would be too much to bear. He then turns the last chorus around to put the spotlight on himself, almost daring her to doubt him in the same way he doubts her. It's clear now that this relationship is past the point of no return and in its death throes; it's just that the audience knows it before the participants do.

But the turmoil isn't over. Springsteen adds an epilogue to let us know how the couple in question is faring, a parting glimpse into the "darkness of our love." We see the man adrift in a cold bed, finally, albeit well too late, coming to terms with the demons inside that have brought him to this point: "God have mercy on the man / Who doubts what he's sure of." It's a line so profound that it should be carved in stone.

In retrospect, we can look at Springsteen's own marital troubles as a possible inspiration here, but that limits the imagination and insight of his songwriting process. If the song teaches us anything, it's that these feelings of uncertainty and doubt are latent within us, ready to strike down a potential good thing at a moment's notice.

"Brilliant Disguise" transcends any one couple's trials and tribulations and serves as a lesson for all those engaged in a relationship. It warns us to beware a counterintuitive yet common conundrum that trips up so many relationships: Two people can be deeply in love and still not believe in each other.

4. "Darkness on the Edge of Town" (From *Darkness on the Edge of Town*, 1978)

"When you got nothing, you got nothing to lose," Bob Dylan once sang. The protagonist of "Darkness on the Edge of Town" takes that theory to the fiercest extreme. Serving as the title track to Springsteen's toughest, rawest album, the song not only serves as a summation of many of the ideas proposed in the previous songs on the record but also as a musical release of all the tension that has been building and waiting to uncoil.

Throughout the *Darkness* album, Springsteen presents an interesting dichotomy between the sometimes crushing nature of life and his contention that the individual has the power to break out and take back the spirit that external pressures attempt to squelch. "Darkness on the Edge of Town" distills these two ideas into a fascinating psychological case study of one man who is willing to give up everything he has just to take back some sort of personal freedom, as destructive as that freedom might actually be.

Much of the song's power lies in the arrangement of the music. In the verses, everything stays quiet and composed, as if to reflect the staid nature of the life the protagonist once knew. In the refrains, called into action by Max Weinberg's furious snares, the music explodes into a lurching powerhouse, with Weinberg banging the house down and Roy Bittan playing like a mad scientist.

Springsteen's vocals are pitched in much the same manner. The verses capture him in a croon so polite as to sound innocent. When he gets to the refrain, it's a serrated cry, the lyrics shouted out as if they're tumors that need to be forcibly excised by the power of his lungs. In the instrumental break, Springsteen punctuates his solo with guttural cries.

The narrator quickly sets up a contrast between the life that he's chosen and the one that his ex now lives. Actually, "chosen" might not be the right word since this separation is described as something that was beyond his control, the product of an innate desire that his wife never had: "Well they're still racin' out at the Trestles / But that blood it never burned in her veins." Instead, she has moved on to a life of "style," a far cry from the street racing that he still favors.

As he has throughout the *Darkness* album, Springsteen is once again shining a harsh spotlight here on those characters that once populated his songs with their wild and innocent exploits. Those characters morph into the man-child at the heart of "Darkness" who clings to that past lifestyle long after the romance of it has faded. He does it now because it's preferable, to him anyway, to the folks who hold in their innermost secret "Till some day they just cut it loose / Cut it loose or let it drag them down."

Say what you will about this guy, at least he is no longer burdened by such hang-ups.

In the final verse, Springsteen crystallizes the conflict that the whole album has been forging. The narrator has shed all of his connections to home and stability: "Well I lost my money and I lost my wife / Those things don't seem to matter much to me now." And as the refrain approaches, he makes his case for a life that many would call reckless, wasted, or doomed. "Tonight I'll be on that hill 'cause I can't stop / I'll be on that hill with everything that I got," he screams, reinforcing the notion that his fate is settled and glossing over the fact that he no longer has anything at stake. His only possessions now are those primal impulses burning inside of him.

So he willingly goes to a place with "lives on the line and dreams are found and lost." And he willingly makes the ultimate sacrifice: "I'll be there on time and I'll pay the cost / For wanting things that can only be found / In the darkness on the edge of town." That "cost" is stability, serenity, maybe even sanity, but he pays it because this world of danger and recklessness is the only thing that now makes any sense to him.

As the music plays out with some delicate piano from Roy Bittan and one last moan from Springsteen, the songwriter leaves his audience with some profound questions. Are we to admire this character or scold him? Are the things he has given away worth what he has gained? And is a life spent on the invigorating yet precarious edge of the abyss preferable to one where the stable ground runs on forever even as the skies press unrelentingly downward?

You'd like to believe there's a happy medium somewhere, but Springsteen's point with this extreme character, and with the entire album, is that life doesn't allow that sometimes, so what can you do? Having already lost it all, this character makes his peace with the fact that for him, it ends in the "Darkness on the Edge of Town," one way or the other.

3. "Incident on 57th Street" (From *The Wild, the Innocent & the E Street Shuffle*, 1973)

To casual Bruce Springsteen fans, his career begins with 1975's *Born to Run*. If they are aware at all of his output before that time, they might know "Rosalita" from reputation and the classic rock airplay it has received over the years. If they're aware of the fact that he actually released two albums in 1973, they might labor under the misconception that these albums are somehow inferior to the rest of his catalog.

Of course, that's not true, but if you play one of those fans just any random song off those first two albums, you might not convince them otherwise. They might wonder where all the huge moments are or why everything sounds a bit muddled. It could create a bit of confusion for those who have seen clips of Bruce with entire arenas or even stadiums pumping their fists in time to one of his anthems.

There is one particular song that indisputably sounds like the future, world-conquering Bruce though, and that's "Incident on 57th Street" from *The Wild, the Innocent & the E Street Shuffle*. This song is the bridge from the 1973 Bruce to the one who has been near or atop the rock-and-roll world for about forty years now. He couldn't have created *Born to Run* without this dry run, albeit a dry run that came out perfect.

"Incident" starts out with a piano intro, seconded in this case by some elegiac guitar from Bruce, that promises something big. In this case, it's a quintessential love story set against a backdrop of violence. Springsteen's innovation is in the way he leaves out the big ending, where the two either get away or tragedy strikes.

What he does give us are the moments between that tell us everything we need to know about these two people to make them seem like real human beings even in this outsized milieu. They are flawed and make poor choices, but we root for them because their connection seems rare and true, something that even a violent end couldn't really ever destroy.

"Spanish Johnny drove in from the underworld last night / With bruised arms and broken rhythm in a beat-up old Buick but dressed just like dynamite," Springsteen sings. With just those two opening lines, he has given us a fully-formed, fascinating character. Seemingly down to his last chance in this hard world of pimps and gangsters, this guy finds redemption in just three words from the heroine, Puerto Rican Jane: "Johnny, don't cry."

With that line, the music, which had been a gentle mid-tempo rumble distinguished by Vini Lopez's hiccupping beat, explodes into life, propelled by Danny Federici's swirling organ. Johnny explains that Jane has to share him with the "golden-heeled fairies" who "pull .38s and kiss the girls good night." Jane can accept this bargain, only if Johnny makes the impossible promise that he can somehow emerge unscathed: "Spanish Johnny you can leave me tonight but just don't leave me alone."

After the music has built up into a thunderous frenzy, it suddenly dissipates, leaving just Garry Tallent's bass to accompany Bruce as he meticulously depicts the two lovers rising in the morning after a night of passion. (It needs to be noted here how brilliant Tallent is in this section, the ever-steady sideman shining in the limelight.) Johnny wistfully watches the kids on the street, seeing in them a familiar rebelliousness. He also watches Jane sleep, knowing that as much as he loves her, that same street will soon beckon.

He leaves, as Jane knew he would, but not before setting a rendezvous for the next night he knows he might not be able to keep: "We may find it out on the street tonight, baby / Or we may walk until the daylight maybe." The refrain is repeated three times: The first is a whisper, the second is more assertive, and the third is a maelstrom of sound, Springsteen singing with majestic desperation as the band crashes all around him.

Eventually, all that remains is just David Sancious's piano, playing a circular figure that might as well be a music box in Jane's bedroom, her only accompaniment as she waits for Johnny to return. She still waits there to this day, a symbol of the sacrifice that love demands even when it can promise no recompense.

It's a thrillingly told tale, accompanied by an endlessly inventive musical arrangement. The music is majestic and ambitious; the lyrics are subtle and concise. There are hooks at every turn, and a refrain that soars into your consciousness.

So if you find yourself defending those first two albums, let "Incident on 57th Street" be Exhibit A. It will silence all arguments.

2. "Jungleland" (From *Born to Run*, 1975)

The word "epic" is thrown around a lot these days, but it should be reserved for those things that truly deserve it. "Jungleland," the closing track on *Born to Run*, is, without question, an epic. It's long, but that's not the reason it deserves the appellation.

It's epic because it creates an entire world in a relatively short time, and yet it still leaves enough open space to fire the imagination. It's epic in musical scope, an endlessly inventive arrangement that showcases every one of the members of the E Street band while also stressing their whole-is-better-than-the-parts aesthetic. Most of all, it's an epic for its fearlessness, the way that Springsteen attempts something on such a grand scale and knocks it out of the park. That's why, for such a long song, you still have the urge to cue it up again when it comes to an end.

Suki Lahav's violin is the first thing you hear, quickly joined by Roy Bittan in a stately dance tinged with melancholy. The violin soon leaves town, leaving just Bittan and his scurrying runs. It's not long before Bruce introduces his two protagonists, the Magic Rat and the barefoot girl.

We meet both through their automobiles, the Rat driving his "sleek machine" to a gang assembly, the girl sitting on the hood of a Dodge. Soon, without even a word passing between them, they are riding off together into a night bursting with an enticing mixture of possibility and danger.

Danny Federici now subtly sneaks in as it's revealed that the Rat has a posse after him. His organ ironically thunders into prominence on the line "From the churches to the jails tonight all is silent in the world." Up until that point, the song is a pure ballad, but that changes when Bruce sings the lines "As we take our stand / Down in Jungleland." The E Street Band gets fully engaged, and the brilliant rhythm section of Garry Tallent and Max Weinberg propel the action into overdrive.

Meanwhile, Bruce's lyrics get more streetwise poetic as the music gets tougher. Every image is vivid and powerful, allowing listeners a front-row seat to this world of alley ballets, turnpike operas, and a cop car that "rips this holy night."

As the song progresses, Springsteen begins to draw parallels between the heightened fantasy world he has created and the fantasy world of rock and roll that he lives every day: "The hungry and the hunted / Explode into rock-and-roll bands." Perhaps he realized that without his talent he could have been one of the charismatic, doomed young characters populating his songs. As if to punctuate this point, he lets loose a furious guitar solo heading into the bridge and the most iconic saxophone solo in rock history.

Springsteen reportedly drove Clarence Clemons to the brink of exhaustion trying to get the perfect feel for the solo, but it was all worth it. Beginning with a sustained note that's like a clarion call for all wounded souls to rally, Clarence somehow manages to play with both force and restraint at the same time. Since Clemons's passing, this solo is even more of a misty-eyed moment than it already was.

When the dust clears, just some sad piano chords remain and Springsteen's voice is a wrecked shell of the powerful instrument it was in the previous parts of the song. He quietly takes us into a random bedroom and its "whispers of soft refusal and then surrender." Yet a tender ending is not in the cards for our hero and heroine. "In the tunnels uptown / The Rat's own dream guns him down," Springsteen sings. What's even more tragic is that no one in Jungleland seems to care, rendering the Rat, for all his charismatic bravado, just another victim, indistinguishable from the rest.

Bittan begins to play with unstoppable power now, and Springsteen laments the indifference of the scene: "And the poets down here don't write nothing at all / They just stand back and let it all be." What becomes of these wayward dreamers? "They wind up wounded, not even dead / Tonight in Jungleland."

The music flares up one more time with Bittan's fast-fingered trills and Tallent's ominous bass notes, while Springsteen lets forth some guttural cries that seem to emanate from the spirits of every character in his pre-"Jungleland" repertoire. Perhaps he sensed that those fantastical folks that rumbled through his first three albums would no longer be such an integral part of his work. Thus he needed to give them the proper send-off with this stunning song.

And so, in those cries, you can hear Go-Cart Mozart's insane ramblings, the ragamuffin gunner's jaded fatalism, Crazy Janey's healing sweet nothings, Zero and Blind Terry's ghostly laughter, Madame Marie's foreboding warnings, and Spanish Johnny's tragically romantic serenade to Puerto Rican Jane. They're all denizens of "Jungleland" in a way, so this is their opportunity to come out to join the Rat and the barefoot girl for one final bow before the curtain closes on both the song and the street anthems from which Springsteen would soon graduate.

Is that epic enough for you?

I. "Born to Run" (from *Born to Run*, 1975)

Sometimes the obvious choice is obvious for a reason.

There are actually countless reasons why "Born to Run" is the finest combination of songwriting excellence and instrumental execution in the Bruce Springsteen canon, not least of which is the fact that it somehow sums up not just his career to that point but all the songs yet to come. The problem with the most oft-played songs is that people hear them so many times that they tend to zone out and don't give them the attention they did when those songs first captivated them.

Listen to "Born to Run" again, really listen to it. Take out your headphones and drink in its multi-tracked glory. Concentrate on those lyrics so that they're not just sounds you've heard blasting out of your car speakers for nearly forty years but instead are once again words fraught with so much feeling that their writer seems about to burst as he delivers them. If you do this, you'll have a hard time coming up with an argument against it, not just as the best song of Springsteen's career, but also as one of the singular achievements in the history of rock and roll.

"Born to Run" begins with the drum snap of Ernest "Boom" Carter, making his only appearance on a Springsteen song and making it count. Then, that riff, that unforgettable riff. It busts down imaginary walls, breaks invisible chains, clears your sinuses, and promises nothing short of infinity.

After that great start, the lyrics could have been a collective anticlimax. Instead, Springsteen begins singing and sums up an entire generation in two lines: "In the day we sweat it out on the streets of a runaway American dream / At night we ride through mansions of glory in suicide machines." Notice how his descriptions are peppered with explosively active phrases: "Sprung from cages on Highway 9 / Chrome-wheeled fuel-injected / And steppin' out over the line." The motion and potency in these words help to form a dead-on description of edgy youth afraid to stand still lest they never be able to start up again.

The narrator has an ulterior motive with all of this fancy talk: He's trying to convince his girl, Wendy, to join him in escaping a town that he depicts as a remorseless entity determined to grind down all hope and promise. As David Sancious's piano swirls around him, he gets to the crux of his argument: "We gotta get out while we're young / 'Cause tramps like us, baby we were born to run." Using the word "tramps" instead of "bums" adds just the right touch of romantic allure to the exploits of his pair and all those like them.

As the next verse begins, the narrator balances a genuinely heartfelt and chaste promise to Wendy with some bawdy talk to appeal to her more prurient side: "Wendy, let me in, I want to be your friend, I want to guard your dreams and visions / Just wrap your legs 'round these velvet rims and strap your hands across my engines." Yet for all of that bravado, this guy quickly reveals himself to be vulnerable and longing, a "scared and lonely rider" who wants to know "if love is real."

After a fast and furious sax solo from Clarence Clemons, the bridge takes on a dreamlike quality, Springsteen sounding like he's sitting on a cloud overlooking the scene. He highlights the undeniable allure of the nightlife, the picturesque scenery, the sounds of the traffic, and the endearing innocence of the kids. In a jaded age when all heartfelt outpourings of emotion are viewed with skepticism, Springsteen embraces unabashed romanticism: "I want to die with you, Wendy, on the streets tonight / In an everlasting kiss."

With that, the band surges upward into the most memorable crescendo in rock since the Beatles contemplated "A Day in the Life." The main riff returns, this time embellished by even more Spectorian grandeur, and Bruce bursts out in a voice so cathartically desperate that it practically cracks on the immortal couplet that follows: "The highway's jammed with broken heroes on a last chance power drive / Everybody's out on the run tonight, there's no place left to hide."

That desperation wasn't a put-on. Springsteen was betting everything on this song, because it might well have been his last chance. With two mediocre-selling albums in his rear view that hadn't matched their hype with earnings, he likely wouldn't have had another shot to go this big again had "Born to Run" flopped. Talk about rising to the occasion.

In the final lines, the possibility arises that these two might not get out; "Someday, girl, I don't know when," Springsteen sings, qualifying his promise to her. It grounds the song in faint sorrow that runs counterpoint to the lofty optimism. He needs to repeat the refrain three times, each time with increasing passion, before the music finally resolves and they emerge triumphant: "Tramps like us / Baby we were born to run."

The title phrase is endlessly meaningful. They're born to run because it's in their nature, an instinct akin to a shark's single-minded quest to eat. They're born to run because inertia is tantamount to death. They're born to run with the grace and beauty of gazelles toward the glorious promise of a future always dangling just out of reach, and they're born to run in a desperate, messy scramble to escape the hellhounds of the past.

That's an awful lot to conjure in four-and-a-half minutes, but that's just what Bruce Springsteen manages with "Born to Run," his most magnificent song. Listen to it again, and prepare to be exhilarated, inspired, heartbroken, hopeful, and spent by the time it's through. Then, while you're at it, go back and listen to the rest of the amazing songs on this list all over again.

I know that's what I plan to do.

...AND 100 MORE

101. "New York City Serenade" (from *The Wild, the Innocent & the E Street Shuffle*, 1973)
102. "Hearts of Stone" (from *Tracks*, 1998)
103. "Devil's Arcade" (from *Magic*, 2007)
104. "Mary Lou" (from *Tracks*, 1998)
105. "Into the Fire" (from *The Rising*, 2002)
106. "Wages of Sin" (from *Tracks*, 1998)
107. "Reason to Believe" (from *Nebraska*, 1982)
108. "My Hometown" (from *Born in the U.S.A.*, 1984)
109. "Johnny Bye Bye" (from *Tracks*, 1998)
110. "Candy's Room" (from *Darkness on the Edge of Town*, 1978)
111. "Rendezvous" (from *The Promise*, 2010)
112. "The Fever" (from *18 Tracks*, 1999)
113. "Walk Like a Man" (from *Tunnel of Love*, 1987)
114. "I'm a Rocker" (from *The River*, 1980)
115. "Magic" (from *Magic*, 2007)
116. "Murder Incorporated" (from *Greatest Hits*, 1995)
117. "Back in Your Arms" (from *Tracks*, 1998)
118. "Shackled and Drawn" (from *Wrecking Ball*, 2012)
119. "Paradise" (from *The Rising*, 2002)
120. "Pink Cadillac" (from *Tracks*, 1998)
121. "Used Cars" (from *Nebraska*, 1982)
122. "Out in the Street" (from *The River*, 1980)
123. "Living Proof" (from *Lucky Town*, 1992)
124. "Seeds" (from *Live/1975–85*, 1986)

125. "Santa Ana" (from *Tracks*, 1998)

126. "She's the One" (from *Born to Run*, 1975)

127. "Sinaloa Cowboys" (from *The Ghost of Tom Joad*, 1995)

128. "Darlington County" (from *Born in the U.S.A.*, 1984)

129. "Nothing Man" (from *The Rising*, 2002)

130. "Local Hero" (from *Lucky Town*, 1992)

131. "I'm Goin' Down" (from *Born in the U.S.A.*, 1984)

132. "Jesus Was an Only Son" (from *Devils and Dust*, 2005)

133. "Long Walk Home" (from *Magic*, 2007)

134. "Fade Away" (from *The River*, 1980)

135. "Roulette" (from *Tracks*, 1998)

136. "Surprise, Surprise" (from *Working on a Dream*, 2009)

137. "The Way" (from *The Promise*, 2010)

138. "Highway 29" (from *The Ghost of Tom Joad*, 1995)

139. "I Wanna Marry You" (from *The River*, 1980)

140. "Last to Die" (from *Magic*, 2007)

141. "Ain't Got You" (from *Tunnel of Love*, 1987)

142. "Fire" (from *The Promise*, 2010)

143. "The Rising" (from *The Rising*, 2002)

144. "My Love Will Not Let You Down" (from *Tracks*, 1998)

145. "My Best Was Never Good Enough" (from *The Ghost of Tom Joad*, 1995)

146. "Lonesome Day" (from *The Rising*, 2002)

147. "Dead Man Walkin'" (from *The Essential Bruce Springsteen*, 2003)

148. "Iceman" (from *Tracks*, 1998)

149. "Queen of the Supermarket" (from *Working on a Dream*, 2009)

150. "You'll Be Comin' Down" (from *Magic*, 2007)

151. "Better Days" (from *Lucky Town*, 1992)

152. "Working on a Dream" (from *Working on a Dream*, 2009)

153. "Youngstown" (from *The Ghost of Tom Joad*, 1995)

154. "My Beautiful Reward" (from *Lucky Town*, 1992)

155. "Land of Hope and Dreams" (from *Wrecking Ball*, 2012)

156. "Kitty's Back" (from *The Wild, the Innocent & the E Street Shuffle*, 1973)

157. "Leah" (from *Devils and Dust*, 2005)

158. "Don't Look Back" (from *Tracks*, 1998)

159. "Does This Bus Stop at 82nd Street?" (from *Greetings from Asbury Park, N.J.*, 1973)

160. "Drive All Night" (from *The River*, 1980)

161. "What Love Can Do" (from *Working on a Dream*, 2009)

162. "Gypsy Biker" (from *Magic*, 2007)

163. "Galveston Bay" (from *The Ghost of Tom Joad*, 1995)

164. "Life Itself" (from *Working on a Dream*, 2009)

165. "Two for the Road" (from *Tracks*, 1998)

166. "When You're Alone" (from *Tunnel of Love*, 1987)

167. "Real World" (from *Human Touch*, 1992)

168. "Matamoras Banks" (from *Devils and Dust*, 2005)

169. "Cadillac Ranch" (from *The River*, 1980)

170. "The Big Muddy" (from *Lucky Town*, 1992)

171. "Ramrod" (from *The River*, 1980)

172. "Soul Driver" (from *Human Touch*, 1992)

173. "It's Hard to Be a Saint in the City" (from *Greetings from Asbury Park, N.J.*, 1973)

174. "Spare Parts" (from *Tunnel of Love*, 1987)

175. "Bishop Danced" (from *Tracks*, 1998)

176. "Blood Brothers" (from *Greatest Hits*, 1995)

177. "Good Eye" (from *Working on a Dream*, 2009)

178. "The Angel" (from *Greetings from Asbury Park, N.J.*, 1973)

179. "Wild Billy's Circus Story" (from *The Wild, the Innocent & the E Street Shuffle*, 1973)

180. "Book of Dreams" (from *Lucky Town*, 1992)

181. "Two Faces" (from *Tunnel of Love*, 1987)

182. "Janey Don't You Lose Heart" (from *Tracks*, 1998)

183. "Dry Lightning" (from *The Ghost of Tom Joad*, 2005)

184. "Empty Sky" (from *The Rising*, 2002)

185. "All That Heaven Will Allow" (from *Tunnel of Love*, 1987)

186. "Reno" (from *Devils and Dust*, 2005)

187. "Crush on You" (from *The River*, 1980)

188. "Night" (from *Born to Run*, 1975)

189. "This Hard Land" (from *Greatest Hits*, 1998)

190. "Save My Love" (from *The Promise*, 2010)

191. "57 Channels (and Nothin' On)" (from *Human Touch*, 1992)

192. "Let's Be Friends (Skin to Skin)" (from *The Rising*, 2002)

193. "Streets of Fire" (from *Darkness on the Edge of Town*, 1978)

194. "I'll Work for Your Love" (from *Magic*, 2007)

195. "Human Touch" (from *Human Touch*, 1992)

196. "You Can Look (But You Better Not Touch)" (from *The River*, 1980)

197. "Something in the Night" (from *Darkness on the Edge of Town*, 1978)

198. "Further On (Up the Road)" (from *The Rising*, 2002)

199. "Mary Queen of Arkansas" (from *Greetings from Asbury Park, N.J.*, 1973)

200. "My Lucky Day" (from *Working on a Dream*, 2009)

NOTES

THE COUNTDOWN

1. Bruce Springsteen, *Bruce Springsteen: Songs* (New York: HarperEntertainment, 2001).

2. James Henke, "The *Rolling Stone* Interview: Bruce Springsteen Leaves E Street," *Rolling Stone*, August 6, 1992, www.rollingstone.com/music/news/the-rolling-stone-interview-bruce-springsteen-leaves-e-street-19920806.

3. Dave Marsh, *Bruce Springsteen: Two Hearts, the Story* (New York: Routledge, 2004), 351.

4. Marsh, *Bruce Springsteen*, 455.

5. David Corn, "Bruce Springsteen Tells the Story of the Secret America," *Mother Jones*, March/April, 1996.

6. Bruce Springsteen, liner notes to *Magic*, Bruce Springsteen, Columbia Records, CD, 2007.

7. Bruce Springsteen, interview with Charlie Rose, *The Charlie Rose Show*, PBS Network, November 20, 1998.

8. Mark Hagen, "Meet the New Boss," *Observer*, January 17, 2009, www.theguardian.com/music/2009/jan/18/bruce-springsteen-interview.

9. Bruce Springsteen, liner notes to *Greatest Hits*, Bruce Springsteen, Columbia Records, CD, 1995.

10. Marsh, *Bruce Springsteen*, 228.

11. Bruce Springsteen, liner notes to *The Essential Bruce Springsteen*, Bruce Springsteen, Columbia Records, CD, 2003.

12. Don Mcleese, "The Bruce Springsteen Interview," *International Musician and Recording World*, October, 1984.

13. Bruce Springsteen, interview with Ian "Molly" Meldrum, *Sunday Night*, Seven Network, November 20, 2010.

14. Joe Levy, "Bruce Springsteen: The *Rolling Stone* Interview," *Rolling Stone*, November 1, 2007, www.rollingstone.com/music/news/bruce-springsteen-the-rolling-stone-interview-20071101.

15. John Steinbeck, *East of Eden* (New York: Penguin, 1952).

16. Dave DiMartino, "Bruce Springsteen Takes It to the River," *Creem*, January 1981.

17. Springsteen, *Bruce Springsteen*.

18. Springsteen, interview with Charlie Rose.

19. Mcleese, "The Bruce Springsteen Interview."

20. Will Percy, "Rock and Read," *Double Take*, Spring 1988.

21. Phil Sutcliffe, "The Greatest Band in the World," *Mojo*, January 1999.

22. Robert Scott and Patrick Humphries, "American Heartbeat: The Bruce Springsteen Interview," *Hot Press*, November 2, 1984.

23. Bruce Springsteen, acceptance speech at the Golden Globe Awards, Santa Monica, California, January 11, 2009, www.springsteenlyrics.com/lyrics/t/thewrestler.php.

24. Judy Wieder, "Bruce Springsteen: The *Advocate* Interview," *Advocate*, April 2, 1996.

25. Bruce Springsteen, liner notes to *Working on a Dream*, Bruce Springsteen, Columbia Records, CD, 2009

26. David Remnick, "We Are Alive: Bruce Springsteen at 62," *New Yorker*, July 30, 2012, www.newyorker.com/reporting/2012/07/30/120730fa_fact_remnick.

27. Springsteen, liner notes to *Greatest Hits*.

28. David Hepworth, "The *Q* Interview: Bruce Springsteen," *Q*, August 1992.

29. Bruce Springsteen, interview with Edward Norton, Toronto International Film Festival, September 24, 2010.

30. Bruce Springsteen, Rock and Roll Hall of Fame induction acceptance speech, New York, March 15, 1999.

BIBLIOGRAPHY

Burger, Jeff. *Springsteen on Springsteen: Interviews, Speeches, and Encounters.* Chicago: Chicago Review Press, 2013. Springsteen has always been extremely thoughtful in describing the motivations and techniques behind his songwriting process, and Burger's book is essential in collecting those descriptions. Not only does Burger gather print interviews from a wide variety of sources, he also includes some excellent television and radio interviews and a few important speeches given by Springsteen over the years. He also does a great job of placing it all into context with brief bits of Springsteen biography, so the book serves as a kind of career timeline.

Marsh, Dave. *Two Hearts: The Definitive Bruce Springsteen Biography.* New York: Routledge, 2004. While there have been many Springsteen biographies written over the years, Marsh's was one of the first and is still, in this author's opinion, the best. There may be no better "you-are-there" description of the recording process of a particular album than the section devoted to the long and sometimes torturous sessions for *Born in the U.S.A.* Although it leaves off in 2003 and Springsteen has continued to release great music after that, no book covers his first thirty years of recording with as much thoroughness and insight.

O'Connor, Flannery. *The Complete Stories.* New York: Farrar, Straus and Giroux, 1971. In the early 1980s, Springsteen's writing took a much darker turn, not just in terms of subject matter, but in the way that his characters were portrayed. His familiarity with O'Connor's work was clearly one of the catalysts for this transformation. Certainly the *Nebraska* album is indebted to the work of this transcendent author and her unforgettable short stories.

Springsteen, Bruce. *Bruce Springsteen: Songs.* New York: HarperEntertainment, 2001. You can take it right from the songwriter's mouth with this wonderful collection of song lyrics that also includes Springsteen's descriptions of what the songs might have meant and the stories behind their recording. Think of this book in terms of a really extensive and elongated set of liner notes entailing the bulk of Springsteen's recorded output. Without any filter, Springsteen's writing really puts you behind the songs.

Steinbeck, John. *The Grapes Of Wrath.* New York: Bantam, 1946. The obvious correlation here is "The Ghost of Tom Joad," Springsteen's 1995 treatise on poverty and hunger that borrows this novel's antihero so he can serve as a kind of benevolent spirit watching over all those struggling in the song. Yet the combination of sharp storytelling against a backdrop of overarching social issues that Steinbeck mastered in this American classic clearly goes beyond just one song in terms of how it influenced Springsteen. Albums like *The Ghost of Tom Joad* and *Devils and Dust* are filled with the spirit of that novel and Steinbeck's writing.

INDEX

ABOUT THE AUTHOR

Jim Beviglia is a featured writer for *American Songwriter* magazine, reviewing new albums and looking back at classic songwriters and songs for both the print and online editions. This is his second book in the Counting Down series, following 2013's *Counting Down Bob Dylan: His 100 Finest Songs*, and Jim continues to maintain his blog at Countdown-kid.wordpess.com, where he delves deep into the musical libraries of rock's finest artists. Jim was born and raised in Old Forge, Pennsylvania, where he currently resides with his mom, his daughter Daniele, and his girlfriend Marie.

CPSIA information can be obtained at www.ICGtesting.com
Printed in the USA
BVOW04*2137240614

357212BV00001B/1/P